Fortran 90

Martin Counihan

University of Southampton

Pitman

PITMAN PUBLISHING
128 Long Acre, London WC2E 9AN

A Division of Longman Group UK Limited

© M Counihan 1991

First published in Great Britain 1991

British Library Cataloguing in Publication Data

Counihan, Martin
  Fortran 90.
  I. Title
  005.362

  ISBN 0-273-03073-6

Printed in England by Clays Ltd, St Ives plc

CONTENTS

(1)   INTRODUCTION

1.1	Fortran 90	1
1.2	Programs and Programming	2

(2)   WHAT IS FORTRAN 90?

2.1	Program Structure	5
2.2	Intrinsic Procedures	6
2.3	Statement Types	7
2.4	What Fortran 90 Isn't	7
2.5	New Features in Fortran 90	8
Notes		10

(3)   GETTING STARTED

3.1	The Character Set	11
3.2	A Simple Program	14
3.3	Arithmetic Operators	18
Exercises 3A		19
3.4	Names and Other Lexical Tokens	20
3.5	Fortran Source Form	21
Exercises 3B		24
Notes		25

(4)   INTRINSIC DATA TYPES

4.1	Integers	26
4.2	Real Numbers	29
Exercises 4A		31
4.3	Simple Form of the Type Declaration Statement	32
4.4	Kinds of Real Numbers	32
4.5	Complex Numbers	33
4.6	Logical Data; Logical and Relational Operators	35
4.7	Characters and Strings	38
Exercises 4B		40
Notes		42

(5)   SOME INTRINSIC PROCEDURES

5.1	An Intrinsic Subroutine	43
5.2	Mathematical Functions	44
5.3	Numeric Functions	46
Exercises 5A		50
Notes		52

(6)   MORE ABOUT CHARACTERS

6.1	Declaring Character Data	53
6.2	Character Constants	54
6.3	Character Operators	55
6.4	Intrinsic Character Functions	56
6.5	Substrings	59
Exercises 6A		61
Notes		62

(7)   ARRAYS

7.1	Declaring Arrays	63
7.2	Using Arrays	65
7.3	Array Constructors	67
7.4	Array Sections	68
7.5	Array Sections, Character Strings and Substrings	70
7.6	Where	72
7.7	Arrays and Intrinsic Functions	73
Exercises 7B		74

(8)   EXECUTION CONTROL

8.1	The "CASE" Construct	76
8.2	The "IF" Construct	80
Exercises 8A		81
8.3	The "DO" Construct	82
8.4	STOP	88
Exercises 8B		88
Notes		89

(9)   FUNCTIONS AND SUBROUTINES (1)

9.1	Functions	90
Exercises 9A		93
9.2	Subroutines	93
9.3	Procedures and Arrays	96
Exercises 9B		99
Notes		100

(10)   MORE INTRINSIC PROCEDURES; STATEMENT LABELS

10.1	Intrinsic Subroutines	102
10.2	Functions for Use with Arrays	104
Exercises 10A		110
10.3	Numeric Inquiry Functions and Floating-Point Manipulation Functions	110
10.4	Statement Labels and "GO TO"	111
Notes		114

(11)   MODULES

11.1	Data Modules	116
11.2	Module Procedures	120
11.3	More About "USE" Statements	124
Exercises 11A		126
Notes		127

(12)   FUNCTIONS AND SUBROUTINES (2)

12.1	Recursive Procedures	128
Exercises 12A		130
12.2	Interface Blocks	131
12.3	Argument Keywords	132
12.4	More About Arguments: "PRESENT"	133
12.5	Array-Valued Functions	134
12.6	Defined Operators	135
12.7	Generic Names	138
12.8	Parallel Processing	141
Exercises 12B		142
Notes		143

(13) THE TYPE DECLARATION STATEMENT

13.1	General Form of the TDS	144
13.2	Character Length Selectors	147
13.3	Attribute Specifications	149
13.4	Array Specifications	152
13.5	The Entity Declaration List	157
13.6	Summary	158
Exercises 13A		159
Notes		161

(14) DERIVED TYPES

14.1	Derived-Type Definition	164
14.2	Structure Constructors	166
14.3	Structure Components	168
Exercises 14A		169
14.4	Structures of Structures	170
Exercises 14B		171
14.5	Functions and Operators with Derived Types	172
14.6	Defined Assignment	174
Exercises 14C		178
Notes		180

(15) ARRAYS AND POINTERS

15.1	Array Element Order; Array Constructors; RESHAPE	181
15.2	Vector Subscripts	184
15.3	Allocatable Arrays	187
Exercises 15A		190
15.4	LBOUND, UBOUND, SHAPE and SIZE	190
Exercises 15B		191
15.5	Simple Pointers	192
15.6	Pointers as Structures and as Structure Components	197
15.7	Pointers and Procedures	204
15.8	Array Pointers	205
Exercises 15C		207
Notes		208

(16)   INPUT AND OUTPUT; DATA FORMAT SPECIFICATIONS

16.1	Data Transfer Statements	209
16.2	The I/O Item List	210
16.3	List-Directed Input	212
16.4	List-Directed Output	216
16.5	Explicit Formats	217
Exercises 16A		219
16.6	Data Edit Descriptors and Character Edit Descriptors	219
16.7	Control Edit Descriptors	223
Exercises 16B		225
16.8	Namelists	226
16.9	Unformatted I/O	228
16.10	The TRANSFER Function	229
16.11	Summary	231
Notes		232

(17)   FILE HANDLING

17.1	Units, Files and Records	233
17.2	Opening and Closing Files	235
17.3	BACKSPACE, ENDFILE and REWIND	240
17.4	Control Specifications for I/O	240
17.5	The 'INQUIRE' Statement	242
17.6	Internal Files	246
Exercises 17A		248
Notes		249

(18)   BITS

18.1	Inside Integers	250
18.2	Bit Logic	251
18.3	A Warning	252
Exercises 18A		253

(19) PROGRAMMING CONVENTIONS AND PROGRAM ARCHITECTURE: PUTTING IT ALL TOGETHER

19.1	Coding Conventions	254
19.2	Towards 'Core' Fortran 90	255
Fortran 90 Recommended Statements		256
Intrinsic Functions		257
19.3	Program Unit Structure	258
19.4	Program Structure	261
19.5	Final Remarks	262

ANSWERS TO SELECTED EXERCISES 263

APPENDICES

A	Fortran 90 Statements	281
B	Intrinsic Procedures	286
C	Intrinsic Procedures: 'Specific' Names	292
D	Argument Keywords in Intrinsic Procedures	294
E	I/O Edit Descriptors	297
F	The ASCII Character Set	301

INDEX 304

Preface

This book provides a comprehensive account of the Fortran 90 computer programming language. It is designed to serve both as a textbook for those learning the language and also as a convenient and complete reference guide for users of Fortran 90. No part of the language has been omitted.

As a textbook this could be used as the basis of a formal course or for individual study. It will be convenient for those converting from languages such as C and Fortran 77. As well as dealing with the vocabulary and syntax of the language, a number of general programming concepts and methods are explained, to encourage the production of comprehensible, bug-free, maintainable code. Fortran 90 is a large language and it provides the programmer with plenty of latitude: it has been made clear that there are obsolete parts of the language and undesirable approaches to programming which should now be avoided, while there are powerful new features (such as derived data structures and modules) which the creative programmer will find enjoyable and beneficial.

Although Fortran 90 includes an impressive set of mathematical functions, and overall is probably the best programming language for scientific and technical computation, it is not intended only for mathematical programming. In fact Fortran 90 handles text and general datasets with the same flexibility that it handles numbers. So, although this book contains numerous mathematical examples, it should also be accessible to non-mathematicians who will be using Fortran 90 to solve problems of other kinds.

To the memory of Florence Frances Counihan

Chapter 1

INTRODUCTION

1.1   FORTRAN 90

Fortran 90 is a new world-standard programming language likely to become dominant for scientific and engineering applications and widely used for general information handling. This book has been written to explain and describe the language, serving both as a textbook for students and as a comprehensive reference book for experienced programmers.

Although 'Fortran 90' is the correct name of the new language, it will often be abbreviated to 'Fortran' in this book. The previous form of the language was FORTRAN 77, spelt by convention with upper-case letters. The word 'fortran' was originally an abbreviation for 'formula translation'.

Programming languages, for many years now, have posed a dilemma to IT strategists and educators. Fortran is a language family that is now about 30 years old, and although it is very widespread it has been available only in the form of the outdated FORTRAN 77 standard or else in non-standard dialects. So, during the 1980's, many people wanting to use an up-to-date and elegant programming language turned away from Fortran. Meanwhile, however, it has become clear that widely-touted alternative languages like Pascal and Ada have their own deficiencies and have not become as popular as was once hoped. Another development during the 1980's was the proliferation of higher-level 'fourth-generation' languages, database systems, and other packages, often menu-driven, which offer powerful facilities for carrying out tasks of specific types. These packages are certainly extremely useful, but they each address a limited domain of problems, they usually run rather inefficiently, and ultimately they can be very complicated to use. For example, a typical modern spreadsheet system is capable of performing sophisticated calculations and can manipulate data in many forms: but it is likely to demand heavy system overheads and to have a command language hardly less complex than Fortran; while there are innumerable things that a spreadsheet cannot do because of its specialised structure. As time has gone by it has become necessary for the well-rounded computer user to be familiar with spreadsheets, statistical packages, graphical interfaces, sophisticated wordprocessors and desktop-publishing systems, and many other things besides, but it has remained necessary to use a Fortran-style programming language to solve general problems in a direct and unconstrained way.

In preference to FORTRAN 77, the language C has become increasingly popular in recent years, and has the virtues of a simple, compact core and good portability. However, C has awkwardnesses that makes it unappealing to many people, and it loses much of its simplicity when the standard procedure library is added and when the language is extended to the more powerful form of 'C++'. Where can we go after C?

1

This brings us to Fortran 90. Fortran 90 has been planned as a fresh route forward: it is a thoroughly modern, powerful, general-purpose language possessing virtually all the conceptual features that users of Pascal and C have come to expect.

Unfortunately Fortran 90 is a large language, retaining all the features of earlier Fortran standards: but this is the price that must be paid for backward compatibility. On the other hand, for the user who is writing fresh programs and is free to ignore the past, Fortran 90 contains an elegant and powerful core language that is intellectually and educationally very appealing. Throughout this book, it is the essential core of modern Fortran 90 that has been emphasised. Older Fortran features whose use is not recommended are relegated to end-of-chapter notes, the appendices, and the index. So this book remains a complete guide to Fortran 90, but the inessential older features are kept clear of the main text and could be ignored by the student.

Fortran 90 is, in a sense, more than just a programming language. It involves concepts and terminology that have become standard in the world of professional software engineering, cutting across programming languages with terms like 'pointer' and 'character' and 'argument'. These terms have precise technical meanings, and are part of the vocabulary that programmers need to use to discuss their work. Beginners should try to get used to the terminology even when it sounds rather pompously long-winded (e.g. 'structure constructor'). This book deliberately uses accurate technical terminology as often as is reasonable, since serious Fortran 90 users will need to become acquainted with the terminology as well as learning the keywords and syntax of Fortran itself.

Up to a few years ago, a book on programming in Fortran would have emphasised facilities and techniques of calculation. The most advanced programming applications tended to involve advanced mathematics. Non-mathematical work was the domain of less sophisticated languages, such as COBOL for business applications. Nowadays things have changed: there are some very sophisticated computer applications outside of the mathematical sciences, and Fortran 90 can deal efficiently and flexibly with non-numerical data. Fortran 90 can be used in applications ranging from linguistic analysis to image processing, with qualitative as well as quantitative results. Calculations can be done not merely with one set of numbers at a time but with large arrays, and compilers can exploit new types of parallel (or 'vector') processors that are now available. In this book mathematical computation takes a vary important place (and in a deep sense all computing is mathematical) but many examples of non-mathematical applications are used as illustrations and exercises.

1.2   PROGRAMS AND PROGRAMMING

A computer program is simply a sequence of instructions to be carried out by a computer. A computer is a composite electromechanical system which works by the transmission of signals and data between components such as magnetic disks, microelectronic memory 'chips', arithmetic processor chips, other chips to control visual display units ('VDU's'), and so on. The internal signals involve codes ('machine code') the details of which will depend on the engineering design of the particular computer.

At the beginning of the history of computing it was vital for programmers to understand computer design so as to make the most of the limited memory available and to make programs run as fast as possible. Memory space and execution time imposed serious limitations on the applications of primitive computers. These limitations still exist today, of course, but at a very much higher level. To minimise demands on memory, and to maximise speed, early programmers often wrote their programs using low-level machine code: a slow and difficult process. Nowadays, machine code is beyond the experience of many programmers, and sophisticated systems have been developed so that very efficient programs can be written straightforwardly using one of the higher-level languages of which Fortran is the prime example. A program written in Fortran 90 will be translated ('compiled') into the appropriate machine code by the computer system itself. This leaves the programmer free to concentrate on solving the real problem in hand, be it in statistics, chemistry, meteorology, aeronautics, economic forecasting or whatever. The programmer can cultivate expertise of the specialist subject, and his or her knowledge of computing need not extend much beyond the strictly defined boundaries of the programming language.

The translation of a program from (say) Fortran 90 into machine code is carried out by a part of the system known as a 'compiler'. A compiler is itself a piece of software, i.e. a computer program, written possibly in machine code or perhaps in some other language. Fortran 90 is a standard language, precisely specified by international agreement, and compilers for it will be found to run on computers of many different types, large and small. This achieves one of the main benefits of a standard language: program portability, whereby a program can be written to solve a problem once and for all and can subsequently be transferred without fuss to a large selection of other machines. Another important benefit is programmer portability!

Although Fortran 90 is a standard language, defined without reference to any particular computer system, any particular implementation of the language may depend somewhat on the details of the system, and in particular on the hardware available and on the characteristics of the compiler. The computer system, including the compiler, is often referred to as the 'processor'. There are a number of examples of processor-dependence within Fortran 90: different screens may display characters in different ways, the data-input device may be a keyboard or an old-fashioned punched-card-reader or something else, the precision of calculations may be better with some processors than with others, and some will let you communicate with more disk files than others. Fortran 90 lays down certain minimum standards, but at the same time helps the programmer to exploit whatever facilities might be available on a particular processor.

Portability has already been mentioned above. Fortran in one form or another has been in use for over 30 years and there is now an enormous investment in existing programs. Consequently, portability in time is as important as portability in space, and Fortran 90 has been designed for backwards-compatibility with the previous standard version, FORTRAN 77. As has been mentioned already, this means that Fortran 90 includes a number of archaic features which would not have been included in the language if it were being designed today without the burden of history. The archaic features should be avoided by a newcomer, they are no longer functionally necessary, and in this book they are mentioned only for the sake of completeness.

One of the archaic features is 'fixed source form', i.e. the old requirement that a program should be broken up into 'lines' exactly 72 characters long, with certain character positions reserved for special purposes. This was necessary when programs were written and stored on 80-column punched cards, but that limitation is no longer with us and the much more flexible 'free source form' should be used.

To use Fortran 90 the programmer has to use compiler software, manipulate and edit files containing Fortran code, and use input/output ('i/o') devices such as a keyboard and a screen. This means that the programmer will be using an operating system and probably some sort of text editor. The command structure of your operating system and editor are not the concern of this book, but you will need a sound understanding of them to use Fortran 90. For example, when you run a Fortran program you may need to use system commands to turn printers on and off, pre-connect disk files, clear your screen, and so on. You should also store your programs systematically on disk files, especially if you build up a personalised collection of general-purpose utilities in the form of 'modules' which can be plugged into different specialised programs.

It was said at the beginning of this section that a computer program is simply a sequence of instructions to be carried out by a computer. The simplest of programs will have a starting point and an ending point, and all the instructions between the start and the end will be 'executed' when the program runs. However, some instructions can permit a program to branch out into alternative paths, and so in practice most programs are not executed in a fixed linear sequence of instructions. There can be branches, loops, conditionally-executed blocks, and other structures, and a program may have several different possible points of termination. In Fortran 90 there are numerous ways in which the flow of a program can be controlled. As an alternative approach, it possible to design a program with the emphasis not on the program flow but on the structure of the data: to do this, Fortran 90 contains simple but powerful facilities for defining data modules and data structures.

This is not a book about the general methodology of program design, but the reader should be aware that there are different philosophies about how to approach the design of a large program. Some approaches are more efficient than others and will lead to more reliable, less error-prone, code. Unfortunately, in a book like this it is only possible to give brief snatches of Fortran 90 code, and some very short programs, but real-life programs often extend to tens or even hundreds of thousands of lines. It must be remembered that Fortran's system of subprograms and modules really only comes into its own with large programs that cannot be directly illustrated here because they would be larger than this entire book. Nevertheless, the principles will all be made clear, and I hope all readers will be able to appreciate the elegance and power of it all. Enjoy Fortran 90!

Chapter 2

WHAT IS FORTRAN 90?

A Subcommittee of the American Nation Standards Institute (ANSI), code-named X3J3, working on behalf of the International Standards Organisation (ISO), had the task of producing Fortran 90 to replace the earlier form of Fortran, FORTRAN 77. X3J3 has a wide international membership and represents computer manufacturers, software companies, research institutes and academics.

X3J3 produced a draft standard for the new language in mid-1987: it included a fresh and updated set of facilities for memory management (arrays and modules), for user-defined data types, and for execution control. A further draft standard was produced in August 1989 specifying additional features such as pointers and procedures for 'bit' data handling. In 1991, after final revisions, the international standard for Fortran 90 was at last adopted officially.

2.1   PROGRAM STRUCTURE

A Fortran 90 program consists, in general, of separate 'program units'. These are:

> (a) A 'main program'. When the program as a whole is run, it always starts at the first statement of the main program.

> (b) An arbitrary number of other program units. These can be called into play by special statements within the main program or within other program units.

A short program could consist only of a main program, but in practice there are usually several program units. Apart from the main program, the other program units fall into two classes, namely:

> (b1) 'modules' (chapter 11) which can, for example, be used to make data accessible to several different subprograms.

> (b2) 'external subprograms', or 'procedures' (see chapter 9).

The difference between a module and a procedure is that a module contains information made permanently accessible to the program unit that invokes it: invocation is by a declarative statement at the start of that program unit. A procedure, on the other hand, is invoked dynamically (and perhaps repetitively) by action statements during program execution.

Procedures can be invoked from the main program or from other procedures. There is even the possibility of 'recursive procedures' that invoke themselves (chapter 12). Procedures fall into two classes, namely 'subroutines' and 'functions', differing according to exactly how they are invoked. Normally, subroutines are used to switch the flow of execution of the program, while functions are used for repeated calculations.

There is another kind of subprogram not so far mentioned, namely 'module subprograms', which are procedures contained within a module. Module subprograms can be a useful way of setting out a group of functions or subroutines that are somehow related to one another and which need access to a shared set of data.

At this stage there is no need to try to remember the different types of program unit. They will be explained gradually as the book proceeds, and a final summary appears in chapter 19.

2.2   INTRINSIC PROCEDURES

'Intrinsic procedures' are a kind of toolkit provided for the programmer in Fortran. They are a general-purpose set of subprograms which can be invoked from any Fortran program. For example, to calculate the square root of a number a program only needs to use the expression SQRT(...) with the number in question provided between the brackets. SQRT is a Fortran 'keyword' which simply causes the square root to be calculated. Procedures like SQRT are just there, waiting in the background in case they are needed. They don't have to be ordered in advance: they are an intrinsic part of the Fortran language. There are well over 100 intrinsic procedures in Fortran 90, and almost all of them (including SQRT) take the form of a 'function', like a mathematical function, and are called 'intrinsic functions'. A function is a procedure that can be referred to simply by mentioning its name, even in the middle of a complicated expression; for example SQRT(21 - SQRT(25)) is an acceptable Fortran expression which uses the SQRT function twice and is equal to 4.

Fortran's intrinsic procedures include several standard mathematical functions such as common trigonometrical and hyperbolic functions. They also include some very useful procedures for frequently-needed numeric manipulations, such as finding the absolute magnitude of a number or picking out the largest from a given set of numbers. There are other intrinsic procedures that operate not on numbers but on strings of characters. Others, again, are useful for checking up on the characteristics of the computer being used: for example the intrinsic inquiry function PRECISION will tell your program what is the limit of your computer's decimal precision. Inquiry functions like this would be unnecessary if all computers were the same, but are very valuable for writing programs to be portable between computers with different characteristics.

There are still other intrinsic procedures that are used for handling vectors and matrices, and for manipulating binary 'bits', and for tasks such as the generating of random numbers. They are introduced gradually through this book, but are all listed together in Appendix B.

2.3   STATEMENT TYPES

A Fortran program consists of an ordered sequence of 'statements', and the statements can carry out different sorts of tasks. Some statements ('assignment statements') give a value to a variable quantity: for example

n = 256

is an assignment statement which sets a variable called n equal (for the time being!) to 256. Assignment statements always have an '=' sign in them. Other kinds of statement are indicated by special keywords, for example a statement that writes out data will begin with the keyword WRITE. Fortran statement types are listed in appendix A; it is a long list, and rather bewildering at first sight, but in practice most programs can be built up predominantly out of statements of relatively few kinds.

2.4   WHAT FORTRAN 90 ISN'T

Fortran 90 is a high-level general-purpose computer programming language. As such, it is ideal for tackling a great variety of analytical and conceptual problems. However, it is not designed as a display tool: Fortran in itself is not a way of displaying graphics or of producing different styles of printed output. On the contrary, it is regarded as a strength of Fortran that it is independent of the particular graphical capabilities that your computer may or may not possess. For the sake of portability between machines, and because data display systems are evolving all the time, Fortran restricts itself to a limited set of characters for the input and output of data. To fully exploit your machine's own display capabilities, it is now usually possible to add an off-the-shelf library of input/output procedures to Fortran. There are many graphics packages that will interface to Fortran programs. Nowadays, probably the majority of professional Fortran programs communicate with the outside world through specialised input/output packages. That is as it should be, and the details of those packages need not concern us here. Fortran has its own input/output facilities, harnessed by the statement keywords READ and WRITE, but since many programmers will bypass them they will not be dwelt upon in this book: the details are deferred until chapters 16 and 17.

Fortran is a language through which a computer may be used to solve an external problem; it is not really intended as a system for controlling the computer itself. So, Fortran is quite different in function from an 'operating system' such as UNIX, or DOS, or IBM's CMS system. However, you are quite likely to find yourself using Fortran through the medium of an operating system such as UNIX. The operating system acts as a kind of gateway, letting the programmer write Fortran programs, edit them, save them, compile them, and what have you; but system commands operate at a different level from the actual Fortran statements and must be distinguished from them. To take an analogy: it's like the difference between the commands that steer your word processing system and the actual text of a letter that you write on it; and like a Fortran program, the letter will in general be designed to solve an external problem that may have nothing to do with computers, such as persuading your bank manager to give you a larger overdraft.

Before starting in earnest in the next chapter, it is convenient to introduce some more terminology here and to briefly describe a few of the innovations that set Fortran 90 apart from previous versions of the language. We will mention arrays, user-defined data types, pointers, modules, and free source form.

Any variable data item has a 'name'. For example, the quantity n in the example in section 2.3 is the 'name' of a data item. In Fortran 90, a very useful feature is that a set of similar data items may be grouped together in an 'array' under a common name. So, it is possible to manipulate large sets of data with very simple statements. Mathematically, these sets of data may be sequences of numbers, or vectors, or matrices, or tensors, or whatever you like, and they may be organised in many different dimensions; they can still be named and handled as single entities. 'Array' is the general term used for a set of data going under a single name. Fortran 90 works very flexibly with arrays of almost arbitrary size, and can be used to exploit vector-processing facilities on computers of advanced architecture. In fact the statement mentioned earlier,

$$n = 256$$

could actually cause a large number of data items each to be set equal to 256 if it had been arranged for the name n to represent an array of numbers. Likewise, most of Fortran's intrinsic mathematical functions will work for arrays: an expression like SQRT(x), if x is the name of an array, will calculate the square roots of all the numbers in the array x.

Data items, whether they have fixed values ('constants') or values that can change during program execution ('variables'), may be of a number of different 'types'. For example, integer numbers and complex numbers are different types. The word 'type' is not used loosely: it is a technical term that refers to the nature, and not the particular value, of a single data item. Most programming languages allow for a few different types of data, but Fortran 90 allows, in principle, for an arbitrary variety of types. This is because of a feature known as 'user-defined types' or 'derived types', by which the programmer may construct a definition of a fresh type of data relevant to the problem in hand. It is easy to draw examples from advanced mathematics: for example, a programmer interested in four-dimensional geometry could define four-component vectors and 4x4 transformation matrices, and could also define what would be meant by the sums and products of such entities. There are also more down-to-earth applications: for example, the latitude and longtitude of a geographical point together comprise a special sort of data item and could be set up as a user-defined type obeying its own rules according to the programmer's wishes. User-defined types can be more flexible than arrays: an array is a set of items all of which must be of the same type, but a user-defined type can be a complicated structure incorporating data of quite different basic types, e.g. mixing numbers and words. So, a single Fortran 'name', like 'x', could in this way refer to a mixed package of data such as a person's name, address, telephone number and age.

Pointers are another new feature in the Fortran language. The concept of a pointer is not easy to appreciate at first, but one way to illustrate the idea is to use the example at the end of the previous paragraph, of a set of data consisting of a person's name, address, telephone number and age. Imagine that we have a large list of information of this sort. Suppose that we want the set of data for each person to include also a cross-reference to the corresponding information for the person's spouse. There are various ways in which this might be achieved. One way might be to give an index number to each person listed, and to include the spouse's index number in the data set for each person who is married. But the simplest method, using Fortran 90, is to include a 'pointer' to a spouse's details together with the information about each person. The pointer would have the appearance of an additional data item encapsulating all the spouse's personal details; but in reality it would simply 'point' to the other area of memory where the spouse's details are already listed in his/her own right. Using pointers, there is no need to take up unnecessary memory space by repeating chunks of data, nor to set up special codes for cross-referencing between data.

Modules are another valuable innovation in Fortran, and have already been mentioned in section 2.1. Like pointers, modules are difficult to appreciate in the abstract. You have to use them, in real programs, to see how effective they can be. Modules are useful in the architecture of large programs or systems of programs, where they can be used to organise plug-in sets of procedures for particular purposes. In smaller programs, modules are most useful for memory access, i.e. for containing data which is to be used from more than one procedure.

'Free source form' is another characteristic of Fortran 90 that programmers will appreciate. It is to do with the way that a Fortran program is laid out by the programmer before being compiled and executed. The programme must be divided into 'lines', but the lines may be of any length up to a maximum of 132 characters. A statement doesn't have to start at any particular position in a line, and it doesn't need any special character to end it. As a rule, blank spaces may be used to space out parts of a statement to improve legibility. If desired, it is possible to have several statements on one line, using the semi-colon as a separator, or to spread one statement over several lines, using an ampersand to mark the break. Also, it is easy to annotate the program with pieces of text (comments) which don't actually form part of the program and will be ignored by the compiler. With free source form, Fortran breaks away from the constraints of the old programming style whose origins lay in the fixed format of the now-vanished 80-column punched card.

9

N2.1 OFFICIALLY OBSOLESCENT FEATURES

Fortran 90 was designed with a view to the inevitable process of future language evolution, and so some features have been officially tagged as 'obsolescent'. This means that they may disappear completely at the next revision of the language. The officially obsolescent features are

(i)   The arithmetic-IF statement (note N10.5)

(ii)   ASSIGN, and the assigned GO TO statement (note N10.3)

(iii)   PAUSE (note N8.1)

(iv)   The use of real expressions for DO loop control (integers should be used as in section 8.3)

(v)   DO loop termination other than on an END DO or CONTINUE statement (section 8.3)

(vi)   More than one DO loop terminating at the same statement (section 8.3)

(vii)   Branching to an END IF from outside an IF block (see chapter 8); you should branch instead to the statement after the END IF)

(viii)   Alternate returns (see note N9.5)

(ix)   Assigned FORMAT specifiers (note N16.2)

Chapter 3

GETTING STARTED

This chapter explains the characters, lexical tokens and source form used in Fortran 90, and introduces the language by discussing a simple example program in detail. The statements encountered here are of various kinds, characterised by the keywords PROGRAM, READ, WRITE, IF...THEN, ELSE, END IF, and END PROGRAM, in addition to which there is the sort of statement called an 'assignment statement' assigning a value to a variable. Arithmetic operators and the intrinsic function SQRT are also discussed in this chapter.

3.1   THE CHARACTER SET

Fortran programs are built up according to a syntax which uses the limited set of characters listed below:

Letters: ABCDEFGHIJKLMNOPQRSTUVWXYZ

Digits: 0123456789

The underscore: _

Special characters:

	Blank
=	Equals
+	Plus
-	Minus
*	Asterisk
/	Slash
(	Left parenthesis
)	Right parenthesis
,	Comma
.	Decimal point or full stop
$	Currency symbol
'	Apostrophe
:	Colon
!	Exclamation
"	Quote
%	Percent

&	Ampersand
;	Semicolon
<	Less than
>	Greater than
?	Question mark

Most of the above characters have specified uses in Fortran. For example, the letters crop up in statement keywords like WRITE or STOP; the digits and decimal point are used to represent numbers; characters like + and - are used in the usual way for mathematical operations; and so on. Virtually all the Fortran standard characters should exist on any keyboard and it should be possible to display them all on a screen or with a printer.

There are just two exceptional special characters, the currency symbol ($) and the question mark (?), which have no particular roles in standard Fortran. However, such characters occur in real life and so they are likely to crop up in programs as elements of character strings, e.g. in the WRITE statement

WRITE (*,*) "What is your name?"

which would cause the standard output device - presumably a screen - to display

What is your name?

The meaning of (*,*) in the WRITE statement will be explained shortly.

With Fortran, output devices will display the characters more or less in the form tabulated above, although the exact font style may vary. The symbol given as a dollar sign ($) is regarded as a general currency symbol and could appear as £ or whatever according to the country.

The example above illustrates an important point: in a specified character string one may distinguish between lower-case and upper-case letters as long as the processor itself recognises a distinction. Almost all modern computer systems do in fact permit the two kinds of letters, but some equipment does not, so Fortran does not insist on the distinction, and no such distinction is made in the syntax of the language itself, e.g. in keywords such as WRITE. This is why lower-case letters were not listed separately at the beginning of this chapter. As far as the processor is concerned, the statement given above could equally well appear as

Write (*,*) "What is your name?"

If the processor is incapable of discriminating between lower-case and upper-case letters, the result of executing the statement might be

WHAT IS YOUR NAME?

However, throughout the rest of this book it will be assumed that the processor can deal with both upper-case and lower-case. It is advantageous for the programmer to develop a style which exploits lower-case and upper-case letters to improve the readability and editability of programs; for example, it is a good idea always to use upper-case letters for statement keywords (like WRITE) and for the names of intrinsic functions, and to use mostly lower-case letters for the names of variables, as in something like

$$x = -b + SQRT(b**2 - 4*a*c)$$

Here, SQRT is Fortran's built-in square root function, mentioned earlier in section 2.2. It should be remembered that a programmer will normally be working through the medium of some sort of text-editor while writing or updating a program. It makes no practical difference to Fortran whether you refer to the square root function as SQRT, Sqrt or sqrt, but it may make a difference to your editor if, for example, a string-search facility is used to find all the usages of that function within a very large program.

Blank spaces are not always relevant to the syntax of Fortran, and can be used to space things out to improve the appearance of a program. The above statement is precisely equivalent to

$$x=-b+SQRT(b**2-4*a*c)$$

but the former version is a little easier to read and to check. But, blank spaces may not be embedded within keywords, etc. The letters of SQRT or WRITE, for example, may not be broken up with blanks. Furthermore, blanks are not ignored when they appear as elements of fixed character strings such as "What is your name?" In program statements, such strings are always enclosed between quotes or apostrophes.

There is one more important point that must be made about characters in Fortran 90. It is that any character representable within the processor may occur in 'character context', i.e. as an element of a character string such as "What is your name?" The lower-case letters are a special case of this rule: but it applies equally to any other unusual characters which were not listed in the table earlier but may be representable by a particular processor and may appear on keyboards and screens. Going further, if a processor is capable of representing the letters of the Greek alphabet, or Japanese kanji characters, or whatever, then they may validly appear in a character context within Fortran 90. The character set shown at the beginning of this section is a minimum set for conformance with the Fortran 90 standard, but a program may display information in other ways depending on the capabilities of the processor.

```
PROGRAM Triangle
WRITE (*,*) "This program calculates the area of a  triangle."
WRITE (*,*) "Type in the lengths of the three sides:"
READ  (*,*) a, b, c
WRITE (*,*) "Check: you have input the following lengths"
WRITE (*,*) a, b, c
s = 0.5 * (a+b+c)                  ! Semiperimeter
areasq = s*(s-a)*(s-b)*(s-c)       ! Square of area
        IF (areasq<0.0) THEN
        WRITE (*,*) "Error: that is not a real triangle"
ELSE
area = SQRT(areasq)
        WRITE (*,*) "The area of the triangle is ", area
END IF
END PROGRAM Triangle
```

Here, the PROGRAM statement serves to introduce the program and to give it a name (Triangle).
The WRITE statements are for the output of data. The statement

WRITE (*,*) "Type in the lengths of the three sides:"

is a Fortran abbreviation for

WRITE (UNIT=*,FMT=*) "Type in the lengths of the three sides."

Ampersands (the '&' character) are used to stitch together two lines into one statement if ever there
is too much to fit comfortably onto one line. For example, instead of the previous statement we
could have had

WRITE (UNIT=*,FMT=*) "Type in values for the lengths of the &
                     &triangle's three sides"

It doesn't really matter where the break between lines occurs. The above statement is precisely
equivalent to

WRITE (UNIT=*,FMT=*) &
"Type in values for the lengths of the triangle's three sides."

The exact rules for continuing a statement from one line to the next are summarised in section 3.5.

In principle WRITE statements may be used to output data onto any of a variety of devices which
may be connected to the processor: printers, a screen, magnetic tape units, or whatever. Fortran
expects each device to have a number, the 'unit number', and the WRITE statement can specify

the unit by including in brackets UNIT=1, UNIT=3, UNIT=9 or whatever. However, to simplify matters any processor is required to have a standard output unit which will automatically be used unless another unit is explicitly specified by number. An asterisk is used to refer to the standard output unit, so we have the specification UNIT=* in the WRITE statement above. In most modern personal computers the standard output device will be a screen, so this WRITE statement will cause the string of characters

Type in the lengths of the three sides.

to appear on the screen.

What about FMT=*? This is to do with the format in which a piece of data is to be output (or, for input, the expected format in which it is to be read). Just as the UNIT keyword gives the programmer access to the range of available input/ouput devices, so the FMT keyword gives freedom to specify precisely in what style the information is to displayed: for example, with how many places of decimals a number will be shown. By using the asterisk in FMT=*, we are taking an easy way out called 'list-directed formatting' whereby the format follows certain default conventions according to the nature of the data item (or items) listed in the subsequent part of the WRITE or READ statement. For the time being, list-directed formatting will be sufficient for us. Format specification is a large topic and will be dealt with in chapter 16.

So, (*,*) in the example above means that standard defaults are being used for the i/o devices and for the i/o formats. Until chapter 16 we will imagine that all input is via a keyboard and all output is onto a screen.

The READ statement in the example program is

READ (*,*) a, b, c

and it means that numbers represented by a, b and c are to be input from the keyboard. 'Real' numbers are expected, i.e. positive or negative numbers which may include decimal fractions, as opposed to integers or complex numbers or people's names or anything more complicated. a, b and c are 'variables', i.e. entities whose values are not necessarily known when the program is written but are determined later on as the program runs. Inputting the numbers with a READ statement is one such way of giving values to the variables a, b and c. Selecting the first three letters of the alphabet as the names of these variables is a completely arbitrary choice. We could have used more or less any letters of the alphabet, or indeed sequences of letters. For example, we could have used instead the statement

READ (*,*) side_a, side_b, side_c

in which case the rest of the program would also have to have a, b and c replaced by side_a, side_b and side_c. Detailed rules for the naming of variables are given in the next chapter. For the time being, it is sufficient to know that Fortran normally expects a variable to be a real number if its name begins with a letter of the alphabet in the range a-h or o-z. Names beginning with i, j, k, l, m or n are expected to represent integer variables. If a variable is of a different type, such as a complex number, Fortran requires this fact to be declared explicitly in advance.

The default (list-directed) format is such that a, b and c in our example can be input from the keyboard in a form such as

> 3, 4, 5

or

> 3,4,5

or

> 3 4 5

or even with the numbers on separate lines as in

> 3(return)
> 4(return)
> 5(return)

The 'delimiter' between the numbers may be a comma, or a blank, or both, or a series of blanks, or it can be the end-of-record code signified by the 'return' or 'enter' button on most keyboards. Decimal points could be included as in

> 3.0, 4.0, 5.0

and obviously the decimal point is mandatory if the variables actually have fractional parts, as in

> 3.333, 4.667, 5

The final number must be followed by a delimiter (e.g. a blank or a 'return') otherwise the processor doesn't know you've finished. More detailed information on the format of 'list-directed' input is given in chapter 16.

Continuing with the example program, Triangle, there are two WRITE statements which display the given lengths of the sides of the triangle as a check. Then we have

> s = 0.5 * (a+b+c)   ! Semiperimeter

This is the first statement of the program which actually does anything mathematical. It is called an 'assignment statement' and it sets the real variable s to be equal to half the sum of a, b and c. (The asterisk is Fortran's multiplication sign.) Assignment statements do not begin with a keyword but are characterised by the '=' sign. In general, on the right hand side of the '=' there must be an expression which the processor can calculate. In this example the processor will just have been given numerical values for a, b and c and these will be used to give a numerical value to s when the assignment statement is executed. It wouldn't matter if the variable s already had a value: if it did, then the previous value would be replaced.

This statement illustrates another feature of Fortran syntax: the use of the exclamation mark to start a comment. The '!' and the text that follows it are treated like blanks by the processor. It is the means by which the programmer can annotate the program.

The next statement is:

areasq = s*(s-a)*(s-b)*(s-c)   ! Square of area

If a, b and c represent the lengths of the sides of a triangle then areasq is the square of the triangle's area. To finish calculating the area we just have to take the square root of areasq, and this is done by calling the function SQRT. SQRT is one of Fortran's 'intrinsic functions', i.e. the set of mathematical and other functions which are part of the language and which form a ready-made toolkit for the programmer.

But there is a potential problem: if the user of the program put in silly values for a, b and c (e.g. 1, 1 and 99, which cannot correspond to the sides of a real triangle) then the variable areasq could come out to have a negative value. Trying to take its square root would then cause the program to fail, since a negative number does not have a real square root. So, the program should first check to make sure that areasq is not negative. The check is carried out by control statements which direct the course of the program so that different statements will be executed according to specified conditions.

The control statements in our example are the IF...THEN, ELSE, and END IF statements. Their meaning should be obvious, but the details are explained in chapter 8. In the IF...THEN statement, the expression

areasq<0.0

is a 'logical expression', that is to say an expression which has not a numerical value but a logical value, i.e. is either true or false. If areasq is less than zero then this logical expression has the value 'true' and control will then pass to the statement following. If areasq is not less than zero then the logical expression has the value 'false' and control will pass down to the statement following ELSE. The END IF statement indicates the end of the blocks of conditional statements. Whatever the value of areasq, control finally passes beyond the END IF statement to the END PROGRAM statement which brings execution of the program to a halt. Note that the conditional statements following IF...THEN and ELSE have been indented to the right purely for cosmetic reasons. Leading blank spaces have no significance in Fortran syntax, but by indenting statements in this way we can make a long program considerably easier to read and understand.

The above example has been discussed in fine detail. We have encountered the statement types PROGRAM, WRITE, READ, Assignment (=), IF...THEN, ELSE, END IF and END PROGRAM. We have discussed numeric variables and the names that can be used to represent them, and used READ and WRITE statements to input and output values of real variables by list-directed formatting on the standard default i/o devices (keyboard and screen). We have encountered real and logical expressions. The real expressions

0.5 * (a+b+c)

17

and

$$s*(s-a)*(s-b)*(s-c)$$

illustrate the use of the arithmetic operators * (for multiplication), + (for addition), - (for subtraction) and brackets to make sure that things are done in the right order (s*s-a*s-b*s-c would be not be same thing at all!). Arithmetic operators in general are described in the next section.

3.3 ARITHMETIC OPERATORS

Fortran's complete list of arithmetic operators is:

**   exponentiation (raising to a power), e.g. 3**4 is equal to 81

* and /   multiplication, e.g. 5*6 is equal to 30; and division, e.g. 7.5/2.0 is equal to 3.75

+ and -   addition, e.g. 9+27 is equal to 36; and subtraction, e.g. 9-27 is equal to -18

These are 'binary operators' in the sense that they go between two numbers and produce a result which depends on the two. (But the minus sign can also be used as a 'unary' operator, applied to just one number, e.g. -b is the negative of b. The plus sign, too, can be a unary operator in the trivial sense that +10 is equal to 10.)

The arithmetic operators above can be combined with variables and constant numbers to form expressions such as b**2-4*a*c.

The descending order of the operators listed above is their order of precedence, i.e. the order in which they are normally carried out when different kinds occur in the same expression. However, brackets are used to over-ride that order of precedence. In the example just mentioned, b**2-4*a*c, b is first of all squared, then 4*a*c is evaluated, then 4*a*c is subtracted from b**2. The result is as if we had instead

$$(b**2) - (4*a*c)$$

When there are two or more operators together on the same level of precedence, the expression is evaluated left to right, i.e. 4*a*c is equivalent to (4*a)*c. With a chain of multiplications, of course, the order doesn't usually make any difference: 4*a*c is the same as 4*c*a. But in many cases the order is significant, e.g.

16/8/2	is equivalent to (16/8)/2, equal to 1
16/8*2	is equivalent to (16/8)*2, equal to 4
12-6-3	is equivalent to (12-6)-3, equal to 3

The left-to-right rule applies to all the above examples, but there is an exception in the case of the exponentiation operator. When a number of exponentiations are strung together they are evaluated from right to left: so 2.0**0.5**(-1) is equivalent to 2**(0.5**(-1)), and is equal to 4.0.

Note that 2**0.5**-1 would not be a permissible expression because the rules of Fortran do not allow two consecutive numeric operators (in this case, **-). Another limitation is that the exponentiation operator should not be used to raise a negative real quantity to a real (as opposed to integer) power: so you should not expect (-3.375)**(0.333333) to have the value -1.5. Expressions of this sort should either be avoided or should be handled using complex numbers (chapter 4).

EXERCISES 3A

3A1   Check which of these are in the Fortran character set:

   #   A $ @   %   [:   ;   >

3A2   Evaluate the following:

(i)	3**2**3	(ii)	4 + 6 / 12 * 2
(iii)	18/4/2**(-1)	(iv)	SQRT(4**3**2)
(v)	9/8*7/6*5/4*3/2	(vi)	9*8/7*6/5*4/3*2
(vii)	6-4+1	(viii)	16.0**3.0/2.0
(ix)	(-1)**0.5**(-1)	(x)	2-1**0.5**(-1)

3A3   If a, b, c, d and e are the names of real variables, write Fortran expressions for

   (i)   The average of a, b, c, d, and e
   (ii)   The root-mean-square of a, b and c
   (iii)   b, expressed as a percentage of the total of a, b, c, d and e
   (iv)   the geometric mean of a and b.

3A4   Input into a computer the example program ('Triangle') given in this chapter. Run the program and test it with different values for a, b and c. Enhance the program to make it calculate and display not only the area of the triangle but also its perimeter.

3A5   Write a program to input two numbers and to output the larger of them. The program should communicate clearly with the user, and should use only the elements of Fortran which appear in 'Triangle' (section 3.2).

3.4   NAMES AND OTHER LEXICAL TOKENS

In the discussion so far we have encountered several of what are called 'names' in Fortran terminology. These examples were as follows:

the name of a program:	Triangle
the names of variables:	a, b, c, s, areasq, area, side_a, side_b, side_c
an intrinsic function:	SQRT

Fortran also permits names for subprograms (user-written functions, subroutines and modules, covered in chapters 9, 11 and 12), for user-defined data types (chapter 14), and for certain other objects such as 'namelist' groups (chapter 16). The general rule is that names must begin with a letter and may consist of up to 31 'alphanumeric' characters. The alphanumeric characters are the letters, the digits, and the underscore.

A blank is not regarded as an alphanumeric character, so blanks may not be included in names, and nor may the other special characters listed in section 3.1.

Names are just one of the six kinds of 'lexical tokens' which Fortran syntax is built up out of. The six are:

Names   (see above)

Keywords   e.g. PROGRAM, WRITE, READ, IF, FMT, UNIT

Constants   e.g. numeric constants such as 1.0, 365 and -66.896; and character-string constants such as "Error: that is not a real triangle" (in quotes or inverted commas)

Operators   e.g. +, -, **, =, and >

Delimiters   e.g. ! and brackets (parentheses)

Statement Labels   (see chapter 10)

It is possible for names to be identical to keywords, but this is best avoided as it could obviously lead to confusion.

We have been using a particular convention for the capitalisation (i.e. upper case or lower case) of letters of the alphabet. This convention is just that - a convention - and is not obligatory within Fortran, but it is extremely important to use some sort of capitalisation convention to achieve orderly, consistent and attractive programming, particularly when teams of programmers are working together. There is nothing worse than a lengthy program in which the use of upper and lower case is arbitrary or inconsistent.

Our suggested capitalisation convention can be summarised as follows:

Upper-case: Statement keywords (such as READ)
Names of intrinsic procedures (such as SQRT)
Keywords for arguments of intrinsic procedures

Lower-case, but with an initial capital letter:

Name of a program or a program unit
Keywords for arguments of non-intrinsic procedures
Namelist group names
Derived types

Lower-case: Names of variables or of constants

Some of the terms mentioned above may not be meaningful to you at this stage, but they are listed here for the sake of completeness. You may of course choose a different convention from this: the important thing is to settle on a convention and stick to it.

3.5   FORTRAN SOURCE FORM

The Fortran 'source form', i.e. the general format according to which programs should appear, can be of two alternative kinds, i.e. 'free' or 'fixed' source form. The latter is now of historical interest only, and is summarised in note N3.2. Free source form has already been mentioned (section 2.5), and used in the examples given so far, and the details are as follows:

(a) A program is divided into records (i.e. 'lines') each up to 132 characters in length. Except as mentioned in (g) below, blank characters have no significance except to make the code more readable, and they are ignored by the processor.

(b) Normally there is one 'statement' per line. A statement may start with a keyword (such as 'PRINT') or it may be an assignment statement (assigning a value to a variable by use of the '=' sign). A statement may be preceded on the line by blank characters (i.e. it may be indented) and it may be followed by blanks. A statement may also be preceded by an integer number used as a 'statement label', a common but generally inelegant feature of Fortran programming discussed in chapter 10.

(c) Comments may be inserted after statements to guide readers of the code. A comment must always be separated from the statement by the '!' character. The '!' terminates the statement as far as the processor is concerned, and everything on that line after the '!' is treated as commentary. A line is permitted to contain only a comment, and no statement at all, if it begins with a '!'. A completely blank line will be ignored. However, it must be remembered that a '!' which occurs within character context, i.e. as part of a character string specified between quotes or apostrophes, does not start a comment.

(d) A statement may be continued from one line to the next. Continuation is indicated by having an ampersand ('&') as the last non-blank character in a line, with the effect that the subsequent line is tacked on to whatever immediately preceded the '&'.

However, a comment cannot be continued in this way: an '&' occurring within a comment has no special effect. Also, an '&' occurring in character context will not normally continue the string on the next line, i.e. it will just be taken as part of the character string, in the same way that a '!' in character context has no special effect. But, in a case where it is necessary to continue a character string to the next line, the effect can be achieved by using two '&'s, putting one at the end of the first line and the other at the beginning of the second.

In fact, it is always acceptable to put an ampersand at the beginning of the continuation line as well as at the end of the preceding line, but unless you are in character context the second ampersand is optional rather than compulsory. When an ampersand starts a continuation line it need not be the first character of the line: there may be leading blanks which the compiler will ignore.

It was mentioned above that the ampersand should be the last non-blank character on a line which is to be continued: but in fact it may be followed by a '!' and a comment except when the continuation is within character context.

(e) A statement may be continued over many lines. The only limitation is that a statement may not contain more than 2640 characters.

(f) It is possible to have more than one statement per line. The semi-colon (';')
then serves to separate one statement from the next. However, a semi-colon in
character context does not have this effect.

(g) Blanks are generally irrelevant to Fortran and they can be used generously
to make a program easy to read. However, blanks are significant in one or two
respects. They may not be embedded in lexical tokens. A keyword adjacent to
a name must be separated from it by a blank. In most double-keyword
combinations (e.g. END PROGRAM) a dividing blank is not mandatory but it
is good practice to include it. Blanks are not ignored in character context.

The following contrived examples, all legal Fortran, should make the rules clear:

```
PROGRAM                     Master                        !Version6

                            READ (*,*) indata

                            WRITE (*,*) "We're off!"

weightedsumofcubes = a * alpha**3              &
                   + b * beta**3               &
                   + c * gamma**3

remark = "When a statement is continued from one line &
&to the next, but not breaking in the middle of a &
&character string like this, it doesn't matter &
&whether or not the continuation line starts with an &
&ampersand."

x=a1 ; y=a2 ; z=a3; sum=x+y+z                  ! 4 statements, 1 line.

this = &                                       ! One statement, two lines
that

!         This & would not make the next line a comment.
```

These are a PROGRAM statement with lots of blank spaces and a comment at the end; READ and
WRITE statements with leading blanks; an assignment statement spaced by ampersands over three
lines; a character-string assignment statement spaced over five lines with pairs of ampersands; a
set of four assignment statements on one line, followed by a comment; an assignment statement
split into two lines and with a comment after the first part; and finally a statement consisting only
of a comment.

EXERCISES 3B

3B1   Which of these are valid Fortran names?

       (i) aramaic   (ii) zhq5   (iii) balance$
       (iv) p998530   (v) 99in   (vi) top_mark
       (vii) bakers dozen   (viii) baker's dozen   (ix) state_population_estimate_1997

3B2   Write a program to read in two numbers and calculate and write the magnitude of their difference as a percentage of their sum.

3B3   Write a program called 'Quad' to solve a quadratic equation which is expected to have real solutions. The coefficients in the equation are to be input, and the two solutions are to be output.

3B4   Write a program ('Mean') which will input six numbers, calculate and display their average, and calculate and display their root-mean-square deviation from that average.

Notes

N3.1   A BLANK AFTER 'END'

In a statement like

    END PROGRAM Triangle

the blank between END and PROGRAM is not strictly necessary, i.e.

    ENDPROGRAM Triangle

would be equally valid. This is the case also for other suffixed END statements which will be met later, such as END SUBROUTINE. However, the name Triangle is a separate lexical token from the keyword END PROGRAM, and so the space immediately before Triangle is necessary.

N3.2   FIXED SOURCE FORM

There is an alternative to the source form described in section 3.5 above, namely 'fixed' source form which was the usual form in earlier versions of Fortran and is therefore retained in Fortran 90 for the sake of backward compatibility. Fixed source form originated when programs were stored on 80-column punched cards, of which the first 72 columns could be used for Fortran. So, in fixed source form each line must contain 72 characters.

In fixed source form, the first six character positions in each line are reserved for the following special purposes:

(i) If the first character is 'C' or '*', the whole line is taken as a comment.

(ii) Characters 1 to 5 may contain an integer statement label (see chapter 10).

(iii) The sixth character is normally blank. A continuation line is indicated by having any non-blank character (other than zero) in sixth position.

Fortran keywords, names, etc. would normally follow after the sixth character. Therefore, in fixed source form, each line may only contain 66 characters of actual code.

Chapter 4

INTRINSIC DATA TYPES

Fortran 90 can deal with data items of many different types: in fact with an indefinite range of data types, since there is a facility for 'derived' (or 'user-defined') data types constructed by the programmer. Derived data types will be explained in chapter 14. Here we will cover the 'intrinsic' data types, i.e. the basic kinds of data defined as part of the Fortran language. The intrinsic types are INTEGER, REAL, COMPLEX, LOGICAL and CHARACTER. This chapter also introduces the simple but invaluable IF statement, and the intrinsic functions ABS, AIMAG, CMPLX, COS, EXP, HUGE, INT, LOG, LOG10, MOD, SIN, REAL, and TRIM.

4.1   INTEGERS

As their name implies, integers in Fortran are the whole numbers 0, 1, 2, 3, 4... and including the negatives -1, -2, -3, ...

Examples of integer constants are

        137
        +365 (the + sign is unnecessary but may be included)
        -9
        0
        299792458

Constant integers may appear explicitly in programs. Integers may alternatively be represented by names. The usual convention is to represent an integer by a name beginning with a letter in the range i-n. Unless otherwise specified (by a type declaration statement, section 4.3 and chapter 13) variables with names like

        istructure
        nyear
        j57
        izero
        mlight
        ides_april

will be therefore be taken by Fortran 90 to be integers.

Arithmetic can be done with integers using the arithmetic operators introduced in chapter 3. If i2=2 and i3=3,

i2**13	has the value 8
i2*i3	has the value 6
i2+i3	has the value 5
i2-i3	has the value -1

and if

i4 = i2/i3   then it has the value 0

The final example arises because of the way the ratio of two integers is interpreted: the exact ratio is calculated, then the fractional part of it is discarded if an integral result is required. Thus, 365/7 has the value 52. Where negative numbers are concerned, the ratio is cut back towards zero, i.e. -365/7 has the value -52. If we had an assignment statement such as

r = i2/i3

with i2 and i3 as above, and r being a real variable, the result would still be zero, because the expression i2/i3 is first interpreted as an integer-valued expression; assigning an integer value to a real variable is something explained in section 4.2.

Fortran has an intrinsic function, MOD, which can be very useful in integer arithmetic. MOD(j,k) is the value of j modulo k, i.e. the remainder when j is divided by k. To be more precise,

MOD(j,k)   is equivalent to   j - ((j/k)*k)

where j/k is the integer quotient calculated according to the rule mentioned earlier. Thus

MOD(365,7)	has the value 1
MOD(-365,7)	has the value -1
MOD(9,5)	has the value 4

Overleaf is an example of a program using the MOD function.

```
PROGRAM Miles

!         Display information and input a number
          WRITE (*,*) "This program converts a large number of inches &
                  &into miles, yards and inches."                  "
          WRITE (*,*) " Type in a distance in inches: "
          READ  (*,*) inches

!         Calculation
          inch   =   MOD(inches, 36)
          nyards =   inches/36
          nyard  =   MOD(nyards, 1760)
          mile   =   nyards/1760

!         Output the results
          WRITE (*,*) "The result is:"
          IF (mile>0)  WRITE (*,*) mile," miles"
          IF (nyard>0) WRITE (*,*) nyard," yards"
          IF (inch>0)  WRITE (*,*) inch, " inches"

          END PROGRAM Miles
```

This program uses statements of the kind introduced in section 3.2, except for the IF statements. An IF statement is simply a conditional form of some other single statement: the keyword IF is followed by a bracketed logical expression, followed by something else (in the above examples, WRITE) which will be executed only if the logical expression is true. Note that an IF statement is not quite the same thing as an IF...THEN construction. Using IF...THEN, we could write

```
IF (miles>0) THEN
          WRITE (*,*) miles, " miles"
END IF
```

but in a case like this, where only one statement is contingent on the IF, it can be put into one IF statement as in the program above.

One may ask how large an integer may be in Fortran. Obviously a finite processor cannot cope with all of the infinite mathematical set of integers. In fact the maximum-sized integer is not specified by the Fortran 90 standard but will depend on the processor. It may therefore be important within the running of a program to check what the processor's largest permissible integer is. For this purpose there is an intrinsic inquiry function HUGE. If i is any variable of type integer, then HUGE(i) returns with the largest integer number representable in the processor. (It doesn't really matter what the value of i is.) For example, the statement

IF (ABS(nyears)>HUGE(1)/100) THEN CALL Error

will transfer control to a subprogram called 'Error' if the variable nyears gets within two orders of magnitude of the largest permissible integer. The keyword 'CALL' is explained in chapter 9. ABS is an intrinsic function that calculates the absolute value of its argument, i.e. a positive number is unchanged but a negative one is changed in sign to become positive. As well as HUGE there is another enquiry function, RANGE, which will return the maximum number of digits allowed. In other words, RANGE(i) = INT(LOG10(HUGE(i))), LOG10 being an intrinsic function calculating the logarithm (to base 10) of its argument, and the function INT being as mentioned in section 4.2 below.

4.2   REAL NUMBERS

'Real' numbers are positive or negative numbers not restricted to integral values, in general having fractional parts. They are sometimes called 'floating point' numbers, and are usually expressed in decimal notation. Real numbers may appear in programs explicitly (i.e. as 'real literal constants') in forms such as:

```
-78.915443
1877724.
+3.000
4.65E-9
-0.3E12
-.1E+6
666E6
```

where the last four examples include the notation of the 'exponent letter' E followed by a power of ten, positive or negative, which is to multiply the number. The last example is therefore equal to 666 million. Note that a + sign is always optional both with the number itself (the 'significand') and with the exponent. A decimal point should always appear somewhere unless there is an exponent letter: otherwise the processor could not distinguish a real number from an integer.

Real variables should normally be represented by names beginning with a letter in the range a-h or o-z.

It is easy to convert integers into the corresponding real numbers, and vice versa, bearing in mind that when a real number is converted into an integer the fractional part will be discarded. One method of conversion is just to use an assignment statement such as

r = i

and then if i=1, r will be set equal to 1.0. With

i = r

we would get i=9 if r=9.9. This works because, according to Fortran's rules for assignment statements, type conversion will automatically take place between real and integer numbers if a variable of one type is set equal to an expression of the other type. More elegantly, there is an intrinsic function INT which always replaces a real argument by the corresponding integer: so the above example is shorthand for

$$i = INT(r)$$

The function INT may of course be combined into expressions, as in

$$ksum = INT(radius\_1) + INT(radius\_2)$$

and you should perceive that this is not necessarily equal to

$$ksum = INT(radius\_1 + radius\_2)$$

To convert integers into real numbers, Fortran has an intrinsic function REAL, and in the example above r=i is exactly equivalent to

$$r = REAL(i)$$

In practice the function REAL is not often needed in Fortran, since implicit type conversion will happen anyway if an integer appears in a context demanding a real number. However, picking up an example from section 4.1, the REAL function is important in a statement such as

$$r = REAL(i2)/REAL(i3)$$

which is not equivalent to r=i2/i3.

It is easy to fall into confusion about how an expression is evaluated if it includes both real and integer numbers. There is a very important rule concerning the effect of a binary arithmetic operator (+, -, *, /, or **) on data of real and/or integer types. Any such operator comes between two 'operands'. That's why it's called 'binary'. The rule is that if both operands are integers, the result is an integer, but if one or both of the operands is real then the result is real. So if we have integers i2=2 and i3=3 as in our earlier example,

$$i2**13$$

is an integer. Because this rule applies to expressions as well as variables,

$$i2*(i2**i3)$$

is also an integer. On the other hand,

$$REAL(i2)/i3$$

is real, because one of the operands is real, and this would be exactly equivalent to i2/REAL(i3)

With an expression like

r1 / i2 / i3

care is needed because the result may depend on the order in which the divisions occur. In fact, because of the left-to-right rule for operators of the same precedence (section 3.3), this statement is equivalent to

(r1 / i2) / i3

The expression in brackets is real (because one of its operands is real) and then the whole expression is real because the first operand of the second division is a real expression. However, if we had

r1 / (i2 / i3)

then the second division would operate first, and would give an integer result because both of its operands are integers. Subsequently the first division, operating between a real variable and an integer expression, would give a real result to the expression as a whole. So, (r1/i2)/i3 and r1/(i2/i3) are both expressions of real type, but of course they have different values.

The lesson to learn from this is that for trouble-free code you should make liberal use of brackets to simplify complicated expressions, and use the REAL and INT functions explicitly, allowing implicit type conversions to occur only in the simplest cases.

EXERCISES 4A

4A1   What are the values of the following integer expressions, if n=-8?

(i)	n**2-2	(ii)	n/2/2	(iii)	MOD(42,n+11)
(iv)	MOD(n,-3)	(v)	ABS(n**3-n)	(vi)	2**n

4A2   Express as ordinary decimal numbers

(i)	666E-3	(ii)	0.024E6	(iii)	1E+1

and use the exponent letter ('E') notation to express the following compactly as Fortran real constants:

(iv)	2700000000.0	(v)	0.0000101	(vi)	10^{-16}

4A3   What are the values of the following real-number expressions, if s=-9.0 and t=14.8?

     (i)   s+t/2-1   (ii)   s**2+t   (iii)   ABS(s+t)
     (iv)   MOD(s,t)   (v)   MOD(t,s)   (vi)   n**2/s, with n=-8
     (vii)   2.0**n, with n=-2

4A4   Write a program to convert a sum of British currency expressed in pounds and new pence to the old-style pounds, shillings and old pence (a pound contained 20 shillings, each of 12 old pence).

4.3   SIMPLE FORM OF THE TYPE DECLARATION STATEMENT

It has been said that integer numbers are represented by variables whose names start with the letters i, j, k, l, m and n, and real numbers by variables starting with other letters of the alphabet. However, this rule can be overridden by a 'type declaration statement' which can take forms like

        REAL :: negentropy
        REAL :: joules, kelvin_temp, energy
        INTEGER :: days, weeks, months

i.e. the keyword REAL or INTEGER, followed by a double colon, followed by a list of one or more names. The variables named are thereby declared to be of real or integer type whatever their initial letters might be.

These REAL and INTEGER statements fall into a special and very important class known as 'nonexecutable' or 'declaration' statements. They are used to define the nature of data objects once and for all when the program is compiled, but do not change anything during execution. Declaration statements must occur at the very beginning of the program (or subprogram, chapter 9) immediately after the PROGRAM statement. Declaration statements may not be mixed up with executable statements.

4.4   KINDS OF REAL NUMBERS

In fact real numbers in Fortran 90 are a little more complicated than the discussion in section 4.2 suggests. The language actually allows for at least two different kinds of real numbers, with different degrees of precision. The first, sometimes called 'default precision', is the sort of real number we have been using so far: it provides ample precision for most calculations and is provided automatically by the processor if the programmer does not explicitly demand still higher precision. The second kind of real number, providing more accuracy, is sometimes called 'double precision' because on many processors it corresponds to doubling the number of bytes used to store a real number (e.g. from 4 to 8 bytes). Double-precision constants can be set up by using a D instead of an E in the exponent-letter notation, as in the examples

```
4.65D-9
-0.3D12
-.1D+6
666D6
0.D0
```

The names of double-precision variables should be declared by means of the REAL statement, the keyword being followed by the specification of a parameter called KIND. For example, this statement could set up five double-precision numbers:

```
REAL(KIND=2) :: splithair, x, y, z, difference
```

It might be possible to use other values of KIND for numbers of still greater precision. However, the actual values of KIND that might be valid may vary from one processor to another. Further details about managing high-precision numbers are deferred to the next chapter.

4.5   COMPLEX NUMBERS

Fortran allows for complex numbers as long as the names of complex variables are declared by statements like

```
COMPLEX :: z1, z2, z3, z4
COMPLEX :: omega
COMPLEX :: i
```

Complex constants can be specified by the usual mathematical notation of giving, in brackets, the real part followed by the imaginary part. Examples are

```
z1 = (3.756, 0.051)
z2 = z1**2 - (0.0, 1.0)
z3 = SQRT(z2) - (0.0, -1.0)
omega = (-1.0, 0.0)**(1.0/3.0)
i = (0.0, 1.0)
```

The brackets are needed even in a case like

```
i = SQRT((-1.0,0.0))
```

because, here, one pair of brackets is needed to set apart the argument of the SQRT function and another to contain the parts of the complex number.

As the above examples show, complex numbers may be combined in expressions using the usual arithmetic operators. The SQRT function works with a complex argument: if the argument is complex, so is the result. In Fortran, the following intrinsic functions are either real functions of real arguments or complex functions of complex arguments, according to the argument types:

SQRT	Square root
SIN	Sine
COS	Cosine
EXP	Exponential function
LOG	Natural logarithm (i.e. base e)

The trigonometrical functions measure angles in radians. The complex SQRT function normally yields the principal value with positive real part, and the complex LOG function yields the principal value with imaginary part between $+\pi$ and $-\pi$. There is one intrinsic function which always has to have a complex argument and a complex value:

CONJG	Complex conjugate

The following functions may have complex arguments but give real or integer values:

REAL	Real part
INT	Real part, truncated to an integer
AIMAG	Imaginary part
ABS	Absolute value

Note that if z is complex, INT(z) is the same as INT(REAL(z)), and that AIMAG((1.0,2.0)) is equal to 2.0, not (0.0,2.0). The function LOG10, which was mentioned briefly in section 4.1 and gives a base-10 logarithm, is not permitted to have a complex argument.

Finally there is a function, CMPLX, which generally has two real arguments and a complex value. It simply forms a complex number, the real and imaginary parts respectively being given as arguments. CMPLX is discussed further in section 5.3.

It is possible to mix complex, real and integer data in Fortran expressions built up out of the arithmetic operators. When each operator takes effect, if either operand is complex then the result of that operation is complex. This is just an extension of what happens with real and integer data, where an operation gives a real result if either operand is real.

'Logical' data is a non-numeric data type which we have already encountered indirectly: for example, the logical expression in brackets within the statement

IF (miles>0) THEN

In general we may have constants, variables and expressions of logical type. They have only two possible values, true and false, and can be thought of as 'bits' of information like binary digits. The names of logical variables must be declared initially using the LOGICAL type declaration statement, e.g.

LOGICAL :: error_flag
LOGICAL :: checksum, kexists, ifmiles

A statement like

ifmiles = miles>0

is a valid assignment statement, setting the logical variable ifmiles to be true or false according to whether or not the integer miles is greater than zero. The IF statement given earlier could then take the form

IF (ifmiles) THEN

Logical constants are written as either '.TRUE.' or '.FALSE.', the surrounding dots being an essential part of the syntax. Logical constants could crop up in code like

```
LOGICAL :: condition_1, condition_2
INTEGER :: j, k
READ (*,*) j, k
condition_1 = .TRUE.   ;   condition_2 = .TRUE.
IF (j>k) condition_1=.FALSE.
IF (k>0) condition_2=.FALSE.
IF (ABS(j+k)>0) condition_1=condition_2
```

There is a set of special operators available for use on logical variables only, namely:

.NOT.	Negation
.AND.	And
.OR.	Or

.EQV.	Logical equivalence
.NEQV.	Logical inequivalence

.NOT. is a unary operator which flips the value of whatever logical quantity follows it. Thus, if checksum is a logical variable, .NOT.checksum has the value .FALSE. if checksum has the value .TRUE., and vice versa. Obviously, .NOT..TRUE. is equal to .FALSE. and .NOT..FALSE. is equal to .TRUE.

The other operators in the list above give results depending on the relationship between two items of logical data. They are binary operators, and stand between the two logical quantities to which they relate. Their meanings are summarised by the following table, with p and q representing logical variables (or logical constants or expressions).

p	q	p.AND.q	p.OR.q	p.EQV.Q	p.NEQV.q
T	T	T	T	T	F
T	F	F	T	F	T
F	T	F	T	F	T
F	F	F	F	T	F

In this table T stands for .TRUE. and F stands for .FALSE. Note that a programmer may avoid the rather clumsy constants .TRUE. and .FALSE. by a declaration like

LOGICAL, PARAMETER :: T=.TRUE., F=.FALSE.

which sets up named logical constants called T and F instead!

The logical operators discussed above may be combined to form more complicated logical expressions like

q.AND..NOT.p.NEQV.q.OR.r

In evaluating such an expression the operators have an order of precedence. .NOT. comes before .AND., which comes before .OR., which comes before .EQV. or .NEQV. That's why they were listed in that order earlier. So, the above example is equivalent to

(q.AND.(.NOT.p)).NEQV.(q.OR.r)

Since .EQV. and .NEQV. have the same level of priority, an expression like

q.EQV.p.NEQV.r.EQV.s

could be ambiguous: but then in a case like this Fortran works from left to right, so it is equivalent to

((q.EQV.p).NEQV.r).EQV.s

Brackets may always be used to over-ride the normal order of precedence, as for the arithmetic operators, and even when brackets are not strictly necessary the programmer should use them to make the meaning of an expression as clear as possible. If brackets are always used, it is unnecessary to memorise the order of precedence!

In addition to the operators discussed above, which operate on logical-type data and produce logical values, there are 'relational' operators which act on numerical data (and, in some cases, character strings) to produce logical values. In fact one or two of these have already been met: in section 3.2 we used the expression areasq<0.0, and in section 4.1 we used expressions such as miles>0. The full set of relational operators that can be used between numerical data are

==	Equal
/=	Not equal
<	Less than
<=	Less than or equals
>	Greater than
>=	Greater than or equals

It is important to realise that these operators, although used to form logical expressions, cannot be used between logical data items. If p and q are logical, we must use p.EQV.q rather than p==q. Also, the double equals sign (==) has a meaning quite different from the single equals sign (=). The = is used in assignment statements, and changes the value of whatever is on the left hand side. The == just compares the existing values of the objects on either side of it, and changes neither.

Using both sorts of relational operator we can form quite complicated logical expressions, as in

IF (((j/=k).AND.(m>k)).EQV.((j+m)==k)) THEN

where j, k and m are integers. Because Fortran has a default order of precedence for all operators it is often possible to get away without all the brackets: the relational operators take precedence over the logical operators, and arithmetic operators take precedence over both, so the above statement is equivalent to

IF (j/=k.AND.m>k.EQV.j+m==k) THEN

but, as said before, the best practice is always to use brackets freely to make the meaning of the code as clear as possible.

4.7   CHARACTERS AND STRINGS

So far we have met the numeric data types INTEGER, REAL and COMPLEX, and the non-numeric type LOGICAL. The next data type for us to deal with is CHARACTER data.

'Character constants' and 'character variables' are not quite the same things as 'characters'. A character is an explicit individual symbol such as a letter of the alphabet. Characters can be drawn from the list given at the beginning of chapter 3, i.e. from the letters, the decimal digits, the underscore, and 21 special characters. In addition, characters could in principle include other more exotic symbols: the total number of permissible different characters is processor-dependent. Usually, upper- and lower-case letters are regarded as distinct characters.

A character constant is an explicit 'string' of characters. For example, "aeiou" is a character constant. In fact we have already met character constants: early in the previous chapter we used "What is your name?", which is a character constant or character string. A character string might be only one character in length; in fact it might have zero length, i.e. have no characters in it at all. In Fortran, character constants are given between a pair of quotes or apostrophes, although in this book we will generally stick to quotes for this purpose.

We can also have character variables, i.e. names which could represent arbitrary characters or strings of characters. We will often use the common term 'character string, or just 'string', to denote any character variable or character constant.

Here is a simple example of how character strings can be manipulated within a program:

```
soft = "aei"
hard = "ou"
vowels = soft//hard
WRITE (*,*) vowels
```

which will yield the output

```
aeiou
```

In this example there are three character variables: soft, hard and vowels. These words are being used as the names of character strings just as they could have been used as the names of numeric variables. The first two statements set the variables soft and hard to be equal to the constants "aei" and "ou". The third statement sets the variable vowels to be the 'concatenation' of soft and hard.

The double-slash (//) is the concatenation operator, making a single longer string out of the two strings on either side of it. The concatenation operator can be used with character variables or with character constants: thus

vowels = "aei"//"ou"

or

vowels = "aei"//hard

or

vowels = soft//"ou"

would all have exactly the same effect as vowels = soft//hard in the above example.

The 'length' of a character string is the number of characters in it (including blanks, which are significant in this context). Strings may obviously have various lengths. Soft, hard and vowels, in the above example, have lengths of 3, 2 and 5 respectively. Before a character variable is used, it must be declared to be of character type: otherwise the name will be assumed to represent a real or integer number. At the same time its length should normally be specified. The example above should therefore be preceded by type declaration statements of the form

```
CHARACTER (3) :: soft
CHARACTER (2) :: hard
CHARACTER (5) :: vowels
```

the lengths of the strings being in brackets after the keyword CHARACTER. The lengths of character variables are, of course, unrelated to the lengths of their names.

In practice we may not know in advance the lengths of character variables, and the declaration statements will need to allow for the maximum number of significant characters that the variable might contain. For example:

```
CHARACTER (20) :: forename, surname
CHARACTER (41) :: name
READ (*,*) "What is your first name?", forename
READ (*,*) "What is your surname?", surname
name = TRIM(forename)//" "//TRIM(surname)
WRITE (*,*) "Thank you.  You are ", TRIM(name)
```

The READ statements here will fill the strings forename and surname with the names which are input, but there will be blank spaces at the ends to make up 20 characters for each. TRIM is an intrinsic Fortran function which takes any string and returns it with trailing blanks removed. The variable 'name' will contain the person's forename and surname with one blank space between them, and with trailing blanks to make up its full length of 41 characters. The WRITE statement will output 'name' without the trailing blanks.

EXERCISES 4B

4B1   Which of these are legal Fortran constants? What are their types?

(i)	.	(ii)	3.	(iii)	3.1		
(iv)	31	(v)	0.	(vi)	+2		
(vii)	-E18	(viii)	'ACHAR(61)'	(ix)	3 500		
(x)	4,800,000	(xi)	"X or Y"	(xii)	"X"//"Y"		
(xiii)	4.8E6	(xiv)	5000E-3	(xv)	"VAT 69"		
(xvi)	6.6_BIG	(xvii)	(1,-1)	(xviii)	007		
(xix)	1E	(xx)	-630958813365				

4B2   Write type declaration statements to declare

(i)   Three real variables called power1, power2 and creeper
(ii)   Two integers called kappa and kappa_prime
(iii)   A KIND=3 real variable called finetune
(iv)   Two strings, each of 4 characters, called v and w

4B3   Using a type declaration statement and three assignment statements, set up complex variables called c1, c2 and c3, and give them the values of the cube roots of -2.

4B4   Write a program to solve a quadratic equation (with real coefficients) allowing for complex roots.

4B5   If gum1 and gum2 are logical variables both with the value .TRUE., what are the values of

(i)   gum1.NEQV.gum2.EQV..NOT.gum1
(ii)   (gum1.NEQV.gum2).EQV..NOT.gum1
(iii)   gum1.OR..NOT.gum2.NEQV.gum1.AND.gum2
(iv)   What is the value of (iii) above if gum1 is .TRUE. and gum2 is .FALSE.?

4B6   Write a Fortran logical expression depending on five integers n1, n2, m1, m2 and k, which will be true if (and only if) the absolute magnitude of the difference between n1 and n2 exceeds that between m1 and m2 by at least the magnitude of k.

4B7   Write a program to read in two strings of 12 characters each and to write out the first if the second is "satisfactory". (If it isn't, write out a message saying so.)

4B8   Write a program to read four real numbers, taken to be the lengths of the sides of a trapezium in cyclic order, and calculate and write out the area of the trapezium.

4B9   With a distance to be travelled being input, produce a table of the journey times for average speeds ranging from 40 to 140 kph (in steps of 10 kph).

4B10   Calculate and display the average of an arbitrary number of input numbers.

N4.1   THE DOUBLE COLON

In type declaration statements we show a double colon between the type keyword and the list of variables. In fact the double colon is optional except in more complicated cases (involving 'attribute specifiers') which will be covered in chapter 13. Nevertheless it is best to use the double colon as a general rule, because it is never wrong to do so and it is distinctive of the type declaration statement.

N4.2   DOUBLE PRECISION

The statement

> REAL(KIND=2) :: splithair, x, y, z, difference

could be written as

> DOUBLE PRECISION :: splithair, x, y, z, difference

In general, DOUBLE PRECISION (or DOUBLEPRECISION) specifies real numbers having a precision greater than the processor's default real kind. DOUBLEPRECISION is equivalent to REAL(KIND=KIND(0.D0)), in terms of the KIND function explained in chapter 5.

N4.3   ALTERNATIVE FORMS OF THE RELATIONAL OPERATORS

The operators ==, /=, <, <=, >, and >= have also the synonymous forms .EQ., .NE., .LT., .LE., .GT., and .GE. respectively.

N4.4   LEN

In a character type declaration statement, the string length may be preceded by "LEN=" as in

> CHARACTER (LEN=5) :: vowels

Chapter 5

SOME INTRINSIC PROCEDURES

'Intrinsic procedures' are facilities provided as a ready-coded adjunct to Fortran and they can be used to carry out a number of commonly-needed tasks and calculations. They include many standard mathematical functions, of which we have already met SQRT, SIN, COS, EXP, LOG and LOG10. Most Fortran intrinsic procedures are 'functions', and a function is invoked simply by a reference to the function name. A function takes on a certain value depending on the argument (or arguments) appearing in brackets after it. Besides the functions, a few intrinsic procedures are 'subroutines', invoked by means of a special keyword, CALL.

5.1 AN INTRINSIC SUBROUTINE

An example of an intrinsic subroutine is DATE_AND_TIME, which can be called by the statement

```
         CALL DATE_AND_TIME                                   &
                 (COUNT=nticks, MSECOND=millisecs,            &
                 SECOND=nsecs, MINUTE=nmins, HOUR=nhours,     &
                 DAY=nday, MONTH=nmonth, YEAR=nyear,          &
                 ZONE=minadvance, ALL=list)
```

This has ten arguments, indicated by the keywords ALL, COUNT, etc., and the effect of this call is to set the integer variables list, nticks, millisecs, etc. to values which will tell the program what the time and date are at the moment the statement is executed. Note that the names nticks, millisecs, nsecs, etc. are arbitrary, and any names for integer variables could be inserted in their place; but COUNT, MSECOND, etc. are Fortran argument keywords which cannot be changed. The advantage of the argument keywords is that they can appear in any order and they need not all be present. For example, we could have a much simpler statement like

```
         CALL DATE_AND_TIME(MONTH=k1, DAY=k2)
```

if we just want to know the month and day. As the keywords suggest, the DATE_AND_TIME subroutine yields the local time and date in milliseconds, seconds, minutes, hours, days in the month, months in the year, and years according to the Gregorian calendar. ZONE gives the number of minutes that local time is in advance of Coordinated Universal Time. COUNT provides a processor-dependent 'stopwatch'. The keyword ALL can provide a neat way of getting all the information of the other keywords: the corresponding argument, which was called "list" above,

43

must be an array with nine elements and would be filled with the values COUNT, MSECOND, etc. in that order. Arrays are explained in chapter 7.

A call to DATE_AND_TIME can be a statement by itself, as in the above examples, or it can be subsidiary to something like an IF statement as in

IF (convergence) CALL DATE_AND_TIME(MSECOND=intime)

Incidentally, a piece of code like

CALL DATE_AND_TIME(ZONE=minutes) ; longitude=minutes/4

could give a very rough indication of where the processor is!

5.2   MATHEMATICAL FUNCTIONS

Fortran's numerous intrinsic functions can be divided into several categories, one being the mathematical functions. A complete list of these follows. The letter X is used to represent the argument: in fact X serves optionally as an argument keyword, although there is nothing to be gained by using an argument keyword when a function has only one argument.

Real or complex argument, and result of the same type:

SQRT(X)	Square root
SIN(X)	Sine
COS(X)	Cosine
EXP(X)	Exponential (power of e)
LOG(X)	Natural logarithm

Real argument and real result:

LOG10(X)	Logarithm to base 10
TAN(X)	Tangent
SINH(X)	Hyperbolic sine
COSH(X)	Hyperbolic cosine
TANH(X)	Hyperbolic tangent
ASIN(X)	Inverse sine (between $\pm\pi/2$)
ACOS(X)	Inverse cosine (from 0 to π)
ATAN(X)	Inverse tangent (between $\pm\pi/2$)
ATAN2(Y,X)	Inverse tangent (in range $\pm\pi$)

The first group (SQRT, SIN, COS, EXP, and LOG) may have either real or complex arguments, and the result of the function will be of the same kind as the argument. So, SQRT((-1.0, 0.0)) is equal to (0.0, 1.0), and in keyword notation the same thing is SQRT(X=(-1.0, 0.0)). The functions SQRT and LOG are not allowed to have a negative real argument, and the argument of LOG may never be zero.

The second group listed (LOG10, TAN, SINH, COSH, TANH, ASIN, ACOS, ATAN, and ATAN2) are all restricted to real arguments such that the function values will be real and finite. Angles are always taken to be in radians, not degrees.

The last function, ATAN2, is unusual in having two arguments. In effect it is very similar to ATAN, but its two arguments can be regarded as the coordinates of a point of which ATAN2 is the bearing and which can lie in the full angular range between $\pm\pi$. Another way of saying this is that ATAN2(y, x) is the 'argument', in the mathematical sense, of the complex number (x, y). In a statement like

$$\text{bearing} = \text{halfpi} + \text{ATAN2(to\_north, to\_east)}$$

the arguments of ATAN2 must be in the correct order to avoid ambiguity and they are called 'positional' arguments. Alternatively, using keyword arguments identified by X and Y,

$$\text{bearing} = \text{halfpi} + \text{ATAN2(Y=to\_north, X=to\_east)}$$

and

$$\text{bearing} = \text{halfpi} + \text{ATAN2(X=to\_east, Y=to\_north)}$$

are equivalent to one another and to the previous example. All Fortran intrinsic functions can be used with keyword arguments. In the remainder of this book, keywords will usually be used whenever a function has two or more arguments that have to be distinguished from one another, but will be omitted when there can only be one argument.

5.3 NUMERIC FUNCTIONS

The 'numeric' functions are a group that carry out simple manipulations of numbers. They include the following, introduced in the previous chapter:

ABS(A)	Absolute value of A (argument of any numeric type)
AIMAG(Z)	Imaginary part of Z (complex argument)
CMPLX(X,Y,KIND)	Form complex number (real or integer arguments X and Y)

INT(A,KIND)	The fractional part of A is removed, giving the integer nearest to A whose magnitude does not exceed the magnitude of A. (Argument of any numeric type, but INT(A) = INT(REAL(A)) if A is integer or complex.)
MOD(A,P)	Remainder if P is repeatedly subtracted from A (real or integer arguments A and P)
REAL(A,KIND)	Converts A to real type (argument of any numeric type)

Most of these will require no further explanation. The function MOD may have either real or integer arguments and the result is of the same type as the argument A. The function REAL can be used to extract the real part of a complex number, or to convert an integer into real type. (This is a different usage of the word REAL from that in a type declaration statement.) The KIND argument is always optional and if present it can specify a non-default kind parameter for the result's type (see section 4.4 for non-default real numbers). For example we could have

$$x = REAL(A=number, KIND=k)$$

and in this example "number" is an integer variable being converted to a real number (x) with a KIND parameter given by the variable k. The REAL function could be used to convert between real types, as in

$$xhigh = REAL(A=xlow, KIND=2)$$

CMPLX can be used to form a complex number as in

$$z = CMPLX(X=horiz, Y=vert)$$

or as in

$$zhigh = CMPLX(X=zlow, KIND=2)$$

converting a complex number from one KIND to another. In short, X and Y may be integer or real, and X may be complex if Y is absent. The other numeric intrinsic functions are:

AINT(A, KIND)	Truncation of A to a whole number (similar to INT, but with real A and real result)
ANINT(A, KIND)	Nearest whole number to A (real A and real result)
CEILING(A)	Nearest integer not less than A (real A but integer result)
CONJG(Z)	Complex conjugate of X (complex argument and result)

46

DIM(X, Y)	Difference (unsigned) between X and Y (X, Y and the result must all be real or all integer)
FLOOR(A)	Nearest integer not greater than A (real A but integer result)
MAX(A1,A2,A3...)	Highest number (indefinite number of arguments)
MIN(A1,A2,A3...)	Lowest number (indefinite number of arguments)
MODULO(A,P)	A modulo P
NINT(A,KIND)	Nearest integer to A (real A but integer result)
SIGN(A,B)	Gives the first argument the sign of the second

AINT simply removes the fractional part of a real number, and ANINT does a very similar job but goes to the nearest whole real number; so AINT(-1.7)=-1.0, AINT(-0.7)=0.0, and AINT(1.7)=1.0, but ANINT(1.7)=2.0.

The CEILING function is very similar, but its result is of integer type: CEILING(A) gives the integer immediately above A in value, i.e. CEILING(1.3)=2 and CEILING(-5.8)=-5.

The function CONJG must have a complex argument and its result is the complex conjugate of it. The DIM function must have two arguments, and they can be either both real or both integer.

FLOOR is another function along the lines of CEILING. The argument of FLOOR must be real, and its result is the integer immediately below. Consequently, if x is any number with a fractional part, FLOOR(x) is equal to CEILING(x)-1. If x has no fractional part, i.e. if REAL(INT(x)) is equal to x, then FLOOR(x) and CEILING(x) are both equal to INT(X).

MAX and MIN are very useful functions which may have any number of arguments; the arguments may be real or integer, but not a mixture of the two types. The result is simply the largest (MAX) or smallest (MIN) of the arguments, i.e. MIN(-9, -5, 0, 2) is -9.

MODULO is subtly different from MOD, the distinction being relevant if either argument is negative. To be precise,

$$MODULO(A,P) \quad = \quad A-P*FLOOR(REAL(A)/REAL(P))$$

whereas

$$MOD(A,P) \text{ is } A-P*INT((A/P)$$

The final two functions listed above, NINT and SIGN, have real or integer arguments and the result is of the same type as the arguments.

47

The precision of real number arithmetic, and the maximum and minimum sizes of real numbers, depend on the processor. To monitor and manage precision, Fortran provides a number of utility functions. We have already mentioned the HUGE function in relation to integers, but real numbers are unfortunately more complicated. The functions listed below are available, X standing for a real argument.

HUGE(X)	Largest representable real number.
PRECISION(X)	An integer equal to the maximum decimal precision, i.e. the maximum number of significant figures.
TINY(X)	Smallest representable non-zero positive number.
RANGE(X)	An integer equal to the order of magnitude of the largest representable number or, if greater, of the inverse of the smallest. So, RANGE(X) is equal to the greater of INT(LOG10(HUGE(X))) and INT(-LOG10(TINY(X))).
EPSILON(X)	A positive real number almost negligible in comparison with unity, convenient when you simply want to use as small a number as the processor will support (e.g. for numerical differentiation).

Different kinds of real number are distinguished by the KIND parameter which we have already encountered. It is a parameter that may be specified in a type declaration statement (see section 4.4 and chapter 13) and it must have a non-negative integer value. When a real constant appears, the KIND parameter may follow the value after an underscore, as in

        -78.915443_normal
        1877724._quad
        4.65E-9_hiprec

where normal, quad and hiprec are named constants given previously in type declaration statements (with the PARAMETER attribute, chapter 13) and having values corresponding to KIND parameters valid for this processor.

The KIND parameter could alternatively be given explicitly, as in

        -78.915443_2

but this sort of code is unsafe as it may not be portable between processors: the actual values of the KIND parameters are not laid down in Fortran. The best thing to do is to use a special intrinsic function, KIND(X), which returns the value of the KIND parameter for the number X. The default KIND parameter is given by, say, KIND(0.0). Real numbers of higher precision can always be specified by a KIND parameter defined by, say,

INTEGER, PARAMETER :: hiprec = KIND(0.0D0)

where 0.0D0 is a 'double precision' number as in section 4.4. It is important to understand that the word KIND can be used in three different ways: as a parameter when real data is declared, as an argument keyword in certain intrinsic functions, and as the name of a particular intrinsic function. Examples of the three sorts of use are the statements

REAL (KIND=hiprec) :: sensitivity
q = REAL(A=k, KIND=2) - AINT(A=1.0, KIND=2)
IF (KIND(r).NE.2) THEN

Another example will be given at the end of this section. In addition to KIND, there is another intrinsic function provided to help control the use of real numbers of different kinds. It is the function SELECTED_REAL_KIND(P,R), which returns an integer equal to the minimum KIND value used by the processor for real numbers of a given precision and range. The argument P is the required decimal precision, and R is the required exponent range, and it is not necessary for both arguments to be present. SELECTED_REAL_KIND could be used in a type declaration statement (chapter 13) such as

INTEGER, PARAMETER :: nreal = SELECTED_REAL_KIND(P=15)

which sets nreal to be a named integer constant equal to the KIND parameter necessary for 15-figure decimal precision. Variables requiring this precision can subsequently be declared by statements like

REAL(KIND=nreal) :: x, y, z

but one should first check that nreal is positive, as the SELECTED_REAL_KIND function will return a negative value if the processor cannot attain the required precision or range. In any program doing serious number-crunching it is advisable for the programmer to decide in advance what precision and range are going to be needed. You could have a statement such as

IF (SELECTED_REAL_KIND(P=15, R=80) &
/= SELECTED_REAL_KIND(0.0)) STOP

to check that non-default kinds are not needed. Or,

$$\text{IF (SELECTED\_REAL\_KIND(P=20, R=100)<0) STOP}$$

to check that kinds of real numbers are available which will be capable of achieving the needed precision and range.

Normally the default precision will be amply good enough for most calculations. Arguably, a program is badly designed if it relies on exceptionally high decimal precision. In the remainder of this book, little more will be said about non-default kinds of data.

Incidentally, intrinsic real functions of a real argument will always return values having the same KIND parameter as the argument.

Among the intrinsic functions discussed in this chapter and in chapter 4 there have been the functions REAL and KIND. It is worth emphasising yet again that these functions should not be confused with the keywords or parameters REAL and KIND that can occur in type declaration statements. The statement

$$\text{REAL(KIND=KIND(0.0D0)) :: giga=REAL(2**30)}$$

is really quite tricky because it uses the keyword REAL, meaning that the data object 'giga' is to be of real type, and also the function REAL which converts the integer 2**30 into a real number; and also there is the KIND function, which yields the parameter needed by this processor to specify a double-precision number such as 0.0D0, and the KIND keyword which applies that parameter to 'giga'!

EXERCISES 5A

5A1   Write programs to read a number from the keyboard and calculate and display the value(s) of its

       (i)   secant (the number being interpreted as an angle in radians)

       (ii)   inverse hyperbolic sine (arcsinh)

       (iii)   logarithm to the base 16

5A2   Write a program to input a sum of money, an interest rate and a time in years, and to calculate what the sum has grown to after that time if the interest is compounded monthly.

5A3   A straight line (chord) divides a circle into two unequal parts. Write a program to calculate the area of the smaller part, given the circle's radius and the length of the chord.

5A4   Write a code fragment to find the current month of the year (using DATE_AND_TIME) and output its name.

5A5   If x is a real variable, write a line of code to calculate the natural logarithm of the complex number whose real and imaginary parts are cosh(x) and sinh(x).

5A6   Write a program which will simulate the tossing of a coin (writing out 'head' or 'tail') using the millisecond counter of DATE_AND_TIME to give an integer of practically random parity.

5A7   Write a program which will input a sequence of ten integers and calculate their average when the largest one and the smallest one are disregarded.

5A8   Write a program to find and write the order of magnitude of the number given by EPSILON on your processor. Also, find out if the square of this number is representable as distinct from zero.

5A9   The intrinsic function SIGN(A,B) gives the first argument the sign of the second. Write a line of code to do this job without using the function.

N5.1   DBLE AND DPROD

There are two intrinsic functions to do with 'double precision' real data. DBLE(A) is like REAL(A) but the result is of double precision. DPROD(X,Y) calculates the double-precision-real product of the default-real arguments X and Y.

N5.2   OTHER (NON-DEFAULT) INTEGER TYPES

Processors may support higher kinds of integer type, allowing integers with more than the normal limit on the number of digits. A function SELECTED_INT_KIND(R) yields the lowest value of the KIND parameter for integers with R digits. If R-digit integers are not supported on the processor, the value returned is -1.

Chapter 6

MORE ABOUT CHARACTERS

More details are given here about characters: how character data is declared, how character constants are formed, and what operators can be used on character data. A large number of intrinsic functions are described which have character strings as arguments (LEN, LEN_TRIM, TRIM, IACHAR, CHAR, LGE, LGT, LLE, LLT, ADJUSTL, ADJUSTR, INDEX, SCAN and VERIFY) or have characters as results (ACHAR and CHAR). At the end of the chapter the concept of a substring is explained, together with the notation for specifying substrings.

6.1   DECLARING CHARACTER DATA

Fortran's handling of character data has already been introduced in preceding chapters. Like the other data types, character data can exist either as constants or as variables. Unlike other data types, character data involves the complication that a single item may be a string consisting of an arbitrary number of individual characters. Character constants are specified simply by putting them between quotation marks or apostrophes. So 9 is an integer, 9.0 is real, "9" is a character, and "Nine" is a character string. A string may be of any length, including zero or one, so a single character is just a special case of a character string. As in the cases of numeric and logical data, names are used to represent variable character data. Names may also be used as a convenience to stand in place of character constants. Apart from cases where an IMPLICIT statement has been used (see the notes to chapter 13) the names of character strings must always be declared at the start of the program or subprogram with a CHARACTER statement. Normally the lengths of the strings must also be specified at that time.

The CHARACTER statement is a special case of the type declaration statement which is explained fully in chapter 13. It can take the form

CHARACTER(length), PARAMETER :: name = expression, ...

where '**length**' is the number of characters in the string (or in each of the strings, if there is more than one) being declared. If 'length' is absent, the length is 1 and only individual characters are admitted. 'length' may be an integer constant or may be a more complex integer expression, a 'specification expression'. Alternatively, 'length' may be the character *, in which case the length of the string is assumed from an actual string given in the same statement or previously. Specification expressions and assumed-length strings normally arise in relation to subprograms, and will be discussed more fully in later chapters.

The specifier 'PARAMETER' is optional. If present, it means that the character strings being declared are not variable but will keep their initial values throughout the execution of the program, i.e. they are 'named constants'.

After the double colon, there follows a list of one or more assignments of the form 'name = expression', separated by commas, each assignment specifying a character string thus:

After the double colon, 'name' is a name constructed according to the basic Fortran rules, just like numeric data, i.e. with up to 31 alphanumeric characters, starting with a letter.

Finally, '= expression' is compulsory if the PARAMETER attribute was specified. Otherwise it is optional. If present it gives an initial value to the variable called 'name'. The 'expression' may be a character constant or it may be a character expression known as an 'initialization expression'.

The following would be valid CHARACTER statements:

```
CHARACTER :: letter
CHARACTER(20) :: forename, midname, surname
CHARACTER(12) :: q = "CONFIDENTIAL"
CHARACTER, PARAMETER :: star = "*"
CHARACTER(*), PARAMETER :: origin = "Made in Thailand"
CHARACTER(nchars+6) :: line1, line2, line3, line4
CHARACTER(*) :: surname = "Spock"
CHARACTER(*) :: title = "Mr. "//surname
CHARACTER :: bell = ACHAR(7)
```

The sixth of these, for example, sets up four character-string variables (line1, etc.) each having a length given by the specification expression nchars+6. At the time this statement is encountered, the integer 'nchars' must already have a determined value.

The meanings of // and ACHAR are mentioned later in this chapter.

6.2   CHARACTER CONSTANTS

In the previous section a number of character constants (as opposed to variables or expressions) were mentioned: "9", "Nine", "CONFIDENTIAL", "*", "Made in Thailand", "Spock" and "Mr. ". Obviously, they are all specified between quotes, as we first saw in chapter 3. But what happens if quote marks are going to crop up in the character string itself? The assignment statement

remark = "Use "==" instead of ".EQ.", please."

does not produce the string

Use "==" instead of "EQ", please."

To get over this problem, there are two additional rules. Firstly, a character constant may be enclosed in apostrophes rather than in quotes, in which case quotes may occur freely between the apostrophes. (Conversely, apostrophes may occur freely in a quote-delimited string.) So, we could have

        remark = 'Use "==" instead of ".EQ.", please.'
        class = 'CONFIDENTIAL'
        quote = '"'
        apostrophe = "'"
        destination = "It's a cul-de-sac"

Secondly, if the delimiting character itself is to occur within the string, this can be achieved (once!) by showing it twice successively. So,

        remark = "Use ""=="" instead of "".EQ."", please."
        quote = """"
        apostrophe = ''''

and

        destination = 'It''s a cul-de-sac'

are equivalent to the corresponding statements earlier. More complicated examples can be contrived, like the character constant

        'Distinguish "it''s" from "its''"'

which actually looks like

        Distinguish "it's" from "its'"

In practice the choice of two kinds of delimiter, and the doubling convention if a delimiter is to appear in the string, together give the programmer plenty of flexibility. In fact it is possible to stick always to one sort of delimiter for all character constants, using the doubling convention when necessary. In this book, quotes will usually be used as the delimiter.

6.3   CHARACTER OPERATORS

There is a concatenation operator, //, which may be used to combine together character strings (explicit constants or names), as in the earlier example of

        "Mr. "//surname

and this may be applied repeatedly, e.g. in the character assignment statement

fullname = "Mr. "//forename//surname

In a statement of this kind the variables fullname, forename and surname must of course have been previously declared in CHARACTER statements, and forename and surname must have been given values. In the above statement, the right hand side is a character string whose length is 4 more than the sum of the lengths of forename and surname. However, the left hand side (fullname) continues to have whatever length was originally declared for the variable fullname. If fullname has a length less than that of the string on the right hand side, then the latter is truncated (from the right) when fullname is given a value. If fullname's length is greater, then the expression will be padded out with blanks (to the right) to make up fullname's value. This is the standard procedure in Fortran whenever a character assignment statement is executed between strings of different lengths.

Other operators that may be applied to character strings are the relational operators ==, /=, >, >=, <, and <=, giving logical results. For example,

(string1=="Sir").AND.(string2>string3)

is a logical expression with the value .TRUE. if string1 is "Sir" (or "Sir ", or "Sir ", or "Sir   ", and so on, but not " Sir"!) and if also string2 is 'greater than' string3. When strings are compared in this way, if their lengths are different then the shorter is first padded out to the right with blanks. Then, strings are compared one character at a time, working from the left, until differing characters are encountered. The 'greater' is then defined by the character which occurs later in the processor's character collating sequence (see CHAR and ICHAR below).

Rather than use >, >=, <, and <= to compare character strings it is usually better to use the special character functions LGT, LGE, LLT and LLE, explained in the next section, which give an ordering according to the ASCII sequence and are therefore processor-independent.

6.4   INTRINSIC CHARACTER FUNCTIONS

There are a number of useful intrinsic functions in Fortran which deal with characters or character strings. They are listed below showing the keywords that may be used with the arguments and with an indication of the types of the arguments and results (C=character, I=integer, L=logical).

Name	Argument Type	Result Type
LEN(STRING)	C	I
LEN_TRIM(STRING)	C	I
TRIM(STRING)	C	C
IACHAR(C)	C	I
ICHAR(C)	C	I
ACHAR(I)	I	C
CHAR(I)	I	C
LGE(STRING_A,STRING_B)	C's	L
LGT(STRING_A,STRING_B)	C's	L
LLE(STRING_A,STRING_B)	C's	L
LLT(STRING_A,STRING_B)	C's	L
ADJUSTL(STRING)	C	C
ADJUSTR(STRING)	C	C
INDEX(STRING,SUBSTRING,BACK)	C's (BACK=L)	I
SCAN(STRING,SET,BACK)	C's (BACK=L)	I
VERIFY(STRING,SET,BACK)	C's (BACK=L)	I
REPEAT(STRING,NCOPIES)	STRING=C, NCOPIES=I	C

The first of these, LEN, simply returns the length of the character string given as the argument. For example, LEN("New Zealand") is an integer with value 11. LEN_TRIM is similar but does not count trailing blanks, i.e. LEN_TRIM("Four ") is 4. The function TRIM returns a character string with the trailing blanks removed, i.e. TRIM("Four ") is "Four". Obviously, LEN(TRIM(c)) is equal to LEN_TRIM(c)for any character string c. TRIM could be used in a statement such as

WRITE(*,*) TRIM(output)," is the answer."

to display some text without having to worry about the number of significant characters in it.

The functions IACHAR and ICHAR convert a character into an integer code, and their arguments must therefore be individual characters, i.e. strings of length one. In the case of IACHAR the resulting integer is the standard ASCII 7-bit code (0-127) corresponding to the character: thus, IACHAR("0") has value 48. The ASCII codes are given in Appendix F. For a character outside the ASCII set the result may be processor-dependent. With the function ICHAR the code may be a different non-ASCII one used by the particular processor. Note that the processor's character set could in principle be much larger than the ASCII set; IACHAR and ICHAR could yield values above 127, and even above 255 if the processor allowed characters to be defined by more than one byte.

ACHAR and CHAR are the inverse functions to IACHAR and ICHAR: they yield a character corresponding to the integer code given as the argument. With ACHAR, the codes are the ASCII codes in the range 0-127, and for larger arguments the result will be processor-dependent. For example, ACHAR(97) is "a", ACHAR(36) is the currency symbol, and ACHAR(13) is a carriage return. With CHAR, the codes may depend on the processor in a sequence consistent with the ICHAR function. For most purposes the IACHAR and ACHAR functions should be sufficient, and ICHAR and CHAR can be avoided.

To illustrate the use of IACHAR and ACHAR, lowercase letters can be converted to uppercase by:

        n=IACHAR(letter)
        IF (n>=97.AND.n<=122) letter=ACHAR(n-32)

Note that ACHAR can be used to specify characters beyond the Fortran standard character set and perhaps not appearing on your keyboard:

        CHARACTER, PARAMETER :: bell=ACHAR(7), cent=ACHAR(91)

The functions LGE, LGT, LLE and LLT are for comparing character strings according to the ASCII codes of the individual characters taken left-to-right. Since the alphabet is a subset of the ASCII set, these functions may be used to test the alphabetical ordering of strings, but it must be borne in mind that uppercase and lowercase letters have different ASCII codes. LGE means 'lexically greater than or equal to', LGT is 'lexically greater than', and so on. For example, LGE(STRING_A="A",STRING_B="Z") is .FALSE. because STRING_A does not follow STRING_B in the ASCII collating sequence, because A does not follow Z in the alphabet. However, lowercase letters follow uppercase ones, so LGE(STRING_A="a",STRING_B="Z") is .TRUE.

Also, LGE(STRING_A="Six",STRING_B="Sixty") is .FALSE., because, in comparing strings of different lengths, the shorter string is extended with blanks to the right to match the length of the longer string, and the blank character (ASCII code 32) comes before any of the alphabet.

ADJUSTL and ADJUSTR are string-to-string functions which replace leading blanks by trailing blanks (ADJUSTL) or trailing blanks by leading blanks (ADJUSTR). Thus the value of ADJUSTL(" Preface ") is "Preface   ", but on the other hand ADJUSTR(" Chapter One ") is "   Chapter One". It is useful that the function-of-a-function TRIM(ADJUSTL(...)) will remove both leading and trailing blanks from a string.

INDEX is a function which carries out the useful job of looking for substrings within strings. (See section 6.5 for substrings.) If c2 is a substring of c1, then INDEX(STRING=c1, SUBSTRING=c2) yields the first starting point (counting characters from the left) of an occurrence of c2 within c1. So the expression

        INDEX(STRING="Birmingham", SUBSTRING="ming")

is equal to 4, and

$$INDEX(STRING="Birmingham", SUBSTRING="i")$$

is equal to 2. INDEX is zero if SUBSTRING is not a substring of STRING. If SUBSTRING has zero length, INDEX is normally returned with the value 1. The optional argument BACK is a logical variable taken to be .FALSE. if it is not otherwise specified, but if BACK=.TRUE., the function looks for the last (instead of first) occurrence of SUBSTRING within STRING; in other words

$$INDEX(STRING="Birmingham", SUBSTRING="i", BACK=.TRUE.)$$

is equal to 5. If BACK=.TRUE. and SUBSTRING has zero length, INDEX is given a value of one more than the length of STRING.

SCAN(STRING, SET, BACK) does a job similar to INDEX, but it looks for any of a number of individual characters within STRING. The argument SET is a string defining a set of individual characters, and INDEX points to the first occurrence of any one of them within STRING. For example, SCAN(STRING="Strength", SET="aeiou") has the value 4. As in the case of the INDEX function, the optional BACK argument will make SCAN look for the position of the last occurrence, i.e. SCAN(STRING="Counihan", SET="aeiou", BACK=.TRUE.) has the value 7.

VERIFY(STRING, SET, BACK) is, in a sense, the opposite of SCAN. It checks to see if all the characters in STRING occur within SET, and if not it yields the position (within STRING) of the first character not found in SET. If BACK is present with value .TRUE., VERIFY gives the position of the last character in STRING which is not in SET. If every character in STRING occurs in SET, VERIFY has the value zero whether BACK is .TRUE. or .FALSE. For example, the logical expression

$$VERIFY(STRING=intprint, SET="0123456789")==0$$

has the value .TRUE. if 'intprint' is the name of a string containing only decimal digits.

Finally, REPEAT is a function that concatenates a number of copies of the same string, i.e. REPEAT(STRING=" ",NCOPIES=80) is a character string consisting of 80 blanks.

6.5   SUBSTRINGS

Any character string can have substrings. A substring is a portion of a string, got by taking a set of adjacent characters within it. Therefore, "ace" and "cent" are substrings of "adjacent".

There is a special notation for indicating substrings in Fortran: the name of the string is followed by a pair of integers giving the positions of the start and finish of the substring within the string. The pair of integers (the 'substring range') is given in brackets and separated by a colon. For example, "adjacent"(4:6)

is "ace", and "cent" is

"adjacent"(5:8)

If one of the integers of the substring range is omitted, it is taken to be the first or last position in the string, e.g. the previous example is equivalent to

"adjacent"(5:)

A string is considered to be a substring of itself, e.g.

"adjacent"(1:8)

is the same as "adjacent". If the substring range is indicated by two equal integers then the substring has length 1, as in

"opposite"(5:5)

which is equal to "s". If the first integer exceeds the second, the substring is taken to be an empty string, e.g.

"hypotenuse"(7:2)

is equal to "". Substring notation may be used with variables as well as constants, as in

initial = name(1:1)

and substring ranges may themselves be integer variables or expressions:

hexdigit = "0123456789ABCDEF"(n+1:n+1)

gap = "_____"(:k)

However, the substring notation may not be applied to an expression other than a constant or a variable. So,

a//b(i:j)

concatenates a string with a substring, it doesn't take a substring of the concatenation of two strings. And it is not permissible to specify a substring of a substring directly as in

p = q(1:m)(n:)

which could actually mean something quite different, as we'll see in the next chapter when arrays are explained.

EXERCISES 6A

6A1   What are the values of

    (i)   LEN("Test_string")   (ii)   TRIM(" ")
    (iii)   ACHAR(111)   (iv)   CHAR(" ")
    (v)   LGE("Q","S")   (vi)   LLE("T","α")
    (vii)   LLE("6","1")   (viii)LLE("5","e")

6A2   What are the substrings

    (i)   "mulligatawny"(7:8)   (ii)   "mulligatawny"(1:4)
    (iii)   "mulligatawny"(6:6)   (iv)   "mulligatawny"(10:8)

6A3   Write code to remove the first character of a string called x if that character is a numeric digit.

6A4   Write type declaration statements to declare

    (i)   A zero-length string called 'null'
    (ii)   Three strings, each of length 24, called 's1', 's2' and 's3'
    (iii)   A character-string constant named 'me' whose value is your surname
    (iv)   A named character constant of length 1 called 'bs' whose
            value is the backslash character (\)

6A5   Write code to trim off all leading blanks, if any, from a string called x, and write the result.

N6.1   NON-DEFAULT CHARACTER TYPES

Just as a processor may support more than one kind of integer, and more than two kinds of real number, it may also support character data of more than one kind. For example, if a processor uses KIND=2 to specify a set of two-byte characters, then we might have for example

CHARACTER(KIND=2) :: runder = 2_"r"

(The kind parameter in a character constant must come in front, opposite to the case with real numbers!)

Chapter 7

ARRAYS

So far we have looked at data which might consist of a real or integer number, a complex number, or a logical element. We have also looked at items of character data consisting of a string of characters. These have all been 'scalar' objects, in the sense that a constant or the name of a variable refers to a single integer, or a single string of characters, and so on. It doesn't matter that a long string of characters can take up many times more memory than a single logical data item: both are regarded as individual scalar data items. An 'array', on the other hand, is an ordered set of data items, all of the same type, which can be referred to collectively by a single name. Arrays are an invaluable feature of Fortran, and in practice only the very simplest of problems are solved without recourse to them.

This chapter begins with how array variables are declared and used. Then 'array constructors' and 'array sections' are explained, followed by the WHERE statement/construct. Finally a number of intrinsic functions for arrays are introduced: ALL, ANY, COUNT, MAXVAL, MINVAL, PRODUCT and SUM.

7.1   DECLARING ARRAYS

In the previous chapter we saw how a statement like

        CHARACTER(30) :: surname

would establish that 'surname' is the name of a variable whose form is a string of 30 characters. It is equally simple to set up instead a list of 50 people's surnames, the declaration statement then taking the form

        CHARACTER(30) :: surnames(50)

By following the name ('surnames') with a positive integer in brackets, it is implied that the variable is a one-dimensional array (sometimes called a 'vector') with that number of members. There is an equivalent alternative notation, namely

        CHARACTER(30), DIMENSION(50) :: surnames

Here the keyword DIMENSION is an 'attribute specifier', specifying that the variable is an array and indicating how many members it has. This form is convenient if you want to declare several similar arrays: for example

CHARACTER(30), DIMENSION(50) :: surnames, forenames, nationalities

sets up three arrays each of 50 character strings, each string being 30 characters long, i.e. 4500 characters in all. Each string is an 'element' of a 50-strong array.

Arrays of other types can be declared in similar ways, e.g.

REAL, DIMENSION(100) :: height, weight
INTEGER, DIMENSION(100) :: kage

However, the attribute DIMENSION may always be omitted if the dimensions of the arrays are given in brackets after their names, as in

CHARACTER(30) :: surnames(50)
REAL :: height(100), weight(100)
INTEGER :: kage(100)
COMPLEX :: roots(25)
LOGICAL :: maskmatrix(32,32)

These are all variations of the type declaration statement (chapter 13). For simplicity it is recommended that the DIMENSION attribute be avoided, and in the rest of this book arrays are indicated simply by specifying their dimensions after their names.

The final example above, the logical array called maskmatrix, is an example of a two-dimensional array, specified by having two integers between the brackets following the name. It may be imagined as a matrix with 32 rows and 32 columns, and therefore with 1024 elements in all. An array's number of dimensions is known as its 'rank', and may be up to seven, i.e. we could have a seven-dimensional array like

INTEGER :: iternary(3,3,3,3,3,3,3)

with 2187 different elements. The total number of elements in an array is called its 'size'. In general an array may have a different 'extent' in each dimension, and the total size is the product of the extents. So,

REAL :: hash(1024,8,26,2)

declares an array of rank 4 and size 425984. Incidentally, an array may have zero size! The set of extents (1024,8,26,2) is known as the 'shape' of the array.

7.2   USING ARRAYS

In the declaration statements given as examples in the above section, the array names are followed by bracketed lists of the extents of the arrays in each dimension. In assignment statements, or in expressions, a similar notation is used to specify a particular single element of an array, e.g.

surnames(12) = "Johnson"

assigns a value to the 12th element of 'surnames'. It does not mean that 'surnames' has rank 12. However, 'surnames' must have rank of at least 12 in order for surnames(12) to exist. To take an example where an array element is on the right hand side,

x = 1.0 - SQRT(hash(98,1,14,2))

uses one element out of the four-dimensional real array 'hash', and uses it to calculate x.

To refer to all the elements of an array it would be possible to use a construct like a DO loop (chapter 8), such as

```
Cuberoots:      DO i=1,30
                      croots(i) = REAL(i)**(1.0/3.0)
                END DO Cuberoots
```

and this would set up a table of cube roots. But this sort of construction is generally not necessary: arrays really come into their own in Fortran because a reference to an array name by itself is equivalent to a reference to all the elements. For example, if x and y are one-dimensional arrays of size 10, then

x = y**2

is equivalent to

x(1) = y(1)**2 ; x(2) = y(2)**2 ; x(3) = y(3)**2 ; x(4) = y(4)**2 ; x(5) = y(5)**2
x(6) = y(6)**2 ; x(7) = y(7)**2 ; x(8) = y(8)**2 ; x(9) = y(9)**2 ; x(10) = y(10)**2

As a rule, array assignment statements may refer to Fortran's intrinsic functions, as in

x = SQRT(y)

which would be equivalent to 10 scalar assignments, and would involve 10 calls to the function SQRT, if x and y both have size 10. Other valid statements would be, for example,

x = SQRT(x)

and

$$x = y/z$$

The variables x, y and z here could be arrays of any shape, but their shapes must be the same. In the latter example, x(1) is set to y(1)/z(1), x(2) to y(2)/z(2), and so on.

An array assignment statement must have an array on the left hand side with the same shape as the array (or array expression) on the left hand side, but an exception to this rule is that we may have a scalar on the right hand side, in which case all elements of the array are set equal to that same value. For example, going back to the first example of this section,

surnames = "Johnson"

would set all elements of the array called 'surnames' to the same string "Johnson". To show how an array might be used in a program, here is something equivalent to the program shown in section 3.2:

```
PROGRAM Triangle
      REAL :: side(3)
      WRITE (*,*) "This program calculates the area of a triangle."
      WRITE (*,*) "Type in the lengths of the three sides:"
      READ  (*,*) side
      WRITE (*,*) "Check: you have input the following lengths"
      WRITE (*,*) side
      s = 0.5 * SUM(side)            ! Semiperimeter
      areasq = s*PRODUCT(s-side)     ! Square of the area
      IF (areasq<0.0) THEN
            WRITE (*,*) "Error: that is not a real triangle"
      ELSE
            area = SQRT(areasq)
            WRITE (*,*) "The area of the triangle is ", area
      END IF
END PROGRAM Triangle
```

This is no shorter than the earlier version of this program, and it uses two intrinsic functions (SUM and PRODUCT) that will be explained at the end of this chapter. But it illustrates how three variables (originally a, b and c) can be referred to under one name (side) so that the program reflects the mathematical symmetry of the problem. Note that READ and WRITE statements can be used with arrays, with the same effect as if each element of the array had been listed. So, the statement

WRITE (*,*) side

is equivalent to

WRITE (*,*) side(1), side(2), side(3)

On the other hand,

WRITE (*,*) side(1)

only writes the first element.

7.3   ARRAY CONSTRUCTORS

So far we have looked at how variables are declared to be arrays, and at how arrays can be used in assignment statements and READ or WRITE statements. But how do we initially set values for the elements of an array? It is possible to set each element individually, as in

```
REAL :: x(3)
x(1) = 3.76  ;  x(2) = -7.4  ;  x(3) = 5.19
```

but for rank-1 arrays there is a simpler construction known as an 'array constructor' which looks like

```
x = (/3.76,-7.4,5.19/)
```

The array has its elements specified as a list between a (/ and a /). This notation can be used in an assignment statement, or it can be used when array variables (or named constants) are initially declared, as in

```
REAL :: x(3) = (/3.76,-7.4,5.19/)
```

or

```
REAL, PARAMETER :: months(12) = (/31,28,31,30,31,30,31,31,30,31,30,31/)
```

The list in an array constructor may include items that are themselves arrays, so

```
INTEGER :: u(3), v(3), w(3), uvw(9)
u = (/1,2,3/)
v = 4
w = (/3,2,1/)
uvw = (/u,v,w/)
```

67

has the effect of giving uvw the value

$$(/1,2,3,4,4,4,3,2,1/)$$

Also, arrays within array constructors may themselves be array constructors, if you see what I mean. For example, uvw above could have been written

$$uvw = (/(/1,2,3/),v,(/3,2,1/)/)$$

Furthermore, a form of implied 'DO' can be used in an array constructor, e.g. an example of the table of cube roots, given in the previous section, is equivalent to

$$croots = (/REAL(i)**(1.0/3.0), i=1,30/)$$

More details of array constructors will be given in chapter 15.

Since an array constructor is a one-dimensional sequence of values, it can be used to construct only one-dimensional (rank=1) arrays. A one-dimensional array can be reshaped into a multidimensional array of the same size, using a special intrinsic function RESHAPE, but details of this are deferred until chapter 15.

7.4   ARRAY SECTIONS

We have so far considered arrays whose elements are labelled by integers ('subscripts') ranging from 1 up to the maximum extent in each dimension. However, subscripts may run from starting points other than 1 using a notation where both the lower and upper subscript limits are given, separated by a colon. For example,

$$REAL :: annual(1900:2025)$$

declares an array with 126 elements, i.e. annual(1900), annual(1901), annual(1902),..., annual(2025). In a case like this items such as annual(1) simply do not exist. This notation can equally well be used for multidimensional arrays, as in

$$LOGICAL :: flipper(-10:10,32,0:20)$$

which is a rank-3 array with total size 21x32x21.

The colon notation is also used to refer to what is called an 'array section', which is a subset of a previously declared array. We could have

REAL :: annual(1900:2025), decade(10)

.
.
.

decade = annual(1981:1990)

where, in the assignment statement, annual(1981:1990) is an array section, i.e. a particular set of ten elements from the larger array 'annual'. The elements of the array 'decade' are being set equal to annual(1981), annual(1982), ..., annual(1990). In fact, for array sections, the notation can be extended to allow sets of elements which are not sequential in the original array, by specifying a 'stride' after a second colon. So,

annual(1904:1996:4)

is an array section consisting of every fourth element starting from annual(1904) and going up to annual(1996). The three bracketed numbers, separated by colons, are a 'subscript triplet' and the general rule is that the processor starts from the first and moves on to the second in steps equal to the third. If 'leaps' is a rank=1 real array of size 24, then

leaps = annual(1904:1996:4)

picks out leap years. The stride may be negative, and if it is equal to -1 the effect is to give an array section with elements in the reverse order from the original array. Note that sections of the same array may occur on both sides of an assignment statement, as in

decade = decade(10:1:-1)

which reverses the order of the elements in 'decade', or

tenfold = tenfold + tenfold(10:1:-1)

where 'tenfold' is a rank-1 array of size 10. This array assignment statement is a bit like

tenfold(1) = tenfold(1) + tenfold(10)
tenfold(2) = tenfold(2) + tenfold(9)
.
.
.
tenfold(10) = tenfold(10) + tenfold(1)

except for the very important difference that when we write it out the long way, with ten scalar assignment statements, the last five statements will have quantities on the right hand side that were changed by the first five statements. The array assignment statement, on the other hand, always uses the original values of all the elements on the right hand side and the result is therefore not dependent on the order in which a processor might evaluate the elements of the array on the left hand side.

An array section may appear on either side of an assignment statement, as in

$$x(1:10) = x(5:15)$$

where x is a one-dimensional array whose subscript range spans at least from 1 to 15.

By applying this notation to each dimension in turn we can form sections of multidimensional arrays. With the rank=3 array given by

INTEGER :: matrices(4,4,200)

it is possible to have sections such as

matrices(1:4, 1:4, 1)
matrices(1:4, 4, 98)
matrices(4:1:-1, 4:1:-1: 200)

The first of these fixes the third subscript to be 1 and so gives a 4x4 (rank=2) array. In the second case both the second and third subscripts are fixed, leaving a rank=1 array of size 4. The final example is like the full array but with the element order reversed along two of the three dimensions.

One final point about array sections: any subscript limit may be omitted, in which case it is taken to be the array's lower bound (before the colon) or upper bound (after the colon). So, with the array 'matrices' as above, the first two examples could be written more compactly:

matrices(:,:,1)
matrices(:,4,98)

7.5   ARRAY SECTIONS, CHARACTER STRINGS AND SUBSTRINGS

It may not have escaped the reader's attention that there is potential ambiguity arising from the fact that array sections are set up using a colon notation very similar to that used for character substrings (chapter 6). If lines(10) is an array of ten character strings, what will the processor understand by lines(1:5)? The answer is, it means the first five elements of the array 'lines'. On the other hand, lines(1)(1:5) would be the first five characters of the first element of the array.

In other words, with an array of character type it may be necessary to follow the array name with two pairs of brackets. The first pair would contain subscript lists to define a section of the array. The second, if present, selects substrings of the elements of the array. We could have

```
CHARACTER(30) :: words(2000), test(25)
CHARACTER(10) :: shorter(2000), check
       .
       .
       .
test = words(176:200)
shorter = words(1:2000)(1:10)
check = words(99)(1:10)
```

The first two of these assignment statements give values to arrays. The third gives a value to the scalar character string 'check'. The last two statements could equally well be written

```
shorter = words(:)(:10)
check = words(99)(:10)
```

since an omitted index is taken to have the lowest or highest value possible, according to whether it is before or after the colon. Similar rules apply to multidimensional arrays, as in

```
CHARACTER(30) :: words(30,60,200), halfpage(30,30)
CHARACTER :: capitals(30,60,200)
       .
       .
       .
halfpage = words(:,:30,57)
capitals = words(:,:,:)(:1)
```

Also, array sections and substrings can be used in array constructors, as in

```
CHARACTER, PARAMETER :: digits(0:9) = (/"01235456789"(k:k), k=1,10/)
CHARACTER, PARAMETER :: octals(0:7) = digits(:7)
```

As a final example,

```
(/"origin","cattle","potato"/)(2:)(4:5)
```

71

is equal to (/"tl","at"/). Incidentally, an array constructor is taken to have the same type as the first element in it, and any other type parameters (e.g. KIND parameters) are also taken from the first element. In particular this means that a character-type array constructor consists of strings whose lengths are all the same as those of the first element. So, the character constant

(/"or","cattle","potato"/)

is exactly equivalent to (/"or","ca","po"/), because the longer elements will be truncated just as they would be if they were given as values to length=2 strings by assignment statements.

7.6   WHERE

Normally, an array assignment statement a=b will set each element of 'a' equal to the corresponding element of 'b'. However, the assignment may be made conditional with a statement such as

WHERE (b>a) a = b

or

WHERE (a<0.0) a = 0.0   ;   a=SQRT(a)

Note that the expression b>a is itself a logical array of the same shape as the arrays a and b, and a<0.0 has the same shape as a. We have not previously given examples of logical arrays, but they follow the same general rules as arrays of numeric variables or character strings. The logical array b>a could be expressed in array constructor notation as

(/ b(1)>a(1), b(2)>a(2), b(3)>a(3), ... /)

The general syntax of the WHERE statement is

WHERE (a) b = c

Here, a must be of logical type: it could be a variable, or a constant, or an expression. If a, b and c are all arrays they must have the same shapes. The assignment b=c then takes place conditionally, element by element, according to whether the corresponding element of a is true or false. The logical object a could be a scalar, in which case the statement is equivalent to

IF (a) b=c

(See chapter 8 for the 'IF' statement.) If c is a scalar and a and b are arrays, then the value of c is given to all the elements of b which correspond to true elements of a.

Here is another simple example:

```
REAL :: angles(500)
WHERE (angles>360.0) angles = MOD(angles,360.0)
```

Going beyond the simple WHERE statement, there is a WHERE construct by which a number of conditional array assignment statements may be tied together. If x, xl and xr are real arrays of the same shape, we could have:

```
WHERE (x.GT.0.0)
      xl = LOG(x)
      xr = SQRT(x)
ELSEWHERE
      xl = -99.0
      xr = 0.0
END WHERE
```

In general, the WHERE construct consists of an opening statement with the keyword WHERE followed just by a bracketed logical array; then there is a sequence of one or more array assignment statements; then optionally there can be an ELSEWHERE followed by assignment statements conditional on the inverse of the original logical array. Finally, the construct is terminated by an END WHERE statement. The WHERE construct forms a unit and must not be interspersed with other types of statement. The WHERE construct may only contain assignment statements and not (for example) WRITE statements.

The WHERE statement, and assignment statements within a WHERE construct, are often called 'masked' array assignments. Note that WHERE constructs, unlike the control constructs we shall meet in the next chapter, cannot be 'nested'.

7.7   ARRAYS AND INTRINSIC FUNCTIONS

Arrays can make use of many of Fortran's intrinsic functions, and in this chapter we have already encountered the SQRT and LOG functions being applied to arrays. Functions that can be applied to arrays are known as 'elemental' functions. Fortran's numeric, mathematical and character functions are all elemental, and so are the bit manipulation functions (chapter 18). However, inquiry functions and so-called 'transformational' functions which operate on whole arrays are not elemental. Examples of transformational functions are

```
ALL(MASK)
ANY(MASK)
COUNT(MASK)
```

MAXVAL(ARRAY)
MINVAL(ARRAY)
PRODUCT(ARRAY)
SUM(ARRAY)

where the arguments are one-dimensional arrays but the results returned are scalars. The use of multidimensional arrays with these functions is a slightly more complicated business treated in chapter 10. MASK and ARRAY are Fortran's keywords for the arguments: MASK must be logical, and ARRAY must be numeric.

The names of these functions make it very easy to remember what they do. The argument of ALL must be a logical array, and the result is of logical type and is true if and only if all elements of the argument are true. The function ANY likewise returns a true result if any of its elements is true. The function COUNT has an integer value equal to the number of true elements in its argument. MAXVAL and MINVAL operate on arrays that may be of real or integer type, and the results are the largest (MAXVAL) or smallest (MINVAL) values to be found among the elements. So,

MINVAL((/5,99,0,-5,1/))

is equal to -5. The functions PRODUCT and SUM operate on arrays that may be real, integer or complex, and the result is the product of all the elements or the sum of them. Thus,

PRODUCT((/(0.0,1.0),(0.0,1.0)/)

is equal to (-1.0,0.0).

EXERCISES 7A

7A1   Write declaration statements, as concise as possible, to set up the following one-dimensional arrays:

(i)   (/-1,-1,...(repeated 30 times)...-1,-1,1,1,...(repeated 30 times),1,1/)

(ii)   (/"a   ","ab   ","abr   ","abra   ", ... ,"abracadabra"/)

(iii)   The first ten powers of π

7A2   Write a program to read a list of ten real numbers (real parts) and then another list of the same length (imaginary parts) and then to form the array of complex numbers comprised by the corresponding real and imaginary parts. Then calculate which of the complex numbers has the greatest magnitude, and write it. (N.B. CMPLX and ABS are elemental functions.)

7A3   Write declaration statements to set up two-dimensional arrays to contain examination marks (0 - 100) and corresponding grades (A - F) for each of 300 students in each of 12 subjects. Write code to rescale all the marks so that the average mark is 60% in every subject, and then convert the marks into grades in a sensible way.

7A4   With

CHARACTER(5) :: s(6)
s = (/"light","trick","witch","hazel","beach","shore"/)

use structure constructors to write down the values of

(i)	s(1:2)	(ii)	s(5:6)	(iii)	s(4:3)
(iv)	s(1:2)(3:4)	(v)	s(1)(4:2)	(vi)	s(5:1)(5:1)

7A5   Write a program to input a string of up to 80 characters which will be interpreted as a line of text. Obtain the words from this string (a 'word' being any sequence of letters with non-letter characters at both ends of the sequence) and search the words for palindromes. A palindrome is a word which reads the same in both directions, like 'boob'. The program should write out any palindromes that it finds.

7A6   Write code to set up a two-dimensional array of the binomial coefficients, i.e. the numbers of ways in which m objects may be selected from n, n being a positive integer up to 50.

7A7   Write code to convert a sequence of x-y-z co-ordinate triplets into the corresponding sequence of radial co-ordinates (r, θ, ϕ), and then write out the radial co-ordinates of the point nearest to the origin.

7A8   Use a WHERE statement to halve all the even elements of an integer array.

7A9   Write a program to input a string of up to 20 characters and replace any blank in the string (but not trailing blanks) by an asterisk. Then write out the string, excluding trailing blanks.

7A10   Write code to take a string which is a series of words (separated by blanks) and reduce it to a string made of their capital letters (e.g. "North Dakota" being reduced to "ND").

Chapter 8

EXECUTION CONTROL

Within any program unit, statements are normally executed in the sequence in which they appear, but very often it is necessary for program execution to branch along different paths or to loop several times through the same set of statements. Moreover, branching and looping may depend on conditions (such as values of data to be read in) which are not known before the program starts to run.

Fortran has three 'constructs' for controlling the flow of execution through different blocks of executable statements: the CASE construct, the IF construct, and the DO construct. Blocks of this sort are not allowed to include non-executable statements such as type declaration statements. Programs generally have numerous control constructs, often 'nested' within one another, and in practice most large programs never run exactly the same way twice.

This chapter covers the statements SELECT CASE, CASE, CASE DEFAULT, END SELECT, IF, ELSE, ELSE IF, END IF, DO, CYCLE, EXIT, END DO, and STOP.

8.1   THE 'CASE' CONSTRUCT

Different blocks of code may be selected for execution according to different possible values of an expression (the 'case expression') which may be of integer, logical or character type. The construct begins with a SELECT CASE statement, then there are one or more blocks each starting with a CASE statement, and finally an END SELECT statement. This very simple example makes a selection according to the value of a logical expression:

```
Switch:  SELECT CASE (input(1:1)=="Y")
                CASE (.TRUE.)
                     .
                     .
                     .          (case block)
                     .
                     .

         END SELECT Switch
```

The case expression is specified in brackets at the end of the SELECT CASE statement. A CASE construct may be given a name, here 'Switch', and if so the name precedes the keywords SELECT CASE and is followed by a colon. Here the case expression is the logical expression

```
input(1:1)=="Y"
```

In this example there is only one case block, following the statement

```
CASE (.TRUE.)
```

and it would be a section of code to be executed if and only if the first letter of the character string 'input' is a Y. The END SELECT statement closes the case construct, and unconditional execution of the program continues. Since the construct has a name, its name must be specified at the end after the keywords END SELECT.

Here is a more complicated example, with a selection being made according to the value of an integer 'nyears':

```
Wars:           SELECT CASE (nyears)
                CASE (1853:1856)
                        war = "Crimean War"
                CASE (1899:1902)
                        war = "Boer War"
                CASE (1914:1918)
                        war = "WW1"
                CASE (1939:1945)
                        war = "WW2"
                CASE DEFAULT
                        war = "Peace"
                END SELECT Wars
```

A character variable (war) is being given different values according to whether the case expression (nyears) lies in certain ranges. The colon notation is used to specify lower and upper (inclusive) limits for the values of the case expression. Both limits need not be present, i.e. CASE (1914:) would be satisfied by any value greater than 1913, and CASE (:1914) would be satisfied by any value below 1915, while CASE (1914) would be satisfied only by the value 1914. In any CASE construct, the ranges satisfied by the different blocks may not overlap, so that whatever the value of the case expression there can be no more than one block selected. A CASE DEFAULT statement may be used to define a default block which will be selected if the case expression matches none of the other blocks. Obviously there can be no more than one default block.

The next example is a section of code with two CASE constructs. The first selects according to the value of an element of a character string, and the second is according to the value of an integer.. The DO construct will be explained in proper detail shortly, but here it means that everything between the DO and END DO statements will be executed repeatedly with the integer i taking the values from 1 up to the length of a character string called 'text'.

```
!          Interpret input text as a number
!          Initialisation
           string = ""            ;           npoints = 0
Text:      DO i = 1, LEN(text)

           Digit:   SELECT CASE (text(i:i))
                           CASE ("0":"9")
                                   string=string//text(i:i)
                           CASE (",")
                                   WRITE (*,*) "NB  Commas are disregarded"
                           CASE (".")
                                   npoints=npoints+1
                                   string=string//"."
                           CASE ("O")
                                   WRITE (*,*) "An O has been interpreted &
                                   &as a zero"
                                   string=string//"0"
                           CASE ("I")
                                   WRITE (*,*) "An I has been interpreted &
                                   &as a 1"
                                   string=string//"1"
                           CASE (" ")
                                   WRITE (*,*) "A blank has been disregarded"
                           CASE DEFAULT
                                   WRITE (*,*) "There is a fatal error"
                                   STOP
                    END SELECT Digit

END DO Text

Points:  SELECT CASE (npoints)
                CASE (0)
                        WRITE (*,*) "Check: There was no decimal point"
                CASE (2:)
                        WRITE (*,*) "There was more than one decimal point"
                        STOP
                CASE DEFAULT
                        WRITE (*,*) "Your number was "//string
                END SELECT Points

text = string
```

The first SELECT CASE statement specifies that the i'th character of the string 'text' is the case expression. In the seven blocks following, different actions are taken if this character is a numerical digit, a comma, a decimal point, a letter 'O' or 'I', or a blank, or something else. When the construct has been executed the required number of times, i.e. after the END DO statement, the character variable 'string' will contain a modified version of the original 'text'. There is then a second CASE construct looking at the number of decimal points that were encountered. The STOP statement is explained in section 8.4 below.

To summarise: in general the case construct takes the form

```
construct-name:  SELECT CASE (case-expression)
                 CASE (case-value-range-list)
                     .
                     .
                 CASE ....
                     .
                     .
                     .
                     .
                     .
                 CASE DEFAULT
                     .
                 END SELECT construct-name
```

where **construct-name** is an optional name, **case-expression** is an expression and **case-value-range-list** is a value, a range of values around a colon, or a set of such values and/or ranges separated by commas. Each value may simply be a constant or it may be an expression of some sort (technically, an 'initialization expression', as mentioned later in chapter 12). Valid CASE statements are

```
CASE (p.NEQV.q)
CASE ("A","E","I","O","U")
CASE (SIZE(array))
CASE (1914:1918,1939:1945)
CASE (10**5+1:10**6)
CASE ("A":"Z","a":"z")
```

The last example illustrates a possible difficulty when the case expression is of character type and a CASE statement specifies a range of values. The problem is that the range is interpreted according to the processor's own character collation sequence, not necessarily the ASCII sequence, and this may differ from one processor to another. For fully portable code, it would be safer to have something like

SELECT CASE (IACHAR(char))

.
.
CASE (65:90,97:122)

to select characters which are upper- or lower-case letters of the alphabet.

8.2   THE 'IF' CONSTRUCT

The IF statement and the IF construct were introduced early in this book. The IF statement can be used by itself to control an action, as in

IF (logical-expression) statement

where 'logical-expression' is any scalar logical expression and 'statement' may be more or less any kind of statement which can stand by itself, except for nonexecutable or declarative statements, and excluding END statements. The statement may not be another IF: if there is a second condition it can be included in the bracketed logical expression as in the example

IF (r>0.0 .AND. s>0.0) qfunc = SQRT(LOG(r)*LOG(s))

The IF construct is rather different from the bare IF statement, although both begin with the keyword IF. The IF construct takes the general form

construct-name: IF (logical-expression) THEN

.
.
ELSE IF (logical-expression) THEN

.
.
ELSE IF (logical-expression) THEN

.
.
.
.
ELSE

.
.
END IF construct-name

As with CASE, a construct name may be included at the front of the IF...THEN statement but it is not essential. After the IF...THEN statement, there follows a block of executable code. After that, there can be any number of ELSE IF blocks. The bracketed logical expressions determine which block, if any, is to be executed. Finally an ELSE block may optionally be included, and this will be executed if none of the expressions controlling the preceding blocks is true. In any IF construct, no more than one block will be executed. If more than one of the logical expressions are true, then only the block controlled by the first of them will be executed. An example of an IF construct is

        IF (initialised) THEN ; I=0 ; J=0 ; K=0 ; END IF

It should be noted that a construct-name may, if the programmer wishes, be appended also to ELSE...IF...THEN and to ELSE statements. Also, IF constructs may be nested inside one another, and in practice often are. When constructs are nested, the use of construct-names is particularly useful for the programmer to keep track of which statements are part of which construct. This is true also of CASE constructs. Here is a simple example of nested IF constructs:

```
Clear:  IF (x<1.0) THEN
              Sign:    IF (x<0.0) THEN
                            x = -x
                            ind = .TRUE.
                       END IF Sign
              x = x + 1.0
        ELSE Clear
              x = SQRT(x)
        END IF Clear
```

EXERCISES 8A

8A1   Write a program, using a CASE construct for execution control, to solve a quadratic equation whose coefficients are real but which may have complex roots.

8A2   Use a CASE construct to look at the initial letter of a character string. If it is a lower-case letter, convert it to upper case. If the string starts with a non-letter character, replace it with an X, but if it starts with a blank just remove it.

8A3   Repeat exercise 8A2 but using an IF construct instead of CASE.

8A4   Given an integer, write code which will check if it is the square or the cube (but not both!) of a smaller integer, and if so write a message saying so.

8.3   THE 'DO' CONSTRUCT

The CASE and IF constructs allow a program to execute one block of statements selected from a set of alternative blocks. The DO construct (or 'DO loop') allows a program to execute a single block of statements repeatedly. The block must be enclosed between DO and END DO statements. In its simplest form, the construct is

```
DO
       .
       .        (block)
       .
END DO
```

and this causes execution to loop through the block an indefinite number of times. The following example calculates the value of the number e by summing an infinite series:

```
e=1.0    ; k=1   ; j=1
DO
          e=e+1.0/REAL(j)  ;   k=k+1  ;   j=j*k
END DO
```

The problem here is that the program will apparently never stop unless there is some way of escaping from the DO loop. In practice, it will keep looping until an error condition arises when j exceeds the processor's range of integers. So how do we get out of a DO loop? There is a special statement, EXIT, which does this and passes control to whatever statement follows the END DO, as in

```
INTEGER :: ifib(100)
ifib(1)=1  ;   ifib(2)=1  ;   i=3
DO
          ifib(i) = ifib(i-1) + ifib(i-2)
          i=i+1
          IF (i>100) EXIT
END DO
```

You can also escape from a DO loop by a STOP (see section 8.4) or, in a subprogram, by a RETURN statement (N12.3). Another construction is

```
        DO WHILE (logical expression)
            .
            .
            .
        END DO
```

Here, each time the program is at the top of the loop, the value of the bracketed logical expression is checked; and if it is not true then the loop will not be executed and control passes to the statement after END DO. The DO WHILE construct is exactly equivalent to

```
        DO
        IF (.NOT.(logical expression)) EXIT
            .
            .
            .
        END DO
```

Note that DO loops, like IF and CASE constructs, may be named. Loop names are not functionally necessary, but it is a good idea to use them as a form of program annotation and self-checking especially when there are nested loops. A loop name, if used, must be given before a colon at the start of the DO statement, and must also appear at the end of the END DO statement. Here is an example of a named DO loop:

```
x = 1.0 ;        y = 1.0 ;        z = 1.0 ;        ncount=0
Lorenz: DO WHILE ((x**2 + y**2 + z**2)<1000000.0)
            xplus = 10.0*(y-x)
            yplus = x*z + 28.0*x - y
            zplus = x*y - 8.0*z/3.0
            test = ABS(xplus) + ABS(yplus) + ABS(zplus)
            IF (test.le.0.000001) EXIT
            ncount = ncount + 1
            IF ((MOD(ncount,20).EQ.0) WRITE (*,*) ncount, " iterations"
            x = x + xplus
            y = y + yplus
            z = z + zplus
            WRITE (*,*) x, y
        END DO Lorenz
```

Another type of statement that is used for DO loop control is CYCLE. The CYCLE statement is a way of jumping to the bottom of the block, and thence back to the top again, but unlike EXIT it does not jump right out of the loop:

```
        DO
                WRITE (*,*) "Type the password"
                READ (*,*) inword
                IF (inword/=password) CYCLE
                WRITE (*,*) "That's right. Now type a new password"
                READ (*,*) password
                WRITE (*,*) "The new password is ",password
                EXIT
        END DO
```

The user never gets out of this loop unless the correct password is typed in.

Another way of controlling a DO loop is with a variable known as a loop index. Historically, this was the usual way of constructing DO loops in earlier versions of Fortran. The syntax is

```
        DO i = i1, i2, i3
                .
                .
                .
        END DO
```

where the loop-control quantities i, i1, i2 and i3 are of scalar integer type. A loop name, of course, may also be included as in the earlier examples.

The first loop-control quantity, here called i, is the 'loop index' and it is a local variable whose name is arbitrary. The integers i1, i2 and i3 may be variables, constants or expressions, but they must have definite values at the start of the loop. The loop is executed for values of i starting with i1 and going up to i2 in steps ('strides') equal to i3. The stride i3 may be omitted from the DO statement, in which case its default value is 1.

Here are two simple examples with constant loop parameters:

```
        WRITE (*,*) "Table of cubes:"
        DO k = 0, 20
                WRITE (*,*) k, k**3
        END DO

        WRITE (*,*) "Table of cubes:"
        DO k = 0, 1000, 5
                r = REAL(k)/1000.0
                WRITE (*,*) k, k**3
        END DO
```

The first of these tabulates the cubes of the integers from 0 to 20, and the second tabulates the cubes of numbers from 0 to 1 in steps of 0.005.

A loop index may have negative stride (i3) if its starting point (i1) is greater than its end point (i2) as in

```
WRITE (*,*) "Table of cubes:"
DO i = 20, 0, -1
        WRITE (*,*) i, i**3
END DO
```

which does the same thing as the earlier example above but in the reverse order. Loop control parameters may also be more complicated expressions, as in

```
DO icount =    MIN(intalpha, intbeta, intgamma), &
               MAX(intalpha, intbeta, intgamma), jumper+1
```

The loop control parameters are set up when the DO statement is first encountered, before looping actually starts, and they cannot be altered by statements within the block. The loop index (i.e. the variable called i or k or icount in the above examples) increases by the 'stride' each time the loop repeats, but it should not be altered by statements within the block.

The nesting of loops is a very useful feature of the language, as in

```
Decades: DO nyear = 1910, 2000, 10
         prod=0.0 ; res=0.0
         Ten: DO n = nyear-9, nyear
                 prod = prod + oil(nyear)
                 res  = res  + found(nyear)
         END DO Ten
         WRITE (*,*) nyear, prod, res
END DO Decades
```

Obviously it is important not to mix up your loop indices and not to have overlapping loops. It is always a good precaution to name the loops, as in the scheme

```
        Outer: DO
            .
            .
      Middle: DO
              .
              .
          Inner: DO
                .
                .
          END DO Inner
                .
                .
      END DO Middle
            .
            .
  END DO Outer
```

The EXIT and CYCLE statements usually have effect with respect to the deepest loop level where they appear, but they can refer to any level if names are appended. If you EXIT or CYCLE from an inner loop to an outer one, the inner loop will be finished and cannot be re-entered without re-initialising the inner loop index. Opposite is a fairly complex structure:

```
Outer: DO
         .
         .
       CYCLE Outer
         .
         .
       Middle: DO
             .
             .
           EXIT Middle
             .
             .
           Inner: DO
                 .
                 .
               EXIT Outer
                 .
                 .
               CYCLE Middle
                 .
                 .
           END DO Inner
             .
             .
       END DO Middle
         .
         .
         .
Outer: DO
```

In this example, CYCLE Outer has the effect of transferring control down to the END DO Outer statement but it does not actually terminate looping at this level. EXIT Middle does stop looping at the middle level because it transfers control to whatever statement follows after END DO Middle (not to END DO Middle itself), and so it leaves only the outer loop operative. EXIT Outer transfers control to the statement after END DO Outer, so no loops remain active. CYCLE Middle transfers control to END DO Middle, terminating the inner loop but leaving the other loops still active.

A complicated example like that is bound to seem confusing at first, but in practice nested loops are extremely useful and the EXIT and CYCLE statements are soon mastered.

8.4   STOP

On the subject of execution control there is one type of statement that still needs to be mentioned. Very simple but very important, it is the STOP statement. STOP halts the execution of the program. The only other statement which should normally halt a program is END PROGRAM, but STOP can appear anywhere within the program and it can be made conditional as in

    IF (time>overrun) STOP

The STOP statement may, optionally, be followed by an 'stop code' or 'access code' consisting of either a character constant or a string of up to 5 digits. The idea is that the stop code should be accessible to the user after the program has stopped and can be used to indicate exactly where it stopped. This is important for debugging lengthy programs that may have numerous STOP statements dotted about them. So, we can have statements like

    IF (time>overrun) STOP "Too Late"

or

    CASE (1999) ;   STOP 1999

Exactly how the stop code is output is a matter for the processor's operating system, not for Fortran, since by definition it happens when the Fortran program is no longer running.

EXERCISES 8B

8B1   Use a DO loop to calculate the factorial of an integer.

8B2   Given a character string which consists of letters of the alphabet, write code to put the letters into alphabetical order and produce a new string consisting of the reordered letters.

8B3   Write code that will calculate an integer value from a character-string sequence of digits, i.e. to calculate the value 10 from the string "10".

8B4   Write code that will find the largest prime factor of an integer.

8B5   Write code to test if a character string would be valid as the name of a Fortran variable.

8B6   Write a program to input a word and write out its vowels.

N8.1 PAUSE

The statement PAUSE can be used to halt execution of the program temporarily, with the possibility of resumption under the user's control. PAUSE can be followed, like STOP, by a stop code.

N8.2 SELECTCASE AND ENDIF

In the cases of the keywords SELECT CASE and END IF, the blanks between the two words are optional.

N8.3 DO LOOPS WITH STATEMENT LABELS

There is a form of the DO loop which uses a statement label (see chapter 10) to indicate the bottom of the loop. In this type of DO statement a statement label follows the keyword DO, and the END DO statement must start with the same label. (Alternatively, the labelled END DO statement may be replaced by a labelled CONTINUE statement.) An example is

```
DO 6 k=1, kmax              ;   sumsq = 0.0
sumsq = sumsq + datum(k)**2  ;   6 CONTINUE
```

which is equivalent to

```
sumsq = SUM(ARRAY=datum(1:kmax)**2)
```

Chapter 9

FUNCTIONS AND SUBROUTINES (1)

We have already come across several of Fortran's intrinsic functions and the intrinsic subroutine DATE_AND_TIME. This chapter will explain how the programmer can write and use additional 'external' functions and subroutines. They are not only useful for carrying out calculations not covered by the intrinsic functions, they are necessary also for the clear organisation and subdivision of any large Fortran program. The program control constructs of chapter 8 are valuable, but should not be pushed too far by themselves: a system of subroutines and functions (or 'procedures') is generally used to organise the flow through any program of more than a few dozen statements.

Usually a complete program will consist of a 'main program' alongside a number of 'subprograms'. A main program is the sort of thing we have been considering so far in this book, i.e. a sequence of statements starting with a PROGRAM statement and finishing with an END PROGRAM statement. Subprograms are other sections of code, ancillary to the main program, and they include functions and subroutines. (Subprograms of another type, 'modules', will be introduced in chapter 11.) The execution of any complete program still begins with the PROGRAM statement at the start of the main program, and subprograms are invoked directly or indirectly from the main program.

This chapter introduces the statements FUNCTION and SUBROUTINE (and type-prefixed variants of the FUNCTION statement) and END FUNCTION, END SUBROUTINE, CALL and RETURN.

9.1   FUNCTIONS

A function subprogram, or 'function' for short, is used to calculate a result whose value will depend on 'arguments' given when the function is actually used. A function is like a mini-program, and has an overall structure deliberately similar to a main program: it starts with a title statement, followed by non-executable declaration statements, and then the series of executable statements finishing finally with a version of the END statement. An example:

```
FUNCTION Cot(x)
REAL :: Cot, x, s, c
IF (x==0.0) THEN
        WRITE (*,*) "Error: cotangent function called with zero argument"
        Cot = HUGE(x)
ELSE
        s = SIN(x)  ;  c = COS(x)  ;  Cot = c/s
END IF
END FUNCTION Cot
```

This piece of code would be provided alongside (not embedded in!) a main program. Whenever there is any reference to Cot in the main program (or for that matter anywhere else in the program as a whole, including other functions) the function will be entered and the cotangent will be calculated. When the END FUNCTION statement is reached, control returns back to wherever the reference to Cot was made.

With the function Cot defined as above, references to Cot must have one argument, and the argument must have a real value. This argument is called x within the function, but elsewhere a reference to Cot can have an argument with any name (or could be a constant or an expression). The name x as it appears above is an arbitrary choice, called a 'dummy' argument. Valid references to Cot (occurring in the main program, for example) could be the expressions

Cot(y)
Cot(0.1)
Cot(pi - SQRT(q**2 + p**2))

or even

Cot(alpha + ATAN((Cot(beta)+Cot(gamma)))

the Cot function being called three times by the last example. In the code for defining the function, x is known as a dummy argument because it stands in place of whatever actual arguments are used in references to the function. It is essential to understand clearly the distinction between 'dummy' arguments and 'actual' arguments. A dummy argument has a name local to the function itself, and should be declared at the start of the function along with other variables used in the calculation of the function's value. An 'actual' argument is supplied at execution time when the function is referred to elsewhere in the program, and the actual argument could be a constant or an expression or a variable.

Leaving aside techniques involving 'modules' (chapter 11), it should be considered that a function's arguments are the only way in which data can enter it. Except as arguments, a function does not have access to data items used elsewhere in the program. Any data items used within a function must be declared within it using appropriate type declaration statements. In our example, after the function statement there is the type declaration statement

REAL :: Cot, x, s, c

affirming that the variables x, s and c are of default real type, as is the function result Cot. Strictly speaking the statement is unnecessary, since the names would correspond to default real numbers by the initial letter convention, but it is nevertheless good practice to include such a statement. To specify that the function Cot itself has a real value there is another method, namely the use of a prefixed FUNCTION statement of the form

REAL FUNCTION Cot(x)

The function name does not then need to appear in a type declaration statement. As a rule it is best always to use type-prefixed function statements. Examples are:

```
INTEGER FUNCTION Nfactorial(n)
COMPLEX FUNCTION Gamma(z)
CHARACTER(20) FUNCTION All_Upper_Case(string)
LOGICAL FUNCTION Cone(z)
```

The function type is not mentioned, however, in END FUNCTION statements.

It has to be understood that the type specified by the FUNCTION statement's prefix is the type of the function's value, and this is not necessarily that of its argument. For example, a logical function Cone could have a complex argument, the function value being true or false according to whether the complex argument z has a real part of greater or lesser magnitude than its imaginary part:

```
LOGICAL FUNCTION Cone(z)
COMPLEX :: z
Cone = .FALSE.
IF (ABS(REAL(z))>ABS(AIMAG(z))) Cone = .TRUE.
END FUNCTION Cone
```

Any function must always arrive at a value for itself before the final END FUNCTION statement is reached. Normally this means that there must be at least one executed assignment statement with the name of the function on the left.

Functions may have more than one argument, as in

```
REAL FUNCTION Average(r1, r2, r3, r4)
REAL :: r1, r2, r3, r4
Average = 0.25 * (r1 + r2 + r3 + r4)
END FUNCTION Average
```

In this example the four arguments are all of the same type, and their order is immaterial, but in general it has to be ensured that the proper order of the dummy arguments is adhered to whenever the function is called. This is obvious from the cases of some of the intrinsic functions already met: for example CMPLX(a,b) is not the same as CMPLX(b,a).

It is best to think of a function as receiving information through its argument and returning information through its value. Therefore, a function should ideally not change the values of its arguments. But, if argument values are changed within a function, then the new values will be passed back to the program unit from which the function was called. When arguments are to be changed, it is usually more appropriate to use not a function but the other type of procedure, namely a subroutine.

EXERCISES 9A

9A1   Write a real function of one argument, calculating the volume of a sphere given its radius.

9A2   Write a complex function to calculate the inverse sine of its (complex) argument.

9A3   Write a function which reverses the digits of an integer!

9A4   Write a function of a real variable which will simply WRITE its value, and explain how this could be used to get around the fact that a WHERE block can only contain assignment statements. Then write code which uses a WHERE block to WRITE the values of the negative elements in a real array.

9.2   SUBROUTINES

Subroutines are simpler than functions. A subroutine is invoked only by a special kind of statement, the CALL statement, as in

```
PROGRAM Process
CALL Read_Data
CALL Analyse
CALL Display_Results
END PROGRAM Process
```

Read_Data, Analyse, and Display_Results are here the names of subroutines to which execution is directed in turn by the CALL statements. Unlike functions, they do not themselves have values. A subroutine can be more or less any block of code, not necessarily calculating anything in particular. At the end of it, control returns back to the calling program at the point immediately following the CALL statement. In the above example three subroutines are called from the main program, but in general any subroutine may be called from anywhere in the program as a whole, including functions and other subroutines.

Information may be passed into and/or out of a subroutine through arguments, as in:

```
PROGRAM Process
REAL :: x(100), y(100), xprime(100), yprime(100)
LOGICAL :: readcheck
CALL Read_Data(x, y, readcheck)
IF (readcheck) CALL Analyse(x, y, xprime, yprime)
CALL Display_Results(xprime, yprime, readcheck)
END PROGRAM Process
```

This illustrates, incidentally, that procedure arguments may be arrays (see section 9.3).

A subroutine is written very much like a main program except that it has arguments after its name and it begins with a SUBROUTINE statement. The above program could call

```
SUBROUTINE Display_Results(a, b, go)
REAL :: a(100), b(100)
LOGICAL :: go
IF (.NOT.go) THEN
        WRITE (*,*) "The data was not input correctly"
ELSE
        .
        .
        (Display a scatter diagram of a against b)
        .
        .
END IF
END SUBROUTINE Display_Data
```

Here, as in a function, we have dummy arguments (a, b and go) whose names are local to the subroutine and need not be the same as the names of the actual arguments in the calling program. The dummy arguments here are associated with the actual arguments x, y, and readcheck by their corresponding positions in the argument lists in the CALL and SUBROUTINE statements.

Subroutines, and functions, may have arguments which are character strings. Fortunately the lengths of character string dummy arguments need not be fixed, but may be assumed from the actual arguments in the calling program using the syntax

```
SUBROUTINE Compare(name1, name2, result)
CHARACTER(*) :: name1, name2
LOGICAL :: result
...
```

The strings name1 and name2 must correspond to actual arguments whose lengths were defined in the calling program. The asterisk in the CHARACTER statement means that the lengths of the dummy arguments name1 and name2 will be decided when the subroutine is called.

The same thing holds good for functions as well as subroutines. In the case of a function, the function value itself may be a character string and may take an assumed length as in

CHARACTER(*) FUNCTION All_Upper_Case(string)

Below is an example of a subroutine, Eicheck, with a character string argument of assumed length. Within the subroutine, the length of the argument can be found simply by using the intrinsic LEN function. The subroutine looks into the string for occurrences of the diphthong ei, and changes them to ie except after c:

```
SUBROUTINE Eicheck(string)
CHARACTER(*) :: string, ei="ei", ie="ie", c="c"
INTEGER :: length
length = LEN(string)
IF (length<3) RETURN
DO ipoint=2, length-1
        IF (string(ipoint:ipoint+1) /= ei) CYCLE
        IF (string(ipoint-1:ipoint-1) == c) CYCLE
        string (ipoint:ipoint+1) = ie
END DO
END SUBROUTINE Eicheck
```

This subroutine includes a statement type that we have hardly come across so far, namely RETURN. The RETURN statement, which may occur in any subroutine or function, has the same effect as jumping down to the END FUNCTION or END SUBROUTINE statement and returning immediately to where the procedure was called from in the calling program. In the case of a function, though, it has to be remembered that the function must have been given a value before you return from it.

So far we have discussed procedures whose dummy arguments are data objects of various kinds. However, it is also possible for a procedure to have, as an argument, the name of yet another procedure. This could be useful if, for example, a procedure is to be written to calculate the integral of an arbitrary function. We could have a subroutine with the structure

```
SUBROUTINE Integrate (Function, alimit, blimit, result)
REAL, EXTERNAL :: Function
REAL :: alimit, blimit, result
     .
     .
     .
     (By references to Function(x), calculate an
     approximation to the integral of that function
     between x=alimit and x=blimit. Set 'result' equal
     to the result.)
     .
     .
     .
END SUBROUTINE Integrate
```

The attribute EXTERNAL in the first REAL statement tells the subroutine that Function is the name of a real-valued external function, i.e. a user-written function of the sort described in section 9.1. The above subroutine could be called with any actual function name as the first argument, as long as that function is also declared EXTERNAL in the calling program and exists as an external function. (It could alternatively be an intrinsic function, in which case it should be declared with the INTRINSIC attribute, but there are awkward restrictions on the names of the intrinsic functions that may be used in this way, so this is best avoided. In most realistic applications a dummy procedure will correspond to an external procedure, not an intrinsic one.)

9.3   PROCEDURES AND ARRAYS

It was mentioned above that procedures may have arguments which are arrays. In the example of the subroutine Display_Results, there were two real arguments which were arrays with 100 elements each. However, for flexibility the numbers of elements need not be specified: if the REAL statement in the subroutine Display_Results took the form

```
REAL :: a(*), b(*)
```

then a and b would be rank-one arrays taking their sizes from the corresponding arrays given as arguments in the calling program, and a and b would be known as 'assumed-size arrays'.

This sort of thing can be done with arrays of characters. Here is a function which could take a sequence of names (e.g. Gerard, Manley and Hopkins) and yield a string of initials (e.g. GMH):

```
CHARACTER(*) FUNCTION Initials(names)
CHARACTER(*) :: names(*)
CHARACTER    :: initial
```

```
        Initials = ""                  !        Preset an empty string
        DO i = 1, SIZE(names)
              initial = names(i)(1:1)
              Initials = ADJUSTL(ADJUSTR(Initials)//initial)
        END DO
        END FUNCTION Initials
```

Here 'names' is an assumed-size rank=1 array of character strings. Not only is the size of 'names' to be assumed, so are the lengths of its elements. Furthermore, the length of the function result itself is to be assumed from the calling program. When the function is called, the argument must be an array of character strings, and remember that the elements of an array of strings must all have the same length. The calling program could contain the code

```
        CHARACTER(20) :: person(5) = ""
        CHARACTER(5), EXTERNAL :: Initials
              .
              .
              .
        Person(1:3) = (/"Gerard","Manley",Hopkins"/)
              .
              .
              .
        WRITE (*,*) Initials(person)
```

Here, the first statement sets up a character string array called 'person', allowing for five elements each of twenty characters' length. The elements are all preset to the empty string, but since we are assigning length=5 strings to a length=0 value the actual effect is to preset 'person' to contain 5 strings each of 20 blanks. The second statement declares 'Initials' to be an external function of character type and length=5. The assignment statement uses an 'array constructor' to specify the array section Person(1:3), and remember that the names will actually be padded out with blanks to make up the full 20-character lengths of the strings.

When 'Initials' is then called, the argument 'person' takes the place of the dummy argument 'names' and the lengths of 'names' and 'Initials' are established within the function. To start with, the statement

```
        Initials = ""
```

actually leaves 'Initials' as a string of five blanks, since its length is five. Then, the DO loop runs through the elements of 'names', takes the initial letter of each, and concatenates them into 'Initials'. In this particular example, the function will return with the value "GMH ".

Assumed-size arrays, using the asterisk notation, are very useful when you want to write a general procedure which will take an array argument of any size. However, it is very easy to get confused between asterisks which stand for array sizes and asterisks which stand for character string lengths. It is often simpler and safer to transmit the size of an array as another argument, as in this function to calculate the root-mean-square deviation of a set of numbers from their average:

```
REAL FUNCTION Rmsd (x, n)
INTEGER :: n
REAL    :: x(n), average, devsq(n)
average = SUM(x)/n
devsq = (x-average)**2
Rmsd = SQRT(SUM(devsq)/n)
END FUNCTION Rmsd
```

The same sort of thing may be done for the lengths of character strings, as in

```
SUBROUTINE Infiltrate (string, nchars)
INTEGER           :: nchars
CHARACTER(nchars) :: string
    .
    .
    .
END SUBROUTINE Infiltrate
```

or even arrays of character strings:

```
SUBROUTINE Worm (string, nchars, nstrings)
INTEGER           :: nstrings, nchars
CHARACTER(nchars) :: string(nstrings)
    .
    .
    .
END SUBROUTINE Worm
```

9B1   Look again at the subroutine Eicheck in section 9.2. Will it always work as intended? What will it do to 'Pompeii'?

9B2   Write a subroutine to arrange three numbers in increasing order of magnitude.

9B3   Write a subroutine with two arguments: firstly a real number, and secondly an arbitrary-length array of real numbers. The subroutine is to rescale the elements of the array so that their average becomes equal to the first argument.

9B4   Write a function to convert a real vector into the scalar consisting of its first element.

9B5   Write a function whose argument is a string of any length, returning a randomly-chosen single character from that string (see the RANDOM function in chapter 10).

9B6   There is a simple way of finding the day of the week for any date in the 20th century. You take the 2-digit year number (i.e. without the '19'), add to it what you get when you divide it by 4 (rounding down to a whole number), add on to that the number of the day within the month, and then add on a "month code" equal to:

0 for January	1 for May	5 for September
3 for February	4 for June	0 for October
3 for March	6 for July	3 for November
6 for April	2 for August	5 for December

Finally, take the result of this modulo 7 (i.e. take the remainder when you divide by 7) and the number you are left with points to the day of the week, i.e. 1 for Monday, 2 for Tuesday, and so on. Write a subroutine to do this. Three arguments should be the integers forming the date (input to the subroutine) and a fourth argument (output) should be the character-string name of the day.

9B7   From two successive complex numbers $z1$ and $z2$, a third is generated by taking

$$z3 = 0.5*(z1 + z2) + c*(z1 - z2)$$

where c is an imaginary constant. Hence, an indefinite sequence of complex numbers can be generated, given two to start things off. Write a program to model what is going on and investigate the convergence of the sequence for different values of c.

N9.1   DOUBLE PRECISION FUNCTIONS

Besides the REAL FUNCTION statement, which introduces a real-valued function, it is possible to use DOUBLE PRECISION FUNCTION in which case the function will have a value of the default higher-precision kind.

N9.2   ENTRY

Usually a procedure is invoked by the name supplied in its first statement, the FUNCTION or SUBROUTINE statement, and it starts executing from that statement; but it is possible to allow a procedure to be entered at different points under different names and with different arguments. This is done by inserting an ENTRY statement at each alternative entry point. A silly example is:

```
SUBROUTINE Powers(x)
REAL : x;                STOP
ENTRY Fifth  (x);        x=x**5;        RETURN
ENTRY Fourth (x);        x=x**4;        RETURN
ENTRY Cube   (x);        x=x**3;        RETURN
ENTRY Square (x);        x=x**2;        RETURN
END SUBROUTINE Powers
```

This is not intended to be called at all under the name Powers, but by statements like CALL Fifth (y) or CALL Fourth (z) which will return with y or z raised to the power 5 or 4. In general an ENTRY statement consists simply of the keyword ENTRY followed by the name by which it will be called, followed by a bracketed list of arguments. Multiple ENTRY statements may also be used in a function subprogram, in which case the appropriate entry names (rather than the overall function name) must be given a value.

N9.3   INTERNAL PROCEDURES

Functions and subroutines are normally either 'intrinsic' or 'external' or are 'module procedures' (chapter 12). A fourth possibility is that of 'internal procedures'. An internal procedure looks very much like an external procedure but is placed inside another 'host' program or subprogram. It must be inserted towards the end of its host, immediately before the host's END statement. The internal procedure(s) must be separated from the rest of the host by a special statement, CONTAINS. An internal procedure may only be accessed from its host, not from other parts of the program.

N9.4   END

It is not strictly necessary to finish a procedure with an END FUNCTION or END SUBROUTINE: a simple END statement will do.

Chapter 10

MORE INTRINSIC PROCEDURES; STATEMENT LABELS

Roughly half-way through this book, we have already dealt with most of the essentials of Fortran: data types, arrays, program control, procedures, character manipulation, and Fortran's repertoire of intrinsic mathematical and numeric functions. Later in the book we will be looking at more advanced aspects of the language, including user-defined data structures, arrays of variable size, pointers, bit manipulation and the details of input and output. This chapter forms an interlude, covering a number of further intrinsic procedures and finally 'statement labels', a controversial language feature that professional programmers love to hate.

The intrinsic procedures met in this chapter are SYSTEM_CLOCK, RANDOM, RANDOMSEED, MAXLOC, MINLOC, ALL, ANY, COUNT, MAXVAL, MINVAL, PRODUCT, SUM, CSHIFT, EOSHIFT, TRANSPOSE, MERGE, PACK, UNPACK, SPREAD, DOTPRODUCT, MATMUL, RADIX, DIGITS, MAXEXPONENT, MINEXPONENT, EXPONENT, FRACTION, NEAREST, SPACING, TINY, and RRSPACING. Two types of statement are introduced: GO TO and CONTINUE.

10.1   INTRINSIC SUBROUTINES

The intrinsic subroutine DATE_AND_TIME was explained in chapter 5. There is another, SYSTEM_CLOCK, also used for timekeeping. It has up to three arguments and is called by a statement of the form

CALL SYSTEM_CLOCK(COUNT=i, COUNT_RATE=j, COUNT_MAX=k)

The arguments are scalar integers (i, j and k are of course arbitrary names) with the keywords COUNT, etc. as shown. The arguments pass information from the processor to the program. The COUNT argument measures time in the processor's own basic units or 'clock counts'. It is the same as the COUNT argument in the DATE_AND_TIME subroutine. COUNT_RATE allows the programmer to connect values of COUNT with real elapsed time, COUNT_RATE being the number of counts per second. COUNT_MAX gives the maximum count after which the clock is reset to zero. If the processor does not possess a clock then COUNT_RATE and COUNT_MAX are returned as zero. SYSTEM_CLOCK could be used by statements like

CALL SYSTEM_CLOCK(COUNT_RATE=nsec)

.
.
.

```
IF (nsec>0) THEN
        CALL SYSTEM_CLOCK(COUNT=n)
        milliseconds = 1000*n/nsec
END IF
```

Note that all three arguments of SYSTEM_CLOCK are optional.

There is a very useful pair of intrinsic subroutines used for generating random numbers, RANDOM and RANDOMSEED. RANDOM has a single argument, of real type, which is returned to the program with a random value in the range between 0 and 1. It doesn't matter what value (if any) the argument had before RANDOM is called. If it is an array variable then an array of different random numbers will be returned. So, if x is a real scalar variable,

```
CALL RANDOM(x)
```

gives x a random value between 0.0 and 1.0. (To be precise, x is less than 1.0 and not less than 0.0.) A more complex usage is the following:

```
REAL :: radvec(3) = 99.0
        .
        .
        .
DO WHILE (SUM(radvec**2)>1.0)
        CALL RANDOM(radvec)
END DO
```

This code finds a random point within the 3-dimensional unit sphere. It does so by picking a point within a cubical volume and checking to see if it is also within the enclosed sphere. The coordinates are preset to a large value merely to satisfy the WHILE condition when the DO loop is first entered: subsequently the loop is repeated until a point within the sphere is found.

The subroutine RANDOMSEED is to do with the initialising of the random number generator that RANDOM will invoke. RANDOMSEED has three optional arguments, but no more than one may be present in a particular call, so we could have

```
CALL RANDOMSEED
CALL RANDOMSEED(SIZE=nints)
CALL RANDOMSEED(PUT=intseedin)
```

or

```
CALL RANDOMSEED(GET=intseedout)
```

Now, RANDOM generates random numbers (or, more technically, 'pseudorandom' numbers) using internally a set of of integers known as the 'seed' and which change from one call to the next. The seed determines the subsequent sequence of random numbers. A call to RANDOMSEED with no argument will simply reset the seed, and might be used at the beginning of a program to make sure that different runs of the same program would give different sequences of random numbers. A call with the argument keyword GET is used to obtain from the processor the current value of the seed. The PUT keyword lets the program specify the seed value. Calls with GET and PUT could be used to record the value of the seed at the start of a simulation, say, and to repeat the run later with the same sequence of random number. A complication is that the seed is not a single integer but a set of them in a rank=1 array. The size of that array (i.e. the number of integers in the seed) is processor-dependent but can be found in a program by calling RANDOMSEED with the SIZE keyword. Obviously the variables used to hold the seed must be arrays of sufficient size, i.e. in the above example, intseedin and intseedout must be of size equal to or greater than nints.

Although RANDOM generates real numbers between 0 and 1, it is a simple matter to scale the results to simulate, say, the throw of a set of seven dice:

```
REAL :: x(7)
INTEGER :: n(7), ntotal
CALL RANDOM(x)
n = 1 + INT(6.0*x)
ntotal = SUM(n)
```

10.2   FUNCTIONS FOR USE WITH ARRAYS

The intrinsic functions described in this section are

MAXLOC	Location of an array's largest element
MINLOC	Location of the lowest element
ALL	True if all an array's elements are true
ANY	True if any element is true
COUNT	The number of true elements
MAXVAL	Value of the largest element
MINVAL	Value of the lowest elements
PRODUCT	Product of all the elements
SUM	Sum of all the elements
CSHIFT	Shift the elements cyclically
EOSHIFT	Shift the elements 'end-off'
TRANSPOSE	The transpose of a matrix
MERGE	Merge two arrays selectively
PACK	Pack an array into a rank-1 array

UNPACK	Unpack a rank=1 array
SPREAD	Replicate an array
DOTPRODUCT	Scalar product of two vectors
MATMUL	Product of two matrices

Each of these in turn will be discussed briefly below, with indications of the argument keywords and their meanings. In many cases it is obvious what the keywords mean, e.g. ARRAY always refers to an array argument. At first reading the descriptions below will inevitably seem very complex, and you may wonder what on earth these functions are really needed for. In fact they can be used for testing, manipulating and reordering the elements of arrays, doing so with great flexibility and conciseness. They are very powerful tools for the programmer who needs to work with arrays of data. However, you may prefer to use this section only for reference.

MAXLOC(ARRAY, MASK) looks into an array of real or integer numbers and returns the set of subscripts giving the location of the largest element. The value of MAXLOC will be a rank=1 array containing the subscripts, so the size of MAXLOC is equal to the rank of ARRAY. MASK is an optional second argument: if present it must be a logical array (or expression) with the same shape as ARRAY, and elements of ARRAY are disregarded if the corresponding elements of MASK are false. For example, if y is (/1946,1932,1945,1949,1936/) then

$$MAXLOC(ARRAY=y,MASK=y<1946)$$

is equal to the array (/3/).

MINLOC(ARRAY,MASK) is exactly like MAXLOC except that it indicates the minimum-valued array element.

ALL(MASK,DIM), and others following it in the list above, were introduced in a simple form in chapter 7. Its first argument is a logical array, MASK. In the simple case where the optional argument DIM is absent, ALL is a logical function true if all the elements of MASK are true. If DIM is present, DIM (short for 'dimension') must be a scalar integer no greater than the rank of MASK, and the function then sees if all the values of MASK are true along the DIM'th dimension: the result is then an array of rank one less than that of MASK. In other words, ALL suppresses the DIM'th dimension of MASK to a value which is true only if all MASK's elements along that dimension are true. For example, if q is a six-dimensional logical array and

$$f = ALL(MASK=q,DIM=4)$$

then f is a five-dimensional array such that $f(i,j,k,m,n)$ is equal to

$$ALL(MASK=q(i,j,k,:,m,n))$$

ANY(MASK,DIM) is like ALL except that the result (or an element of the result) is true if any of MASK's elements (or its elements along a particular dimension) is true.

COUNT(MASK,DIM) also operates on logical arrays. In the simple case when the optional argument DIM is absent, the function has an integer (not logical) value equal to the number of MASK's true elements. If DIM is present, then (as for ALL and ANY) the result COUNT is an array whose shape is reduced from that of MASK by the elimination of the DIM'th dimension: and continuing the previous example

$$\text{ntrue} = \text{COUNT(MASK=q,DIM=4)}$$

gives an array such that ntrue(i,j,k,m,n) is equal to

$$\text{COUNT(MASK=q(i,j,k,:,m,n))}$$

MAXVAL(ARRAY,DIM,MASK) operates on an array of type integer or real and looks for maximum element values. MASK is an optional logical array which, if present, must be of the same shape as ARRAY and causes the function to ignore elements of ARRAY corresponding to false elements of MASK. If DIM is present it has an effect similar to that for the functions ALL, ANY and COUNT, and the result is an array.

MINVAL(ARRAY,DIM,MASK) is similar to MAXVAL but finds the minimum-valued element, or elements, of ARRAY.

PRODUCT(ARRAY,DIM,MASK), just like MAXVAL, has optional arguments DIM and MASK which make it possible to do more complicated things than were mentioned when we introduced this function in chapter 7. For example, if

$$\text{kit} = (/1,0,6,-5,3,0,0,-2,10/)$$

then

$$\text{PRODUCT(ARRAY=kit,MASK=kit/=0)}$$

is equal to 1800.

SUM(ARRAY,DIM,MASK) is just like PRODUCT except that it adds rather than multiplies.

CSHIFT(ARRAY,DIM,SHIFT) is a function we have not encountered before. It operates on an array of any type. The result CSHIFT is also an array, and it is of the same type and shape as ARRAY. In the simplest case, where ARRAY is one-dimensional, DIM must be equal to 1 and the effect of the function is to perform a circular shift of the elements of ARRAY. The shift is through SHIFT places, SHIFT being a scalar integer. So,

$$
\begin{aligned}
&y = (/"a","b","c","d","e","f"/) \\
&z = \text{CSHIFT(ARRAY=y,DIM=1,SHIFT=2)/\&} \\
&\qquad \text{/CSHIFT(ARRAY=y,DIM=1,SHIFT=-1)}
\end{aligned}
$$

gives

$$(/"eb","fc","ad","be","cf","da"/)$$

If ARRAY has more than one dimension, then shifting will take place along the dimension specified by DIM. DIM must be a scalar integer lying in the range from 1 up to the rank of ARRAY. In this case, SHIFT may be a scalar integer and all elements of ARRAY will be shifted by SHIFT places around the DIM'th dimension; but alternatively the different sections

$$ARRAY(i,j,k...,:,...)$$

(where a colon appears in the DIM'th position) may be shifted DIMwise by different numbers of places, SHIFT then being an array whose shape is reduced from that of ARRAY by the suppression of the DIM'th dimension (cf. ALL, ANY etc. above).

EOSHIFT(ARRAY,DIM,SHIFT,BOUNDARY) is just like CSHIFT except that the shifting of elements is not circular, i.e. elements disappear when they fall off one end of a dimension and are not transferred to the other end. EOSHIFT is an acronym for 'end-off shift'. With an array y defined as previously,

$$EOSHIFT(ARRAY=y,DIM=1,SHIFT=2)$$

is equal to

$$(/" "," ","a","b","c","d"/)$$

i.e. as we move the array to the right, vacancies are created on the left and these are filled with blank strings of the appropriate length. In the case of numeric or logical data, zero or .FALSE. is inserted. If different infill values are required, they can be specified through the optional argument BOUNDARY, which like SHIFT may be a scalar or an array. For example, if

$$n = (/k, k=1,10/)$$

then

$$EOSHIFT(ARRAY=EOSHIFT(ARRAY=n,DIM=1,SHIFT=4, \&$$
$$BOUNDARY=0),DIM=1,SHIFT=-2,BOUNDARY=10)$$

is equal to $(/0,0,1,2,3,4,5,6,10,10/)$.

TRANSPOSE(MATRIX), by contrast with the above functions, is extremely simple. It obtains the transpose of a matrix, in the mathematical sense. MATRIX, the only argument, must be a rank=2 array and may be of any type. If MATRIX is an array m with shape (n1,n2) and elements m(i,j), and t=TRANSPOSE(m), then t has shape (n2,n1) and elements t(i,j) = m(j,i).

MERGE(TSOURCE,FSOURCE,MASK) is an elemental function returning either TSOURCE or FSOURCE according to whether MASK is true or false. MASK must be of logical type; TSOURCE and FSOURCE may be of any type, but the same, and if they are arrays they must have the same shape. If MASK is an array it must have the same shape as TSOURCE and FSOURCE. If TSOURCE and FSOURCE are logical, then MERGE is equivalent to

(TSOURCE.AND.MASK).OR.(FSOURCE.AND..NOT.MASK)

The MERGE function acts as a sort of switch, as in the expression

MERGE(TSOURCE=1,FSOURCE=0,MASK=veracity)

which could be used to convert a logical variable ('veracity') into integer type.

PACK(ARRAY,MASK,VECTOR) can transform an array whose rank is 2 or more (ARRAY) into a rank=1 array. This can be done selectively, keeping only those elements corresponding to MASK being true. In other words, PACK is constructed by forming the elements of ARRAY into a one-dimensional list. The order is determined by running through the subscript values of ARRAY from the left as in:

ARRAY(1,1,1,...),
ARRAY(2,1,1,...),...,
ARRAY(1,2,1,...),....

This is called 'array element order'. It is permissible for ARRAY to have rank 1, in which case PACK will be very similar to ARRAY but excluding elements for which MASK is false. Thus, the expression

PACK(ARRAY=characters,MASK=(characters/=" "))

eliminates all the blanks from an array of single characters.

The size of PACK will be the number of elements in ARRAY for which MASK is true, but to get a result of predetermined size the optional argument VECTOR can be used: it must be a rank=1 array whose size will be the size of PACK and whose latter elements provide values to pad out PACK in default of sufficient MASK=.TRUE. elements from ARRAY. For example,

PACK(ARRAY=(/5,4,3,2,1/),MASK=.TRUE.,VECTOR=(/k,k=1,10/))

has the value

(/5,4,3,2,1,6,7,8,9,10/)

UNPACK(VECTOR,MASK,FIELD) can be regarded as the inverse of PACK. If VECTOR is a rank=1 array of any type, its elements will be distributed into the array FIELD to form the result

UNPACK. FIELD may have any shape, but its type must be the same as VECTOR's. The unpacking of VECTOR into FIELD is done under the control of MASK. Running through the elements of FIELD in the usual array element order (see PACK), elements from VECTOR are inserted sequentially to replace those elements of FIELD for which MASK is true. Where MASK is false, or where the elements of VECTOR have already been used up, FIELD is unchanged. To take a simple example, if there is such a thing:

```
UNPACK(VECTOR=(/1,2/),&
        MASK=(/.TRUE.,.FALSE.,.FALSE.,.TRUE./),&
        FIELD=(/9,8,7,6/))
```

is

```
(/1,8,7,2/)
```

SPREAD(SOURCE,DIM,NCOPIES) will replicate the array SOURCE by adding an extra dimension of extent NCOPIES; each element of SOURCE is repeated NCOPIES times along the new dimension. The argument DIM indicates in which position the new dimension is to be inserted in the list of extents defining the shape of SOURCE. So, if the shape of g is (4,4,200),

```
SPREAD(SOURCE=g,DIM=3,NCOPIES=10)
```

has the shape (4,4,10,200). A more complicated example: the code

```
v1 = .FALSE.
v2 = EOSHIFT(ARRAY=v1,DIM=1,SHIFT=1,BOUNDARY=.TRUE.)
m1 = SPREAD(SOURCE=v2,DIM=2,NCOPIES=d)
m2 = CSHIFT(ARRAY=m1,DIM=2,SHIFT=(/i-1,i=1,d/)
m3 = 0.0
diagonal_matrix = UNPACK(VECTOR=vector,MASK=m2,FIELD=m3)
```

where the v's are size=d vectors and the m's are dxd matrices, is a way of forming a diagonal matrix from the elements of 'vector'.

DOTPRODUCT(VECTOR_A,VECTOR_B) forms the dot product (or 'scalar product') of the two vectors which are its arguments. If the vectors are integer or real numbers, the dot product is the sum of the products of corresponding pair of elements. If they are complex (to be more precise, if VECTOR_A is complex) then the complex conjugates of the elements of VECTOR_A are multiplied with the elements of VECTOR_B. If the vectors u and v are of logical type, then DOTPRODUCT(u,v) is equivalent to ANY(u.AND.v).

MATMUL(MATRIX_A,MATRIX_B) forms the matrix product of two numeric matrices. The shapes of the two arguments must fit together, i.e. if MATRIX_A has shape (i,j) and MATRIX_B has shape (j,k) then MATMUL has shape (i,k). Alternatively, one of the two arguments may be a vector, in which case MATMUL takes the product between the vector and the matrix in the conventional way. MATMUL may be used with logical instead of numeric data: if u and v are logical matrices, and w=MATMUL(u,v), then w(i,j) is ANY(u(i,:).AND.v(:,j)).

EXERCISES 10A

10A1   Using RANDOM, write an integer function that will simulate the throw of two dice, adding their results. If a double is thrown, an extra throw is allowed in addition.

10A2   Under the MERGE function, a way was pointed out for converting an item of data from logical to integer type. Write an expression to do the converse, i.e. to convert a binary digit into logical type.

10A3   Being consistent with the account of MATMUL given above, express as clearly as you can in words what MATMUL(x,y) would mean if x were a logical vector and y a logical matrix.

10.3   NUMERIC INQUIRY FUNCTIONS AND FLOATING-POINT MANIPULATION FUNCTIONS

The next set of intrinsic functions to be looked at are to do with the way in which numbers are represented internally within the computer. Although we almost always work with numbers displayed in decimal form, the computer itself may use a base other than 10. There is an intrinsic inquiry function RADIX(X) which returns an integer equal to the internal number base being used for real numbers (if X is real) or for integers (if X is an integer). In fact, most computers use the binary (base 2) system. Below, it is assumed that RADIX is equal to 2.

The processor represents a real number X in a form that may be modelled as

$$X = \pm 1 * 2^{**}e * 0.1...$$

where the exponent e is a positive or negative integer and 0.1... is any binary fraction in the range 0.1000... to 0.1111... (i.e 0.5 to almost 1.0 in decimal). The integer e might typically be formed from 8 bits and could then range from -126 to +127. To represent the case of X=0, e and all the digits in the binary fraction are set to zero. The binary fraction might run to, say, 24 places, and since the first place is always 1 this corresponds to 23 bits of information. With the sign bit and the 8 bits forming e, we therefore have 32 bits representing a real number. This is a common system for representing default-real data in processors with 32-bit 'words', but real data of higher-precision kind may use, say, 64 bits and have a higher exponent range and more significant figures.

To find out the situation on a particular processor, for numeric data of particular type and kind, there are intrinsic inquiry functions DIGITS(X), MAXEXPONENT(X) and MINEXPONENT(X) as well as the function RADIX(X) already mentioned. The argument just specifies the type and kind of data (e.g. DIGITS(0.0) specifies default real data). DIGITS returns the number of significant binary digits, while MAXEXPONENT and MINEXPONENT return the maximum and minimum values of the exponent e. The function TINY(X) returns the value of the smallest positive number which can be represented on the processor.

Other functions give details of the representation of particular numbers. EXPONENT(X), for real X of a specific value, gives the (integer) value of the exponent e as defined above. FRACTION(X) gives the value of the binary fraction 0.1... defined above, but expressed as a real decimal fraction. NEAREST(X,S) returns the real number that the processor will allow nearest to (but not equal to) X; the real argument S is a flag to indicate whether NEAREST is to be above X or below it, according to whether S positive or negative. SPACING(X) returns the minimum spacing between two real numbers in the neighbourhood of X. (If SPACING is too small to be represented itself, TINY(X) is returned instead.) Another function, RRSPACING(X), returns the very large number which is the reciprocal of the relative minimum spacing between two real numbers near X. The definitions are such that

$$RRSPACING(x) * SPACING(x) = ABS(x)$$

There is a function SCALE(X,I) which scales up a real number X by the I'th power of the processor's internal base, i.e. usually by $2**I$. Finally, there is SETEXPONENT(X,I), a function which changes the exponent part of X to the power I; in other words, e is replaced by I in the expression for X given near the start of this section.

10.4   STATEMENT LABELS AND 'GO TO'

All the Fortran statements that we have met so far must start with a letter of the alphabet. However, before that (i.e. before the first keyword, at the beginning of the line) it is possible to have a sequence of digits serving to label the statement, as in the examples

```
1   n=1+INT(x)
341 CALL RANDOM(x)
90 nh6 = Firstroot(g1,g2,g3,g4,g5,g6)
```
and
```
8 i=0 ; 9 j=0 ; 10 k=0
```

A label must have at least one nonzero character, it must be separated by at least one blank from the start of the statement itself, it must be unique within its program unit, it may not consist of more than five digits, and it may not have blanks embedded in it. Labels need not be in numerical sequence, although in the examples below they are ordered in the natural way. Labels can be used in Fortran in a number of minor ways which add nothing to the functionality of the language, but they have one important use: to redirect the flow of execution through a GO TO statement, which has the simple form

GO TO 341

or whatever might be the number labelling the statement you want to go to at that point. The keyword GO TO must be followed by an actual label, not by an expression or variable name. The GO TO statement may be contingent on an IF, as in

```
26 IF(x<0.0) GO TO 27
   y = SQRT(x)
```

It can sometimes be handy to have a 'do-nothing' statement to hang a label onto; a special statement, CONTINUE, exists for this purpose, so for example

27 CONTINUE

could follow the previous example.

GO TO statements can be used to write extremely opaque code very concisely, as in

```
READ (*,*) j
j = MAX(1,ABS(j))  ;  k=0
1  If(MOD(j,2).EQ.1) GO TO 2
j=j/2  ;  k=k+1  ;  GO TO 1
2  j=j+k  ;  IF(MOD(j,3).EQ.1) GO TO 3
GO TO 1
3  j=(j-1)/3
WRITE (*,*) j
```

or as in the following program:

```
PROGRAM Find_A_Prime
INTEGER :: j, k
1  READ (*,*) j
        j=ABS(j)  ;  k=2
2  IF(k.GT.SQRT(j)) GO TO 4
IF(MOD(j,k).EQ.0) GO TO 3
k=k+1  ;  GO TO 2
3  WRITE (*,*) "Divisible by ",k  ;  GO TO 1
4  WRITE (*,*) j, " is prime"
END PROGRAM Find_A_Prime
```

Note that there is scarcely any point in ever labelling non-executable statements (such as the INTEGER statement in the last example). It would be an error to GO TO a non-executable statement such as a type declaration statement.

It is arguable that the GO TO statement does nothing that can't be done with more clarity in Fortran in other ways (e.g. by calling a subroutine). However, GO TO is seductively simple to use and really comes into its own when you want to stitch a modification into a previously existing program. For example,

                GO TO 999
                    .
                    .
                    .
            999 CONTINUE

will simply bypass all the code between those two statements and could be a useful trick when debugging a program. However,

            Bypass: IF (.FALSE.) THEN
                    .
                    .
                    .
            END IF Bypass

does much the same thing.

Notes

N10.1 SPECIFIC NAMES OF INTRINSIC FUNCTIONS

Fortran's intrinsic functions have been introduced under names which are 'generic'. This usually means that the function can accept arguments of more than one type, and that the function result has the same type as the argument. For example, SIN(X) is real if X is real, complex if X is complex, and has 'double precision' if X has double precision. SIN is therefore said to be a 'generic' function name. Likewise, HUGE is 'generic' because HUGE(X) is a large integer if X is an integer, and a large real number if X is real. However, Fortran also allows for a number of 'specific' names, i.e. names under which functions may be referenced when the argument is restricted to being of a specific type. In the case of the SIN function, there are specific names CSIN and DSIN which can be used if the argument and result are to be restricted to complex or double-precision-real types respectively.

In Appendix C there is a complete list of specific names for generic Fortran functions. As a rule there is no point in using specific names, and they are a hangover from earlier versions of Fortran in which different function names had to be used for arguments of different types.

However, a complication arises if the name of an intrinsic function is to be used as the argument of an external procedure. In this event, the name used must be a specific one, because the function's name must predetermine its type. The specific names CSIN and DSIN could therefore be used as arguments of a procedure. In fact, when used in this way SIN is also interpreted as a specific name, i.e. of real type. On the other hand, going back to our other example, there are no specific names for the HUGE function and HUGE cannot therefore be used as a procedure argument.

What we mean by 'specific' and 'generic' names can cause confusion. The situation is that all intrinsic functions have a generic name. In many cases (especially the non-mathematical functions like HUGE and ACHAR) there is only the generic name. Furthermore, the fact that the name is 'generic' doesn't necessarily mean that arguments or results of more than one type are possible: for example ACHAR by its nature can only be a character function of an integer variable, but this is still regarded as a 'generic' function name. At the same time, some generic names can also be used as specific names when the context demands it: SIN is an example. And there is one final complication: in spite of the remarks above about using specific names as procedure arguments, some specific names cannot be so used - an example is ICHAR, which is a generic name and a specific name but has a character-type argument and may not be used as a procedure argument!

Since these complications only arise when we wish to use intrinsic function names as procedure arguments, a usage which crops up only very rarely, the simplest practice is to avoid using any intrinsic function names in this way.

N10.2   GOTO

In the GO TO statement it is not essential to have a space between the GO and the TO.

N10.3   ASSIGNED GO TO

A special statement, ASSIGN, can be used to associate a particular statement label with an integer variable, as in

ASSIGN 10 TO ipoint

The integer variable could subsequently be used instead of a statement label in a GO TO statement, or instead of a format statement label in an i/o statement (see note to chapter 16).

N10.4   COMPUTED GO TO

GO TO may be followed by a bracketed list of statement labels, and then by an integer expression, as in

GO TO (100, 31, 41, 51) kchoice

and the effect is that control passes to the first, second, third, etc. statement in the list according to whether the integer expression (kchoice in that example) has value 1, 2, 3, etc. If the integer is larger than the number of labels listed, or is less than 1, nothing happens.

N10.5   ARITHMETIC IF

A statement such as

IF (handle) 20, 30, 40

transfers control to the statement labelled 20, 30 or 40 according to whether 'handle' is negative, zero or positive. The labels 20, 30 and 40 in this example are arbitrary, but there must be a list of three (not necessarily distinct) labels. The name 'handle' is also an arbitrary example: any real or integer expression may appear between the brackets.

Chapter 11

MODULES

This chapter deals with a Fortran feature which can be enormously useful in communicating data between subprograms and in organising the overall architecture of any large program. It is a new type of program unit, called a 'module'.

So far we have considered only three different kinds of program units, namely the main program, subroutines, and functions. As we have seen, program execution always starts with a main program, from which subroutines and functions (collectively called 'procedures') may be called. Procedures may call on other procedures in turn. Whenever a procedure is called, a list of arguments is used to pass data in either direction between the two program units, the calling and the called. In the case of functions, of course, the function name itself transfers data back from the function. If a procedure is written to carry out a simple self-contained operation, like calculating a simple mathematical function, then data transmission by argument-passing may be good enough, but in general it can be very useful if not essential to have a way in which program units can share larger sets of data in a more flexible and open way. Modules provide a method of doing this.

Modules are important not only for sharing data-access between program units, they are also useful for access to entities such as derived type definitions (to be met in chapter 14) and to grouped sets of procedures known as 'module procedures'.

This chapter introduces just four very simple new statements: MODULE, END MODULE, USE and CONTAINS. They are deceptively powerful.

11.1   DATA MODULES

Normally a name given to a variable (or to a named constant) is meaningful only within a particular program unit. A declaration like

CHARACTER(80) :: line(60)

is only known to the main program or procedure in which it appears. If this statement were to be repeated in different program units, the processor would assume that it referred to different things, and distinct areas of memory would be allocated. In other words the names of variables in Fortran are usually 'local' entities. Using modules, however, it becomes possible for the same sets of data to be accessible to a number of different program units.

Suppose, as an example, that a program needs to use an array of character strings representing a page of text together with some integer and logical data items related to it. The form of the data might be specified by the declaration statements

```
CHARACTER(80) :: line(60)
INTEGER :: linelength, linesperpage, numpage
LOGICAL :: checkin, checkspell, checkout
```

To have access to this data in different procedures, these declaration statements could be encapsulated in another kind of program unit called a 'module', consisting simply of the statements above topped and tailed by MODULE and END MODULE statements:

```
MODULE Textpage
CHARACTER(80) :: line(60)
INTEGER :: linelength, linesperpage, numpage
LOGICAL :: checkin, checkascii, checkspell, checkout
END MODULE Textpage
```

The module can then be invoked in any other program unit simply by supplying the statement

```
USE Textpage
```

The name Textpage is of course arbitrary. The general form of the MODULE statement is simply the keyword MODULE followed by a name which may be chosen according to the usual Fortran rules, like the name of a variable or a procedure. The END MODULE statement is similar, just like an END FUNCTION or END SUBROUTINE statement, and it is not compulsory to repeat the module's name; in fact 'END' by itself would suffice. As will be seen later, the USE statement can be a little more complicated than is indicated here, but basically it consists of the keyword USE followed by the name of a module.

A program may include many different modules as long as they have different names. A particular program unit may invoke a number of modules by having a series of USE statements. USE statements are nonexecutable, and they must appear at the very beginning of a program unit immediately following the PROGRAM (or SUBROUTINE, etc.) statement and before any other nonexecutable statements. A module may itself invoke a further module, e.g. we could have

```
MODULE Textpage
USE Language
CHARACTER(80) :: line(60)
INTEGER :: linelength, linesperpage, numpage
LOGICAL :: checkin, checkascii, checkspell, checkout
END MODULE Textpage
```

but it is not permissible for a module to invoke itself, directly or indirectly. So, the module 'Language' may not have a 'USE Textpage' statement, or a circularity would be created.

The next example is a data module containing information about metals, and it shows that a module can be used to hold a database of fairly complex design. It must be stressed that this module does not actually 'do' anything. It has no executable statements. Its purpose is to declare the structure of a set of data that can subsequently be utilised in other program units.

```
MODULE Metals
INTEGER :: number_of_metals, namelengths(100)
CHARACTER(20) :: metal_name(100)
REAL :: weight(100), density_0(100), density_100(100),&
        meltpoint(100), conductivity_0(100),&
        conductivity_100(100), pricerange(2,100)
LOGICAL :: data_has_been_read_in
END MODULE Metals
```

This could be invoked (by the statement 'USE Metals') in different subroutines to carry out tasks like reading the data from a disk file, modifying the data, rewriting the disk file, and making calculations which need access to this dataset. For example, to estimate the conductivity of a metal at a particular temperature we could write a function such as

```
REAL FUNCTION Conductivity (metal, temperature)
USE Metals
REAL :: temperature, c0, c100
CHARACTER(20) :: metal
Conductivity = -99.0  ! unrecognised metal
DO i = 1, number_of_metals
        IF (metal/=metal_name(i)) CYCLE
        c0 = conductivity_0(i)
        c100 = conductivity_100(i)
        Conductivity = c0 + temperature*(c100-c0)/100.0
        EXIT
END DO
END FUNCTION Conductivity
```

This is obviously much simpler than transmitting all the data through a long list of arguments.

With a module, a large or complex set of data need only be designed and declared once. This saves memory, keeps programs shorter, avoids error, and avoids passing clumsy long lists of arguments to procedures. In fact subroutines need have no arguments at all. A main program could simply look like

118

```
PROGRAM Economic_Prediction
CALL Startup
CALL Calculate
CALL Display
END PROGRAM Economic_Prediction
```

with the associated subprograms being, say,

```
SUBROUTINE Startup
USE Basedata
USE Workspace ....


SUBROUTINE Calculate
USE Workspace
USE Results ....


SUBROUTINE Display
USE Results
USE Output_Formats ....


MODULE Basedata ....


MODULE Workspace ....


MODULE Results ....


MODULE Output_Formats ....
```

In this example the four modules could contain all the data declarations and the subroutines could contain only executable statements after the USE statements. The program as a whole consists of eight program units. This sort of design can give the programmer great flexibility: for example, the module called Output_Formats could be written in two or three different versions, to interface with different display devices that could be connected to the processor.

Modules encourage a systematic approach to the design, management and use of a program or system of programs. When important data is kept in modules, the programmer's work can become focussed more on the careful design of the data structures rather than on procedures. Modules take on a life of their own, central to how we perceive the program, while procedures can be regarded as mere ancillaries that carry out operations on the data modules. In many application areas that depend on large data sets, this sort of programming style ('declarative', or 'data-oriented' programming) is far more appropriate than the 'stream-of-consciousness' style that concentrates on the flow of control between subroutines and functions.

This section was headed 'Data Modules' and we have seen that a module may contain a number of data declarations. The declarations may be type declaration statements of any kind (see chapter 13). We shall see later that modules may also contain declarations of derived types (chapter 14), procedure interfaces (chapter 12) and namelist groups (chapter 16). They may also include procedures, as explained in the next section.

11.2   MODULE PROCEDURES

The procedures we have so far met have been 'external' procedures, i.e. subroutines and functions which are external to the main program. External procedures are extremely useful, and in practice they form the bulk of almost all large Fortran programs. They have the incidental advantage that they need not necessarily be supplied in the Fortran language: in principle it is possible for a Fortran program to call external procedures that are in another language or in precompiled machine code. Almost everything that can be achieved with Fortran can be done using a set of external procedures, a main program, and data modules.

Nevertheless, Fortran allows for another kind of procedure, 'module procedures', which are specified within modules. Like external procedures, module procedures are either of the 'subroutine' or the 'function' variety; they look very similar to external procedures and are invoked in the same way by CALL statements or function references. However, a module procedure may only be invoked from parts of the program to which the module is plugged in by USE statements. Module procedures must always be supplied in Fortran.

There are a number of reasons why module procedures can be useful. If a module defines the structure of a special set of data, and if there are also some specialised procedures needed for operating on that data, then it can be appropriate to include the procedures as well as the data in the one module. Even if no special data set is involved, it can be handy to use a module to hold a 'library' of related procedures, such as functions used to make actuarial calculations. A programmer may create a set of procedures with a frequently-encountered problem in mind (e.g. reading disk files in various formats) and put them into a module which could be copied and used in a number of different programs. Another point is that procedures with the same name can sit in different modules, and then the programmer can switch between different versions of the same procedure just by changing the USE statement.

A special statement, CONTAINS, is required when a module contains module procedures. The general form of a module is

```
MODULE ....

    USE statements

    declaration statements

CONTAINS

    module procedures

END MODULE ....
```

When this module is invoked by a USE statement in any other subprogram, that subprogram has access to the data sets declared in the module and may call any of the procedures that follow the CONTAINS statement. It also has access to the additional modules, if any, identified by USE statements at the beginning of this module. The declaration statements may be a mixture of type declaration statements and the other kinds of declaration mentioned at the end of the last section, but may not include executable statements.

After CONTAINS, there is a set of one or more module procedures. Module procedures are exactly the same in form as external subroutines or functions, each starting with a SUBROUTINE (or FUNCTION) statement and finishing with a suitable END statement. All the sorts of subroutines and functions explained in chapters 9 and 12 may occur as module procedures rather than as external procedures.

There is one very important difference between module procedures and external procedures, namely that a module procedure has direct access to the data declared in the module before the CONTAINS statement. This is called the 'host association' of data, and the module is said to be the 'host' of its module procedures. Entities declared before the CONTAINS statement are shared by host association among all the module procedures following.

Here is an example of a module with data and procedures:

```
MODULE Polynomial
REAL :: c(0:3)

CONTAINS

SUBROUTINE Show_Coefficients
WRITE (*,*) c
END SUBROUTINE Show_Coefficients

REAL FUNCTION Poly(x)
REAL :: x
```

```
        Poly = c(0) + x*(c(1) + x*(c(2) + x*c(3)))
        END FUNCTION Poly

        REAL FUNCTION Inverse_Poly(y)
        REAL :: y, scratchpad(4)
            .

            .
        (find an approximate real solution to the cubic equation y=Poly(x), with
        Poly as defined as above)

            .

        Inverse_Poly = ....
        END FUNCTION Inverse_Poly

        SUBROUTINE Switchback
        c(0:3) = c(3:0:-1)
        END SUBROUTINE Switchback

        END MODULE Polynomial
```

The subroutines Show_Coefficients and Switchback, and the Functions Poly and Inverse_Poly, can be accessed by any other program unit that has the statement

        USE Polynomial

These module procedures may also access one another: for example the function Inverse_Poly could include calls to Poly. Moreover, the data declared at the beginning of the module above (the array c) is also directly accessible to all the module procedures and to other parts of the program using the module.

At the same time, a module procedure may have data items internal to itself and not accessible outside it. This the situation if a module procedure has some type declaration statements of its own: the items declared will be 'local' variables and will not be accessible by host association outside the module procedure. For example, the function Inverse_Poly above includes a data array called scratchpad, and this is a local variable not accessible anywhere else. The argument y in Inverse_Poly, and also the argument x in Poly, are names local to those procedures and not accessible to the rest of the module, but they are also dummy arguments and are therefore accessible (by 'argument association', not 'host association'!) wherever the functions are called from.

Note that if one of a module's data declarations is repeated within a module procedure, the effect is to set up a separate local variable, and therefore to prevent the module procedure from accessing the module's data. Consequently,

```
MODULE Pointless
REAL :: x
CONTAINS
SUBROUTINE Double
REAL :: x
x = 2.0 * x
END SUBROUTINE Double
END MODULE Pointless
```

will do nothing because, within the subroutine, x is a local variable and is not the same piece of data as the x declared before the CONTAINS statement! If the subroutine's REAL statement were removed then its x would be host-associated to the original x, and a statement 'CALL Double' would double the value of x.

To make all this a little clearer, notice that data items can be regarded as falling into a number of different categories according to their 'scope', i.e. over how much of the program they can be used. It is useful to distinguish the following possibilities:

(a)   **'Local' variables** may be declared by one type declaration statement and are used within the main program or within one subprogram and have no significance whatsoever outside it. A local variable need not be declared at all if it is a scalar of real or integer type (according to the initial-letter naming convention). It is usual not to declare DO-loop variables or the implied-DO variables that can be used in, say, array constructors.

(b)   **Arguments of procedures** allow data to be passed between program units as the program is executing. Just as a door has two sides, an argument exists both as a 'dummy' argument in the procedure itself and as an 'actual' argument in a calling program. When a procedure is invoked, there is 'argument association' between the actual arguments and the dummy arguments. In the case of a function, a similar thing happens with its value. Although 'argument association' passes a value between one program unit and another, the names of arguments should be declared separately in the two program units.

(c)   When variables are declared at the beginning of a module which also contains module procedures, then the variables are shared between the module procedures by **'host association'**. The host-associated variables' declarations must be separated by a CONTAINS statement from the module procedures.

(d)   When a USE statement connects a module to a subprogram, the variables declared at the start of the module (i.e. before any CONTAINS statement) are said to be **'use associated'** to the subprogram.

The three kinds of association (argument, host and use association) should be kept quite distinct from one another. A crucial point is that argument association happens dynamically as the program executes, with values being passed from one memory location to another. By contrast, host association and use association are static relationships which are established once and for all when the program is compiled. Host association and use association do not involve any copying or duplication of data: they are merely forms of shared access to particular memory locations.

11.3   MORE ABOUT 'USE' STATEMENTS

USE statements are nonexecutable statements which must be positioned before anything else after a PROGRAM, SUBROUTINE, FUNCTION or MODULE statement. Each USE statement points to a module and gives the subprogram access to a set of data and/or module procedures. This could, potentially, give rise to problems if the same names have been used to represent different variables in different parts of the program. If there is a data module such as

```
MODULE Coordinates
REAL :: x(60), y(60), z(60), units
REAL :: xlimits(2), ylimits(2), zlimits(2)
REAL :: scalex, scaley, scalez
INTEGER :: npoints
LOGICAL :: provisional(60)
END MODULE Coordinates
```

then there would be a conflict if it were used by another subprogram which already had other variables called (say) x and y. To avoid this sort of problem, the USE statement may specify a different local name for data within a module. There is also a form of the USE statement which limits access to a chosen subset of the things in the module. The following examples show the syntax:

```
USE Coordinates, nplaces => npoints
USE Coordinates, xhere => x, yhere => y, zhere => z
USE Coordinates, x => y, y => x
USE Coordinates, ONLY : xlimits, ylimits, zlimits
USE Coordinates, ONLY : z
USE Coordinates, ONLY : zhere => z
```

The first of these gives full access to the module coordinates, but a different local name (nplaces) is to be used here in place of the module's name (npoints) for that particular data item. After this USE statement, the name npoints would not refer to the data in the module at all, and could be used for something completely different. The combination => is used to link the new local name with the module name. This is similar to the notation we will come across later for pointer assignment (chapter 15). In the second example above, the local names xhere, yhere and zhere are linked to the data objects known in the module as x, y and z. Incidentally, when a local name is set up in this way, there is no need to mention it in a type declaration statement in the same subprogram: it is assumed to have the same properties as were declared in the module. So, xhere, yhere and zhere are 60-element arrays.

It is permissible for a program unit to have more than one USE statement referring to the same module, and it is possible for one data object to have more than one local name. If the first three statements above were put together at the top of the same subprogram, the effect would be to give access to all the module's data items but with npoints having the local name nplaces, x having the local names xhere and y, y having the local names yhere and x, and z having the local name zhere; and all the other data items in the module would keep their original names.

The fourth, fifth and sixth examples above show how the keyword ONLY is used to give partial access to a module. The fourth would be used in a subprogram where access is wanted only to the variables xlimits, ylimits and zlimits. The fifth gives access only to z. The sixth also gives access only to z, but imposes the local name zhere. A USE statement with ONLY does not cancel out another less restrictive USE statement; if a program unit has a USE statement without the ONLY qualifier for a particular module, then all parts of the module are accessible even if the same module is also invoked by a USE...ONLY statement. A set of USE...ONLY statements gives access to all the items named. If the three final examples above occurred together, the combined effect would be to give access to xlimits, ylimits, zlimits, and z, the latter having the local name 'zhere' as well as the name z.

All that has been said above about local names and partial access to modules applies not only to data but also to module procedures (and other entities, such as interface blocks, which will be met in later chapters). This means that the statement

    USE Polynomial, Tell => Show_Coefficients

(referring to the example in section 11.2) gives full access to the module Polynomial but the subroutine Show_Coefficients is to be referred to locally as Tell. The statement

    USE Polynomial, ONLY : Tell => Show_Coefficients

means that no other parts of the module, apart from this subroutine, are accessible here.

As a rule it is a good idea to avoid renaming data and other entities in USE statements. When the same item is referred to by different names it generally leads to confusion rather than clarity. On the other hand, USE statements with the ONLY keyword are a useful form of 'positive vetting' to ensure that data sets in different parts of the program are not inadvertently confused, and they make it easier for the programmer to remember exactly what is to be accessed in each module. For example,

    USE Iocontrol, ONLY : Printer, printer_output_format

could be used to select a printing function (Printer) and associated format data (printer_output_data) from a library of data and module procedures for input and output (Iocontrol).

EXERCISES 11A

11A1   Write a data module to contain in a convenient form the names of the days of the week, the names of the months, and the usual numbers of days in the months. With this data module in mind, write a USE statement giving access just to the names of the months.

11A2   Write a data module to contain the mathematical constants π and e and the first twenty powers of 2.

11A3   A database is to consist of a set of up to 3000 names, postal addresses, and telephone numbers, in addition to each of which there is a 12-character code for administrative purposes. Design a data module to contain this information in a suitable form. Then, write specifications (in English, not Fortran!) for a number of module procedures that could operate on the database to carry out as many useful tasks as you can think of in ten minutes.

11A4   Write a data module containing a two-dimensional 'spreadsheet' of 30 rows and 10 columns, each cell containing data in the form of a string of 12 characters. An ancillary array is to contain single-character indicators to say which cells contain values and whether the values are to be interpreted simply as words or as integers or real numbers.

11A5   To the module in 11A4, add a module procedure. It is to be an integer function, yielding the integer value if that is what is represented by the character string in a given cell of the spreadsheet. You can use an internal READ statement (chapter 16) to transform a character string into an integer!

N11.1   PRIVATE AND PUBLIC

The PRIVATE and PUBLIC data attributes would normally be specified in a type declaration statement (see chapter 13) in a module. However, they may alternatively be specified by separate statements such as

>   PUBLIC :: This, That
>   PRIVATE :: The_Other

and the statement

>   PRIVATE

by itself changes the normal default (by which all variables are usually PUBLIC) to PRIVATE.

N11.2   COMMON

There is an alternative to using a data module for 'sharing' data between different program units. The alternative, an old construction that goes back to Fortran's early days, is the 'COMMON block'. An example of the syntax is

>   COMMON /Pool/ mums(10), arr(3,3,3), intflag

Between slashes, Pool is the (arbitrary) name of the common block and can be used in different program units to refer to a single shared area of memory. Data are to be found there according to the ordered list of names and array shapes that follows: in this example, some arrays of real numbers and integer with the local names mums, arr and intflag. The data does not need to appear also in type declaration statements unless further specifications have to be given. The data in a common block can have different local names in different program units, i.e. the names and array shapes which follow the slashes can vary, but they will everywhere refer to the same items of data.

The name of the common block can be omitted, in which case the statement refers to a special area of memory known as 'blank common'. The syntax is like this:

>   COMMON // mums(10), arr(3,3,3), intflag

Chapter 12

FUNCTIONS AND SUBROUTINES (2)

External procedures, i.e. functions and subroutines, were first introduced in chapter 9. In chapter 11, we dealt with how 'module procedures' may be contained within modules. This chapter covers a number of more advanced facilities, starting in section 12.1 with 'recursive' procedures.

When a program unit invokes a procedure, for many purposes it is necessary for the program unit to include first a special block declaring more detailed information about the procedure. This is known as an 'interface block' and the idea is introduced in section 12.2. Most of the remainder of this chapter is then devoted to special features which require the use of interface blocks: procedures with argument keywords, procedures which may be used with variable numbers of arguments, functions with array-valued results, how to have assumed-shape arrays as arguments, functions that define new operators, and how to give a set of procedures a single generic name. Finally, section 12.8 indicates how function calls in Fortran 90 could in principle support parallel processing.

The new statement types introduced here are EXTERNAL, INTERFACE, MODULE PROCEDURE, and END INTERFACE, and we meet a new intrinsic inquiry function, PRESENT.

12.1   RECURSIVE PROCEDURES

Normally a procedure may not invoke itself, either directly or indirectly. In some circumstances, though, it can be convenient to let this happen, and it is made possible by putting the keyword RECURSIVE before the procedure's name in the first line of the procedure. This can be applied both to functions and to subroutines, but in the case of a function an extension has to be made to the syntax of the FUNCTION statement: if, for example, an integer function called Iris is to be made recursive, its first line could be

> RECURSIVE INTEGER FUNCTION Iris (juniper) RESULT (berry)

or, equivalently,

> INTEGER RECURSIVE FUNCTION Iris (juniper) RESULT (berry)

the order of the first two keywords being irrelevant. The meaning of RESULT (berry) is explained below. Subroutines are simpler, just requiring the keyword RECURSIVE as in

> RECURSIVE SUBROUTINE Metamorphosis (jekyll, hyde)

How can recursive procedures be used? An example is this subroutine to put a sequence of characters into alphabetical order:

```
RECURSIVE SUBROUTINE Order (caps)
CHARACTER :: caps(*), store
LOGICAL :: disorder = .FALSE.
DO kount = 1, SIZE(caps)-1
        IF (LGT(caps(kount),caps(kount+1)) THEN
                store = caps(kount)
                caps(kount) = caps(kount+1)
                caps(kount+1) = store
                disorder = .TRUE.
        END IF
END DO
IF (disorder) CALL Order (caps)
END SUBROUTINE Order
```

This works by putting a disordered sequence into something closer to alphabetical order and then calling itself again. The next example is a recursive subroutine which will show the running total of an indefinite series of input numbers:

```
RECURSIVE SUBROUTINE Add_In (k)
INTEGER :: k, knew, number
READ (*,*) number
IF (number==0) RETURN                    ! A zero terminates (see N12.3)
knew = k + number
PRINT (*,*) knew
CALL Add_In (knew)
END SUBROUTINE Add_In
```

This is started by CALL Add_In(0), and finished when a zero is input.

In the case of a recursive function, to avoid a possible ambiguity, the function's result value must be given a name different from that of the function itself. The result name that will be used within the function must therefore be specified in brackets after the keyword RESULT at the end of the function statement. Then, within the function, any reference to the actual function name is taken as a recursive call to the function.

A popular textbook example of a recursive function is the factorial, which can be written:

```
RECURSIVE INTEGER FUNCTION Factorial (n) RESULT (nfac)
INTEGER :: n
SELECT CASE (n)
CASE (1)
        nfac = 1
CASE DEFAULT
        nfac = n * Factorial (n-1)
END SELECT
END FUNCTION Factorial
```

Here the result is being called 'nfac', as declared in the first line. There is no need for nfac to appear in any type declaration statement as it is taken to have the same type as 'Factorial', i.e. it is an integer. The name 'Factorial' can only occur as a call to the function and is not used to assign a value to the function.

Recursive procedures can sometimes make life simpler for the programmer, but they can lead to inefficient code and it is usually possible to carry out the task in another way. The factorial function above can be calculated much more simply by the one-liner

$$nfac = PRODUCT ((/i, i=1,n/)) !$$

EXERCISES 12A

12A1   Write a recursive function to calculate a definite integral of the function $\sin^n(x)$, the arguments being the power n and the limits of integration.

12A2   Write a recursive subroutine which will find a solution of the equation $x - 3\cos(x) = c$. It should work by starting from a rough estimate of the solution, finding a better estimate, and then calling itself again, until the estimate is very close to the exact solution. The subroutine's arguments should be the number c and the current estimate of the solution of the equation.

12A3   The Ackerman function, ACK(m,n) is a function of two non-negative integers. It is defined by:

$$ACK(0,n) = N+1$$

$$ACK(m,0) = ACK(m-1,1)$$

$$ACK(m,n) = ACK(m-1,ACK(m,n-1)) \text{ if neither m nor n is zero}$$

Write a function to give ACK(m,n), and use it to investigate the function's properties.

12.2   INTERFACE BLOCKS

A procedure's interface block is something that occurs not in the procedure itself but in another part of the program from where the procedure may be referenced. An interface block specifies the characteristics of the procedure and of its arguments, giving details that the compiler could not necessarily deduce merely from the form of a reference to the procedure.

There are a number of technical reasons why it is a good idea to provide interfaces for procedures. For one thing, if an external procedure is precompiled or is in a language other than Fortran, the Fortran compiler may simply not have access to the procedure definition itself and therefore may not 'know' all the characteristics of the procedure's arguments. And, even when a procedure is supplied in Fortran, it can be very time-consuming for a compiler to have to scan through an entire program to find a procedure so as to get information needed to compile a quite separate program unit. Interfaces mean that different program units may, to a large extent, be compiled independently and with a substantial saving of time.

An interface block is nonexecutable and must be placed among the other nonexecutable statements (type declaration statements, etc.) at the beginning of the program unit before any executable statements. A very simple interface block is:

```
INTERFACE
REAL FUNCTION Triangle_Area (x1, x2, x3, y1, y2, y3)
REAL :: x1, x2, x3, y1, y2, y3
END FUNCTION Triangle_Area
END INTERFACE
```

i.e. it starts with the statement INTERFACE, finishes with the statement END INTERFACE, and between them there is a repetition of the FUNCTION (or SUBROUTINE) statement, argument type declaration statements, and END FUNCTION (or END SUBROUTINE) statements that would be given elsewhere in the procedure definition itself. An interface block may contain interfaces to more than one procedure, as in

```
INTERFACE

REAL FUNCTION Triangle_Area (x1, x2, x3, y1, y2, y3)
REAL :: x1, x2, x3, y1, y2, y3
END FUNCTION Triangle_Area

REAL FUNCTION Quad_Area (x1,x2,x3,x4,y1,y2,y3,y4)
REAL :: x1, x2, x3, x4, y1, y2, y3, y4
END FUNCTION Quad_Area

END INTERFACE
```

However, interface blocks as simple as those would not be mandatory unless the argument names (x1, x2, etc.) were being set up as argument keywords. Argument keywords in external procedures are our first example of a feature for which interface blocks are compulsory, and are the subject of the next section.

12.3   ARGUMENT KEYWORDS

The idea of argument keywords has already been explained in the context of intrinsic procedures. When a procedure has several arguments, keywords are a foolproof way of avoiding confusion between them, instead of relying simply on the order in which they are specified. With user-written procedures, keywords are not set up in the procedure definition itself, they are set up in an interface block, by listing the desired keyword names in the order of the arguments in the FUNCTION or SUBROUTINE statement. So, with a function like

```
REAL FUNCTION Distance (x1, x2, y1, y2)
REAL :: x1, x2, y1, y2
Distance = SQRT( (x1-x2)**2 + (y1-y2)**2 )
END FUNCTION Distance
```

we could use an interface such as

```
INTERFACE
REAL FUNCTION Distance (Xa, Xb, Ya, Yb)
REAL :: Xa, Xb, Ya, Yb
END FUNCTION Distance
END INTERFACE
```

and, in any program unit containing that interface, the function could be called by a statement such as

```
s = Distance (Xa=1.576, Ya=34.88, Xb=pt3x, Yb=pt3y)
```

As this example shows, the arguments need not have the same names in the interface block as in the procedure itself (they are all 'dummy' arguments) although they must correspond in order. Where the function is actually called using the keywords, the arguments can be in any order. It is suggested, as a convention, that argument keywords be given an initial capital letter.

Note that a procedure may be given two (or more) different interface blocks in different parts of a program; this means that different keywords may be used in different places for the same procedure!

Where an interface block makes it possible for argument keywords to be used, they may nevertheless be omitted, but not beyond a point in the argument list where the arguments' order differs from that specified in the procedure itself. Thus, the statement above is equivalent to

$$s = Distance\ (1.576,\ Ya=34.88,\ Xb=pt3x,\ Yb=pt3y)$$

and to

$$s = Distance\ (1.576,\ pt3x,\ Yb=pt3y,\ Ya=34.88)$$

Notice that it is only by the occurrence of an '=' sign that the processor knows that a keyword is being used, and it is only through the interface that the name of the keyword is specified.

Whenever writing and using external procedures that have multiple arguments, it is good practice to supply interfaces with argument keywords. In fact, one interface block could be put together containing interfaces for all the program's external procedures. This block could be put into a module, and accessed by a USE statement at the start of every program unit.

12.4   MORE ABOUT ARGUMENTS; 'PRESENT'

One use of argument keywords is to control a situation where not all (or, indeed, perhaps none) of the procedure's arguments need necessarily be present each time it is invoked. (A good example of this is the intrinsic subroutine DATE_AND_TIME, described in chapter 5.) An argument which need not be given is known as an 'optional' argument, and in an external procedure it would be declared by having a special attribute, OPTIONAL, in the type declaration statement. We could have a function starting with

```
INTEGER FUNCTION Addemup (k1, k2, k3, k4, k5, k6)
INTEGER :: k1, k2
INTEGER, OPTIONAL :: k3, k4, k5, k6
        .
        .
```

which means that the arguments k3, k4, k5, and k6 need not actually be present. In other words, Addemup may be called with between two and six arguments. Within such a function it is usually necessary to have some way of knowing whether or not an optional argument has actually been specified, and this is done with an intrinsic inquiry function, PRESENT, which should be called from within the procedure. If A is the name of an argument, PRESENT(A) is a logical function which is true if and only if A has been specified in this particular call to the procedure. The above function could therefore be completed with the statements

```
            .
            .

        Addemup = k1 + k2
        IF (PRESENT(k3)) Addemup = Addemup + k3
        IF (PRESENT(K4)) Addemup = Addemup + k4
        IF (PRESENT(k5)) Addemup = Addemup + k5
        END FUNCTION Addemup
```

If a procedure has any optional arguments, an interface must be supplied. An interface block for the above function could be

```
        INTERFACE
        INTEGER FUNCTION Addemup (K1, K2, K3, K4, K5)
        REAL :: K1, K2
        REAL, OPTIONAL :: K3, K4, K5
        END FUNCTION Addemup
        END INTERFACE
```

and valid forms of reference to the function would be, for example,

```
        Addemup(1,2)
        Addemup(1,2,3)
        Addemup(K1=1,K2=2,K5=9)
        Addemup(3,4,5,6,7)
        Addemup(K1=mheathrow, K2=mgatwick, K3=mluton)
```

Note that keywords do not necessarily have to be used when there are optional arguments; but without keywords it would only be possible to omit a series of arguments from the back end of the procedure's argument list. So, in the example of Addemup(1,2,3) above, it is K4 and K5 that are not present.

12.5   ARRAY-VALUED FUNCTIONS

A function's result need not just be a scalar: it may be an array. However, in that case the shape of the array must be specified as part of a type declaration statement within the function, and

134

therefore there is no need for the function's type to be prefixed to the FUNCTION statement itself. An array-valued function must have an interface.

This function has an array as its argument and as its value:

```
FUNCTION Inverse_Vector (v)
REAL :: Inverse_Vector(3), v(3)
Inverse_Vector = v/DOTPRODUCT(v,v)
END FUNCTION Inverse_Vector
```

and a suitable interface would be

```
INTERFACE
FUNCTION Inverse_Vector (v)
REAL :: Inverse_Vector(3), v(3)
END FUNCTION Inverse_Vector
END INTERFACE
```

then, Inverse_Vector((/1.0,0.0,3.0/)) = (/0.1,0.0,0.3/).

12.6   DEFINED OPERATORS

User-written external functions can be regarded as a supplement to Fortran's own set of intrinsic functions, and likewise it is possible to have user-defined operators to supplement Fortran's intrinsic operators (+, -, *, **, //, >, etc.). Most of Fortran's intrinsic operators are 'binary' operators, i.e. they operate between two quantities to produce one result. Sometimes the operation is symmetrical, as for multiplication (*) or addition (+),and sometimes it is not, e.g p**q is not the same as q**p. There are two or three 'unary' intrinsic operators, operating on a single quantity (+ and - may be used as unary operators, and the logical operator .NOT. is always unary).

Any external function of one or two arguments may be referenced through a user-defined operator with the help of an interface block. The INTERFACE statement then takes the form

INTERFACE OPERATOR (....)

with the required operator being given in the brackets. A defined operator must consist of a series of up to 31 letters, surrounded by a pair of dots. Taking again the last example of the previous section, if we had the interface

```
INTERFACE OPERATOR (.Inv.)
FUNCTION Inverse_Vector (v)
REAL :: Inverse_Vector(3), v(3)
END FUNCTION Inverse_Vector
END INTERFACE
```

then .Inv. is defined as a unary operator which can be applied to any real array of rank=1 and size=3. So, .Inv.(/1.0,0.0,3.0/) is equivalent to (/0.1,0.0,0.3/). Note that this is a unary operator, with one argument, although the argument is an array.

With one argument there may be little to choose between a function-name reference and a defined-operator reference, but with two arguments the usefulness of a defined operator is more apparent. Consider this example:

```
REAL FUNCTION Vector_Multiplication (v1, v2)
REAL :: v1(*) , v2(*)
Vector_Multiplication = DOTPRODUCT(v1, v2)
END FUNCTION Vector_Multiplication
```

with interface

```
INTERFACE OPERATOR (.X.)
REAL FUNCTION Vector_Multiplication (v1, v2)
REAL :: v1(*) , v2(*)
END FUNCTION Vector_Multiplication
END INTERFACE
```

This means that expressions like r.X.t or x.X.(/1.89,-5.71,20.04/) can be used freely to calculate the dot product of any pair of real vectors.

When the two arguments are not treated symmetrically in a procedure, then with a binary operator the first argument comes before it and the second comes after it as one would expect.

Besides defining operators of a new form (.Inv. and .X. in the examples above) it is possible to redefine Fortran's existing intrinsic operators. If in the example immediately above we had the INTERFACE statement

```
INTERFACE OPERATOR (*)
```

this would have the effect of turning the ordinary multiplication operator into a dot product operator in the case of real vectors. This technique is known as 'overloading'.

It must be emphasised that defined operators (like keywords) arise not as a feature of the procedure itself but of the interface. Since different program units may in principle have different interfaces to the same procedure, different operators could be used for the same task in different parts of a program, or conversely we could have the same operator being used for different tasks. And, with overloading, it is possible to completely confuse Fortran's intrinsic operators: for example the functions of * and / could be interchanged! Unless it is your objective to produce cryptic code, it is best to avoid overloading intrinsic operators and to put all the interfaces to defined operators into one module accessed by the whole of your program.

In the evaluation of Fortran expressions, defined unary operators take higher precedence than any other operators, just as if they were single-argument function-name references. By contrast, defined binary operators have a lower precedence than other operators. Naturally, parentheses can and should be used to avoid any ambiguity in the order of evaluation.

As another example, the following procedure and interface make it possible to concatenate strings using a plus sign (+) as an alternative to the usual // operator:

```
FUNCTION Concat (c1, c2)
CHARACTER (*) :: c1
CHARACTER (*) :: c2
CHARACTER ( LEN(c1) + LEN(c2) ) :: Concat
Concat = c1//c2
END FUNCTION Concat


INTERFACE OPERATOR (+)
FUNCTION Concat (c1, c2)
CHARACTER (*) :: c1
CHARACTER (*) :: c2
CHARACTER ( LEN(c1) + LEN(c2) ) :: Concat
END FUNCTION Concat
END INTERFACE
```

Note that an interface is always required if, as in this example, we have a character function whose result is not of constant length and cannot be assumed from the program unit which calls the procedure. Although the lengths of the arguments c1 and c2 are assumed from the call, the length of Concat itself is got from the specification expression LEN(c1)+LEN(c2) and this fact can only be revealed to the calling program by means of an interface.

12.7 GENERIC NAMES

Procedure interfaces can be extremely useful if we want to use a single name (or a single operator) to invoke any of several different procedures, the choice depending on the nature of the arguments. This is what happens with intrinsic functions when a 'generic' name is used and when the result's type depends on the argument's type. To take a very simple example, suppose we want a procedure to 'multiply' a character by an integer, and to work whichever way round the arguments are given. This would require two functions:

```
FUNCTION Multcn(c,n)
CHARACTER :: c
INTEGER :: n
CHARACTER (n) :: Multcn
Multcn = REPEAT(c,n)
END FUNCTION Multcn

FUNCTION Multnc(n,c)
CHARACTER :: c
INTEGER :: n
CHARACTER (n) :: Multnc
Multnc = REPEAT(c,n)
END FUNCTION Multcn
```

but either could be invoked through the name 'Mult' as long as there is the generic interface

```
INTERFACE Mult

FUNCTION Multcn(c,n)
CHARACTER :: c
INTEGER :: n
CHARACTER (n) :: Multcn
END FUNCTION Multcn

FUNCTION Multnc(n,c)
CHARACTER :: c
INTEGER :: n
CHARACTER (n) :: Multnc
END FUNCTION Multcn

END INTERFACE
```

When Mult is referred to, control will pass either to Multcn or to Multnc according to the order of the arguments. In general, any set of procedures may be referenced by one generic name as long as (a) they are all functions or all subroutines, and (b) the characteristics of the arguments will narrow the choice down to one specific procedure from among the set, so that there is ultimately no ambiguity. The 'characteristics' of the arguments means their types, keywords, shapes (if arrays) and whether they are present or not!

Not only can a set of procedures be referenced by a single generic name, but alternatively they may (if functions) be referenced by a single generic operator. The following enables 'multiplication' to be defined between integer and logical variables:

```
INTEGER FUNCTION Pnm (n, m)
INTEGER :: n, m
Pnm = n*m
END FUNCTION Pnm

INTEGER FUNCTION Pnq (n, q)
INTEGER :: n
LOGICAL :: q
Pnq = n ;         IF (.NOT.q) Pnq = -n
END FUNCTION Pnq

INTEGER FUNCTION Pqn (q, n)
INTEGER :: n
LOGICAL :: q
Pqn = n ;         IF (.NOT.q) Pnq = -n
END FUNCTION Pqn

LOGICAL FUNCTION Pqr (q, r)
LOGICAL :: q, r
Pqr = q.AND.r
END FUNCTION Pqr
```

The interface being headed by

```
INTERFACE OPERATOR (*)
```

and containing all the declarative parts of the function definitions above. This would permit the asterisk to be used freely between integer and logical data, either way round, with the meaning as defined.

To summarise: the INTERFACE statement may simply take the form

```
INTERFACE
```

in which case the interface may be specifying the names of procedures, the types and shapes of function results, and the types, shapes, keywords and optionalities of the arguments. The number of procedures specified is arbitrary and there need be no connection between them. Alternatively, the statement may take the form

INTERFACE name

where 'name' is a 'generic name' for a set of two or more related procedures specified in the block. The third possibility is

INTERFACE OPERATOR (op)

where 'op' is the name of an operator, either of the form .XYZ.... or of the same form as an intrinsic operator being 'overloaded'. The interface block must then contain one or more functions, and no subroutines, and the functions must have either one or two arguments (unary or binary operators). If there is more than one function, the operator is a 'generic' one.

In the above examples, the sets of functions being given generic names were external functions. The same sort of thing holds good also for external subroutines. However, things can be done differently in the case of module procedures, because it is not necessary to have explicit interfaces for module procedures within the same module. Instead, an interface block which provides a generic name or operator for a set of module procedures may be of the form

```
INTERFACE ....
      MODULE PROCEDURE list
END INTERFACE
```

where 'list' is just a list of the names of the module procedures being bundled together. Going back to the earlier example, if the functions Pnm, Pnq etc. had been module procedures in the same module, the interface to define the operator could have been

```
INTERFACE OPERATOR (*)
      MODULE PROCEDURE Pnm, Pnq, Pqn, Pqr
END INTERFACE
```

The MODULE PROCEDURE statement can also be used in the context of defined assignment (see section 14.6).

12.8 PARALLEL PROCESSING

Parallel processing is a feature of advanced computer architectures which is becoming increasingly important as time goes by. Unlike vector processing (which permits the same things to be done at the same time with different pieces of data, and is implicit in Fortran's array facilities) true parallel processing permits a program to follow two or more quite different paths at the same time. Since parallel processing machines are still relatively unusual and do not operate in a standardised way, parallelism is not an overt option within Fortran. If it were, programs would not be portable between parallel and non-parallel machines. Therefore, it is generally expected in Fortran that statements will be executed one an a time. To permit parallel processing there can be special extensions to the Fortran language: however, this is not strictly necessary, since in a statement with more than one function call, such as

$$y = Function\_A(x) + Function\_B(x)$$

the standard Fortran language does not require that Function_A be called before Function_B, and they may be called in parallel if the compiler and the hardware are capable of supporting parallel processing. Thus, a statement like

$$CALL\ Parallel\ (Strand\_A,\ Strand\_B)$$

could act as a general-purpose parallel branch point in the program, with Strand_A and Strand_B being the names of separate subroutines, if supported by a module such as

```
MODULE Split
CONTAINS
        SUBROUTINE Parallel (Ra,Rb)
                EXTERNAL Ra,Rb
                LOGICAL :: y
                LOGICAL, EXTERNAL :: F
                y = F(Ra).AND.F(Rb)
        END SUBROUTINE Parallel

        LOGICAL FUNCTION F(R)
                EXTERNAL R
                CALL R
                F=.TRUE.
        END FUNCTION F
END MODULE Split
```

Here Ra, Rb and R are dummy subroutine names. The values of y and F are irrelevant: the construction is arranged simply so that the subroutine Parallel may be called with two arbitrary subroutine names as its arguments.

EXERCISES 12B

12B1 Write a subroutine with six optional arguments representing the lengths of the sides and the internal angles of a triangle. Use the argument keywords Side1, Side2, Side3, AngleA, AngleB and AngleC. The subroutine should do its best to calculate values for those not present.

12B2 Write a function which can be called with up to a dozen integer arguments. Its value is to be the integer closest to their average.

12B3 Write a function, calling it Vector, to do a job similar to what an array constructor does (see section 7.3). The function is to have up to 12 optional arguments each of scalar integer type, and its result is to be a rank=1 array of size 12 whose first elements (up to the number of actual arguments) are equal to the actual arguments in order. If some arguments are not present, the corresponding elements are to be left zero.

12B4 Write a real array-valued function, called Cross, with two arguments both of which are also real arrays. The arrays are of rank=1 and size=3, representing three-dimensional vectors, and the result is to be the vector product ('cross product') of the two arguments.

12B5 Write a function called whose argument and value are both character strings of (different) variable lengths. The argument is to be any word, and the result is to be the same word but with the vowels removed.

12B6 An operator is needed which, acting between two real numbers, gives their geometric mean. Write a function and interface to do the job. (What can you do about the case where the two numbers are of opposite signs?)

12B7 Write a function and interface with a defined operator so that any real number (including a negative one) can be raised to an arbitrary real power. If the result is mathematically a complex number, the function's value is to be equal to its real part. Use the symbol ** as the defined operator, i.e. overloading the intrinsic exponentiation operator.

12B8 Extend the solution of exercise 12B3, providing functions with a generic interface so that the function can be called with either integer, real or complex type.

N12.1   BLOCK DATA (BLOCKDATA, END BLOCK DATA)

There is another sort of program unit in Fortran, known as BLOCK DATA, intended merely to preset the values of data items. The syntax is

> BLOCK DATA
> .
> .
> END BLOCK DATA

where the keyword DATA may optionally be followed by a unit name. The final statement may be abbreviated to END. Between the two statements shown, one or more COMMON blocks may appear (see note N11.2) and data items from them may be specified by type declaration statements and/or by DATA statements (see note 13.2).

N12.3   RETURN

The statement

> RETURN

may be included in any procedure, if necessary more than once, and it returns control to where the procedure was called, i.e. RETURN has the same effect as if END FUNCTION or END SUBROUTINE were encountered. The RETURN statement may be conditional, as in

> IF (ncalls>maxcalls) RETURN

N12.4   STATEMENT FUNCTIONS

Within a program unit it is possible to have a sort of simplified one-line function which can be used only within that program unit. It is specified by a non-executable statement which might typically look like this:

> Fun_name(x, y, z) = x/y + y/z + z/x

i.e. an arbitrary function-name, followed by a bracketed list of arguments, followed after an '=' by an expression giving the value of the function in terms of the arguments. All arguments and other quantities must be scalars or single elements of arrays. Here is another example:

> Croot (a) = a**(1.0/3.0)   !   Cube Root Function

Chapter 13

THE TYPE DECLARATION STATEMENT

A simple form of the type declaration statement (TDS) was introduced back in section 4.3, and since then several elaborations of it have been mentioned when necessary. At this point it is appropriate to give complete details of the syntax of the Fortran TDS, although there are still one or two features that will not be fully explained until later chapters. In its various forms the TDS is probably the second most common statement type in Fortran (after the assignment statement) and it is essential to understand it well.

Several technical terms are used here (e.g. 'entity declaration list' and 'automatic array') and although they may at first seen cumbersome they are a standard terminology and the reader should try to get used to them.

13.1   GENERAL FORM OF THE TDS

The purpose of a TDS is to declare the characteristics of data items. The statement may at the same time serve the additional purpose of giving initial values to the data items.

In general a TDS consists of three parts in this order: firstly a single 'type specification', secondly an optional list of 'attribute specifications', and thirdly an 'entity declaration list'. The type specification and the attribute specifications which may follow it are separated by commas. The attribute specifications are separated by a double colon from the entity declaration list. In the simplest cases where there are no attribute specifications and initial values are not given to any data, it is permissible for the entity declaration list to follow the type specification without the intervening double colon. However, it is recommended that the double colon should always be used.

A simple example of a TDS is

        LOGICAL, SAVE :: a, cq, cr

where LOGICAL is the type specification, SAVE is an attribute specification, and the entity declaration list contains the three names a, cq, cr. A more complicated example is

        CHARACTER(2), PARAMETER :: unit(3) = (/"mm","cm","dm"/)

and here the type specification is CHARACTER(2), there is one attribute specification, PARAMETER, and the entity being declared is the array called unit(3). Initial values are being given to the elements of unit(3).

The primary purpose of a TDS is to declare the existence of data objects of a certain type. A single TDS must refer to a single type. The type is given by the type specification and it must be one of the following:

```
INTEGER (KIND=...)
REAL (KIND=...)
COMPLEX (KIND=...)
DOUBLE PRECISION
LOGICAL (KIND=...)
TYPE (type-name)
CHARACTER (selector, KIND=...)
```

The parameters which can occur here (KIND, etc.) are part of the type specification. After the type specification there can be the following range of possible attribute specifications, which will be discussed in turn in section 13.3:

```
PARAMETER
SAVE
PUBLIC
PRIVATE
EXTERNAL
INTRINSIC
OPTIONAL
INTENT (specification)
POINTER
TARGET
ALLOCATABLE
DIMENSION (specification)
```

Finally, there are the entities actually being declared. The entity declaration list at its simplest is a series of the names of entities which are of the type given in the type specification and which have special qualities indicated by the attribute specifications. These entities are usually variables, but could be constants or functions. Their names must follow the usual Fortran naming rules given in section 3.4. A name in the entity declaration list of a TDS may have additional information appended to it if it is an array or if it is of character type, and it may be given an initial value. These possibilities are detailed in section 13.5.

Returning to the type specification, we have the following possibilities, of which one and only one may occur in one TDS:

INTEGER (KIND=...)

This indicates that the data declared here is of integer type. There may be a KIND parameter if the processor may support integers of unusual precision (see note 2, chapter 5) but Fortran does not require this to be possible, so this specification will almost always consist simply of the keyword INTEGER. An example:

INTEGER :: i, j, k, input_unit, gamma

REAL (KIND=...)

This indicates data of real type. The bracketed KIND parameter will rarely be needed, but it allows for real numbers of unusual precision (see section 4.4). Examples:

REAL :: estimate_1, estimate_2, result, error
REAL (KIND=KIND(0.0D0)) :: &
        hairsbreadth_x, hairsbreadth_y

For simple scalar data objects of real and integer type, whose names fit the initial-letter convention (sections 4.1 and 4.2) and which have no special attributes, there is no need to use a TDS at all.

COMPLEX (KIND=...)

The data following this would be complex numbers. The KIND parameter, if present, means that each complex number is equivalent to two real numbers of the specified kind of precision. Example:

COMPLEX :: omega1, omega2, i, z

DOUBLE PRECISION

It is never necessary to use this specification (see N4.2).

LOGICAL (KIND=...)

This specification indicates data of logical type. The KIND parameter, as in the case of integers, allows for processors to have more than one way of representing such data, but KIND would generally be meaningless and we can disregard it. Example:

LOGICAL :: decision

TYPE (type-name)

This type specification makes it possible to declare data objects of special user-defined types, or 'derived' types. Derived types are the subject of chapter 14.

CHARACTER (length-selector, KIND=...)

This indicates data of character type. Whenever character data is declared, the length of each item must be indicated, and this can be done by means of a length selector following the keyword CHARACTER. The selector specifies a length which will apply to all the items listed later in the statement.

This length-selector is not mandatory, because the same job can be done by means of a selector appended to each item's name in the entity declaration list. There is a superficial advantage in specifying character string lengths in the entity declaration list, because then strings of different lengths may be declared in the one statement. However, on balance, it is recommended that the lengths should be specified after CHARACTER even if this demands more statements, since the syntax can otherwise become more confusing. Section 13.2, below, will be devoted to character length selectors.

A KIND parameter may be specified with the CHARACTER keyword if the processor supports non-default character sets (see N6.1).

13.2   CHARACTER LENGTH SELECTORS

The CHARACTER keyword, with the length selector following it, may take any one of the forms below:

CHARACTER

```
CHARACTER (expression)
CHARACTER (LEN=expression)
CHARACTER *(expression)

CHARACTER *constant

CHARACTER (*)
CHARACTER (LEN=*)
CHARACTER *(*)
```

The first of these, with no length selector, would be used to declare length=1 character strings, i.e. individual characters.

The following group of three forms are equivalent, and one may as well stick to the first form, i.e.

```
CHARACTER (expression)
```

Here, 'expression' must be an expression of non-negative scalar integer type. It may simply be a constant, or a constant expression, or it may be a more complicated expression involving variables. However, if it involves variables then they must be accessible and have values when this TDS appears. Accessibility could be through a data module, or (within a procedure) through a dummy argument, or by reference to an intrinsic function. We could have, for example,

```
CHARACTER (128)
CHARACTER (64*128)
CHARACTER (n)
CHARACTER (1 + LEN(TRIM(z)))
```

as long as the integer n, and the character string z, have been previously made accessible. In this way, lengths of strings can be set dynamically rather than fixed when the program is compiled. When a nonconstant expression is used to declare the length of a string which is not a dummy argument, the string is known as an 'automatic' data object.

Another form listed above was

```
CHARACTER *constant
```

and here 'constant' would simply be a non-negative integer value. In other words, lengths can be specified by things like

```
CHARACTER *128
```

but this notation offers no advantage over

CHARACTER (128)

and is best avoided. The list of forms given above ended with three more which are equivalent to one another, i.e.

CHARACTER (*)
CHARACTER (LEN=*)
CHARACTER *(*)

all of which use an asterisk to mean that the length of the character string is to be assumed from elsewhere. Sticking to the first and simplest of these forms,

CHARACTER (*)

should be used

(a) when the length can be taken from an explicit initial value given to the string later in this statement, or

(b) in a procedure, to declare a dummy character argument whose length will be taken from the program unit where the call is made, or

(c) in a character-valued function, to declare the name of the function if its value's length is to be assumed from where it is called.

In cases (b) and (c), the length will therefore be determined not on compilation but on execution, and could be different each time the procedure is actually called.

Here are a few more examples of character TDS's:

CHARACTER :: initial1, initial2, initial3
CHARACTER(20) :: name_of_state, name_of_city
CHARACTER(12*nwords + 24) :: page
CHARACTER(*) :: input_data

13.3   ATTRIBUTE SPECIFICATIONS

The set of possible attribute specifications in a TDS was listed in section 13.1. Each attribute may be specified no more than once in one TDS. Many of the attributes are mutually exclusive, and many can apply only to certain sorts of data (e.g. to procedure arguments) so in practice it is unusual for a TDS to include more than one or two attribute specifications. When there is more than one attribute specification, they may be given in any order. The meaning of each attribute is explained below:

PARAMETER

A data object with the PARAMETER attribute has a fixed value, i.e. it is a 'named constant' which will not be changed during the running of the program. The value must be appended to the name in the statement's entity declaration list (section 13.4). Examples:

REAL(KIND=2), PARAMETER :: e = 2.718281828459045235
CHARACTER(*), PARAMETER :: country = "Lithuania"

SAVE

This is an attribute that may apply to data items (other than arguments) occurring in subprograms. It means that the items will retain their values after the subprogram has executed. In other words, SAVE is a way of retaining the value of data between subsequent calls to a function or subroutine. The SAVE attribute has no effect if it is specified in a main program. Example:

INTEGER, SAVE :: number_of_times_called

PUBLIC and PRIVATE

These two 'accessibility attributes' are only applicable to data items declared in a module. PRIVATE means that the items are not accessible (via a USE statement) to any other program unit outside the module. It could be advisable for data to be declared PRIVATE if it is used only within module procedures and if there could be an unintended clash of names with other data in program units using the module. PUBLIC means the opposite, i.e. that the data is accessible by another program unit using the module, but this is the usual default situation so it is rarely necessary to use PUBLIC. Example:

REAL, PRIVATE :: input_buffer(1025)

EXTERNAL

This is applicable not to ordinary data items but only to the names of functions. It indicates an external function. It is important to declare the EXTERNAL attribute with a function name if that name is to be passed as an argument to another procedure. Within a procedure, EXTERNAL may indicate a dummy argument which is a function name, i.e. an argument which will later correspond to an external function name. Example:

REAL, EXTERNAL :: Integrand
CHARACTER, EXTERNAL :: Alphabet(32)

Here, Alphabet is an array-valued function with 32 elements.

INTRINSIC

The INTRINSIC attribute means that a function name is that of a Fortran intrinsic function. If it is a specific (as opposed to generic) function name, it permits the name to be passed as a procedure argument. Not recommended.

OPTIONAL

This attribute can be used when the dummy arguments of procedures are declared. It indicates arguments which need not necessarily be included in the actual argument list when the procedure is called (see section 12.4). A procedure with optional arguments must have an interface. Examples:

COMPLEX, OPTIONAL :: croot1, croot2
REAL, OPTIONAL, EXTERNAL :: Smoothing_function

INTENT (specification)

Like OPTIONAL, this is an attribute that may apply to procedures' dummy arguments. INTENT permits the programmer to ensure that an argument is used (a) only for data coming in to the procedure, or (b) only for data going out, or (c) for data flowing both ways. This is done by a specification, in brackets, which may be IN, OUT or INOUT respectively. An argument with INTENT(IN) cannot be changed by the procedure, and one with INTENT(OUT) is initially undefined and must be defined by the procedure. The attribute INTENT(INOUT) embraces both possibilities and need not be used except as a form of program annotation. Example:

REAL, INTENT(IN) :: vector(3), rotation_matrix(3,3)
REAL, INTENT(OUT) :: new_vector(3)

POINTER and TARGET

These two attributes can apply when pointers are being used; they will be covered fully in chapter 15.

ALLOCATABLE

The ALLOCATABLE attribute is applicable only to arrays. It will be dealt with in chapter 15.

DIMENSION (specification)

The DIMENSION attribute is used only with arrays. DIMENSION indicates that array variables are being declared, and it is followed by a bracketed specification of the shape of the arrays.

Alternatively, shapes may be given for individual arrays as part of the entity declaration list, in which case they override a shape specified with DIMENSION. The situation is rather like that for character strings, where string lengths may be given globally, for the whole set of entities declared in a statement, or individually.

Because arrays may be declared simply by specifying a shape for each array in the entity declaration list, the DIMENSION attribute is not actually necessary at all. So, the TDS

COMPLEX, DIMENSION(4,4) :: gamma1, gamma2, gamma3, gamma4, gamma5

is equivalent to

COMPLEX :: gamma1(4,4), gamma2(4,4), gamma3(4,4),&
gamma4(4,4), gamma5(4,4)

Array specifications following DIMENSION, and array specifications following an item in the list, can be constructed in exactly the same ways. These ways are covered in more detail in the next section.

13.4 ARRAY SPECIFICATIONS

The simplest kind of array specification is the sort shown in the above example, where the shape of the array is given by a list of its extents in each dimension. A shape (4,4) means that there are two dimensions, i.e. a rank of two, and a total of 16 elements making up the whole array. This is a simple example of an 'explicit shape' specification list. In fact Fortran distinguishes between four different sorts of specification list, namely 'explicit shape', 'assumed shape', 'deferred shape' and 'assumed size'.

EXPLICIT SHAPE

Explicit shape specification lists such as (4,4) or (3,3,3) or (100) or (4,20,2) declare arrays whose elements would be referenced by indices running from 1 to 4 (twice), 1 to 3 (three times), 1 to 100, 1 to 4, 1 to 20, and 1 to 2. Alternatively, starting points different from 1 can be set using the colon notation introduced in section 7.4. In that notation, the shape (4,4) is equivalent to (1:4,1:4). For each dimension, the lower bound and upper bound are given separated by a colon. If we have

    REAL :: alpha(-3:3,0:9)

then the array's rank is 2 and there are 70 elements, and individual elements can be referenced by expressions such as array(n,m) with n taking any integer value from -3 to 3 and m from 0 to 9 inclusive. It is possible to have mixed declarations in which some but not all dimensions are given with the colon notation:

    REAL :: alpha(-3:3,0:9), beta(20,0:1), gamma(20,20)

Moreover, the bounds need not be given as specific integers. A declaration like

    REAL :: xyz(3,npoints), r(npoints,npoints), checksum(0:k)

is possible if npoints and k are the names of integer constants. In fact, when the declaration is made in a procedure and the object is not a dummy argument, the bounds need not even be constants: they can be integer variables or expressions as long as they will have ascertainable values when the TDS is encountered. The array is then known as an 'automatic array', since its shape is not fixed until the procedure is called (and may differ from one call to another). Here is an example:

    SUBROUTINE Falsetto (n, w)
    USE Printer_data
    INTEGER, INTENT(IN) :: n
    CHARACTER(*), INTENT(IN) :: w
    REAL :: r(0:n-1,0:n-1)
    CHARACTER :: ch(2*LEN(w))
    CHARACTER :: page(linelength, pagelength)
        .
        .

This subroutine uses the argument n to fix the bounds of both dimensions of a rank=2 array r, and it uses the length of the character string argument w in order to determine the size of an array ch containing single characters. The dimensions linelength and pagelength are presumably specified within the module Printer_data.

The bounds of explicit-shape arrays may be given by fairly complicated 'specification expressions', but there are certain restrictions. In particular, a specification expression may not involve a reference to any non-intrinsic function. In the example above, LEN is of course an intrinsic Fortran function. Obviously, in order to have a definite value a specification expression must include only variables that are accessible as dummy arguments, as module data, or by host association (section 11.2).

ASSUMED SHAPE

So far here we have been discussing 'explicit shape' arrays. Something a little different is an 'assumed shape' array. A dummy argument in a procedure may have an assumed shape, which means that its rank is known but its shape is taken from that of the corresponding actual argument whenever the procedure is called. An assumed shape is specified by giving a series of colons, one colon for each dimension. In the following example there are two dimensions, i.e. the array being declared has rank=2, but the extents in each dimension will be determined only as and when the function is called. The extents need not be the same, i.e. this need not be a square matrix:

```
INTEGER FUNCTION N_positive_elements (matrix)
REAL :: matrix(:,:)
   .
   .
```

With an assumed shape array it is possible to specify that a lower bound other than 1 will be used in the procedure, by giving the lower bound before the colon. So,

```
REAL :: matrix(0:,0:)
```

means that the lower bounds are both 0, but this does not affect the numbers of elements.

DEFERRED SHAPE

The third kind of array specification is a 'deferred shape' specification, but this involves allocatable arrays or pointers and it would be premature to give details here. Deferred shape specifications are explained in chapter 15.

ASSUMED SIZE

The fourth and final class of array specification is the 'assumed size' specification. Like an assumed shape, an assumed size is a possible feature of a dummy argument array in a procedure. The notation for declaring an assumed size includes an asterisk. To take the simplest example,

```
REAL FUNCTION Chi (a, b, z)
REAL :: a, b, z(*)
       .
       .
```

means that the arguments a and b are scalars but z is an array. Within the function, z has rank=1, but the corresponding actual argument could be an array of any rank. The rank of the actual argument is not passed on and does not become the rank of the dummy argument z. The array z always has rank=1. However, z is given the same total number of elements as the actual argument had, i.e. z assumes the size of the actual argument.

In the above example the lower bound of z's dimension would be 1, but as we have previously seen it is possible to give a different lower bound before a colon: with

```
REAL :: a, b, z(1025:*)
```

the array z has elements z(1025), z(1026), z(1027), and so on up to an index which will exceed by 1025 the size of the actual argument corresponding to z.

There are one or two further possibilities with assumed-size arrays. For one thing, the actual argument need not be the name of an array but could just be an array element, in which case what is passed is the series of elements starting at the one given and going on to the end of the array (in normal array element order, see chapter 15). In other words, with

```
klap = (/2,5,7,1,1,0,7,9,5,4,0,0/)
n = 6
CALL Turn (klap(n))
       .
       .
SUROUTINE Turn (k)
INTEGER :: k(*)
       .
       .
```

the dummy argument array k in the subroutine will have size 7 and the value (/0,7,9,5,4,0,0/).

Things can get a little more complicated with assumed-size character arrays, since the elements of the actual and dummy arguments may be character strings of different lengths! Then, the size assumed for the dummy argument will be whatever is needed to accommodate all the characters in the actual argument array. Suppose we have the following code:

```
toffee = (/"and","pat","cob","try","owl"/)
CALL Twist (toffee)
        .
        .
SUBROUTINE Twist (tripe)
CHARACTER (5) :: tripe(*)
```

then tripe will be (/"andpa","tcobt","ryowl"/), i.e. with size=3. As with non-character data, the first part of an array can be left out by giving, as actual argument, one element (or a substring of an element) to be taken as the starting point of what is passed to the procedure:

```
toffee = (/"and","pat","cob","try","owl"/)
CALL Twist (toffee(3)(2:3))
        .
        .
SUBROUTINE Twist (tripe)
CHARACTER (2) :: tripe(*)
```

Here, the actual argument is a substring ("ob") consisting of the second and third characters from the third element of toffee. The subroutine will receive the contents of toffee starting from that substring, giving tripe the value (/"ob","tr","yo","wl"/). The call

```
CALL Twist (toffee(3)(2:2))
```

would have had exactly the same effect.

So far, in our examples of assumed size specifications, we have had dummy argument arrays of rank=1. Arrays of greater rank are possible, but then all dimensions except the last must be specified as in an explicit shape specification. Only the last dimension is left indeterminate with an asterisk. In the example immediately above, if we had had

```
CHARACTER (2) :: tripe(2,*)
```

then tripe would have been a rank=2 array taking the shape (2,2).

156

Having dealt with type specifications and attribute specifications, it only remains to describe the entity declaration list that comes at the end of a TDS. The task is made easy because the most complicated aspects of entity declaration are those to do with character string lengths and array shapes, and these have already been covered exhaustively above.

For scalar data of non-character type, the entity declaration list will simply consist of a series of names separated by commas, each possibly being given an initial value by an 'initialization expression' following an '=' after the name. The following are examples of valid lists:

> a, b, c, d=0.0, e=5.5, f
> karavan = 4520988765, k2 = 2**64, kstore1, kstore2, kstore3
> check1=.TRUE., check2=.TRUE., check3=.TRUE., checksum
> q = (0.39967, -1.03847)

There are a number of restrictions to the use of an initialization expression in a TDS. Initialization expressions are compulsory whenever the PARAMETER attribute is present. An initialization expression is forbidden when declaring a dummy argument, function name, or automatic object (sections 13.2 and 13.4), and it is also incompatible with the ALLOCATABLE and POINTER attributes. Any data object that is declared with an initialization expression will be saved, in the sense that it is given the SAVE attribute even if SAVE was not explicitly included in the attribute list. Note that data initialization takes place once and for all before program execution: data in a procedure are not re-initialized each time the procedure is called.

Initialization expressions are subject to a number of technical restrictions. They may not involve variables, and the only functions allowed are intrinsic integer or character functions, inquiry functions (except ALLOCATED), and the transformational functions REPEAT, TRIM, TRANSFER, and RESHAPE. Defined operators are not allowed and the exponentiation operator ('**') is only allowed with an integer power.

When declaring arrays, array constructors may be used as initialization expressions (if necessary with implied-DO variables) as in

> kpow(32) = (/2**m, m=1, 32/)

When declaring character data, initialization expressions may involve substrings and character functions, e.g.

> alphabet = (/"abcdefghijklmnopqrstuvwxyz"(j:j), j=1, 26/)
> blank_page = REPEAT(" ",1750)

It was mentioned at the end of section 13.1 that the length of character data may be specified alongside the name in the entity declaration list. The notation is similar to that which can be used to do the same job after the CHARACTER keyword (section 13.2) but is a little more limited. The permissible forms are

charname*(expression)
charname*constant
charname*(*)

where 'charname' is the object's name, 'expression' is an integer expression as in section 13.2, 'constant' is a specific integer, and the '*(*)' notation is similar in effect to CHARACTER(*). With any of these forms, an array specification could also be inserted between 'charname' and the character length specification. In an extreme case, we could therefore have a specification such as

CHARACTER :: chimera(*)*(*)

which is an assumed-size assumed-length character array equivalent to

CHARACTER, DIMENSION(*) :: chimera*(*)

but the simplest notation is

CHARACTER(*) :: chimera(*)

This variety of different notations arises from the history of Fortran and is not an attractive feature of the language. To keep things simple and clear, it is strongly recommended that you always give character length specifications with the CHARACTER keyword, and always give array shapes with the arrays' names, avoiding the use of the DIMENSION keyword.

13.6   SUMMARY

Leaving aside some relatively unimportant options, the type declaration statement should begin with one of

INTEGER
REAL or REAL(KIND=KIND(0.0D0)
COMPLEX or COMPLEX(KIND=KIND(0.0D0)
LOGICAL
CHARACTER(...)
TYPE(...)

158

In the case of CHARACTER, the brackets contain the length of the strings, determined either by a constant expression or by a nonconstant expression ('automatic' data) or by an asterisk ('assumed length'). TYPE is dealt with in chapter 14. The type specification may be followed by optional attribute specifications:

> PARAMETER or SAVE for ordinary variables
> EXTERNAL or INTRINSIC for function names
> INTENT and/or OPTIONAL for dummy arguments
> ALLOCATABLE, POINTER, and TARGET: see chapter 15

Then there is an entity declaration list consisting of variables' names separated by commas. There may be an array specification after each name. An array specification will be of one of these kinds:

> Explicit shape (including 'automatic' arrays)
> Assumed shape (for dummy arguments, using colons)
> Deferred shape (see chapter 15)
> Assumed size (for dummy arguments, using an asterisk)

Finally, the name of a variable may be followed by an '=' sign and an initialisation expression, giving a starting value to the object named. If the PARAMETER attribute is specified an initialisation expression is compulsory and the object is technically a 'named constant' rather than a variable.

EXERCISES 13A

13A1   Write a TDS to declare an array (called 'zbanks') of 30 complex numbers.

13A2   Write a TDS to declare three optional logical dummy arguments in a procedure. Call them check1, check2 and check3.

13A3   Write a TDS, intended for use in a procedure, for a 20x20 matrix of real numbers and also a vector of 45 real numbers. All are to have their values saved between calls to the procedure.

13A4   A procedure has a character-type dummy argument to be called 'thread'. Write a TDS declaring it to be an assumed-size array of individual characters, the idea being that the procedure can be called with the actual argument being a character string or an array of strings of any length.

13A5   Write a TDS for an array of 100 named integer constants, called 'squares', with the index running from 0 to 99, fixing their values to be equal to the squares of the integers from 0 to 99.

13A6   Write a TDS for a dummy argument which is of length=12 character type. Its name is to be 'julius' and it is an assumed-shape array of rank=2.

13A7   Write a TDS for an array of 201 real variables called 'inverse_squares', the indices running between ±100. They are to be given the initial values of the inverse squares of the integers ranging from -100 to 100.

13A8   Write a TDS for a scalar character constant whose value is your name. Call it 'moniker'.

N13.1 STATEMENTS EQUIVALENT TO DATA ATTRIBUTE SPECIFICATIONS

All the data attributes (PARAMETER, SAVE, etc.) which may occur in a TDS may, equivalently, be given by separate statements, 'attribute specification statements' (ASS's). An ASS does not specify the data objects' types, which must still be given in a TDS or assumed from the initial letter of the names. An ASS may not duplicate or contradict an attribute already given in a TDS. Examples of ASS's are given here:

```
SUBROUTINE Integrate (Rfunction, g, h, i, j, name)
REAL :: Rfunction
EXTERNAL Rfunction                   !Double colon forbidden!
INTEGER :: g, h
INTENT (IN) :: g, h, i, j            !Double colon optional!
CHARACTER(*) :: name
OPTIONAL :: name                     !Double colon optional!
SAVE :: ncalls                       !Double colon optional!
DIMENSION iflags(6)                  !Double colon forbidden!
PARAMETER del=0.0002                 !Double colon forbidden!
```

In addition, in a module there may be a PRIVATE statement such as

```
PRIVATE :: workspace                 !Double colon optional!
```

This may happen without any list of variables, i.e. just the PRIVATE keyword by itself:

```
PRIVATE
```

which means that all data declared in the module are PRIVATE. Subsequent to this, a PUBLIC statement

```
PUBLIC :: x, y, z                    !Double colon optional!
```

will make the named objects accessible outside the module again.

N13.2 THE DATA STATEMENT

As an alternative to initialising data in a TDS or in a PARAMETER statement, or in an ordinary assignment statement, there is a special statement type, DATA, which exists in order to give initial values to variables. It works only for ordinary variables, i.e. not for dummy arguments, automatic objects, and the like. As an example, to illustrate the details of the syntax, suppose that variables have been declared by the TDS

$$\text{INTEGER :: i1, i2, kappa(4), mult(20), \&}$$
$$\text{ncells(-10;10,-10:10)}$$

Then initial values could be declared by

$$\text{DATA i1, i2, i3 /0,0,20/, kappa /14,71,0,33/, \&}$$
$$\text{mult /20*1/, ((ncells(i,j),i=-10,10),j=-10,10) /361*0/}$$

which is hardly less complicated than it looks. The DATA statement consists of a list of sets, the sets in the above example being

$$\text{i1, i2, i3 /0,0,20/}$$
$$\text{kappa /14,71,0,33/}$$
$$\text{mult /20*1/}$$
$$\text{((ncells(i,j),i=-10,10),j=-10,10) /441*0/}$$

Each set consists of a list of names followed by a list (between slashes) of initial values. The first set puts i1, i2 and i3 equal to 0, 0 and 20 respectively. The second set gives values to the four elements of the array kappa. The third set illustrates a 'repeat' notation in the list of values, where an integer before an asterisk is equivalent to that number of occurrences of the value; the 20 elements of the array mult are all set to 1. The final set in our example shows how an implied DO notation can be used to run through elements of an array.

The DATA statement does nothing that cannot be done in other ways (especially with array constructors) and it should be avoided.

N13.3   IMPLICIT

Unless declared by a TDS to be of a different type, variables are assumed to be of integer type if their names begin with letters of the alphabet in the range i-n. Otherwise, they are assumed to be real. This initial-letter convention may be changed within a program unit by a special nonexecutable statement, IMPLICIT. An IMPLICIT statement must come immediately after USE statements and before any other statements. Some examples will make its use clear:

$$\text{IMPLICIT REAL (a-z)}$$

means that all variables are interpreted by default as real numbers.

IMPLICIT INTEGER (a, e, i, o, u), REAL (b-d, f-h, j-n, p-t, v-z)

means that names starting with a vowel are to be taken as integers, and others as real numbers.

IMPLICIT CHARACTER (a-z)

means that all names (unless individually specified otherwise) are taken to be the names of character strings.

IMPLICIT Encrypt (a-z)

means that all names will refer by default to the data type ENCRYPT. Since ENCRYPT is not one of Fortran's intrinsic types this must be a special user-defined type (see chapter 14). Finally,

IMPLICIT NONE

means that there is no initial-letter data type convention imposed in this part of the program, and therefore that the programmer will specify explicitly the types of all variables.

IMPLICIT statements could be provided in a module and used throughout a program. For example,

```
MODULE Precision
IMPLICIT REAL (KIND=KIND(0.0D0)) (a-h,o-z)
END MODULE Precision
```

could be used to change, at a stroke, the precision of all the real numbers used in a program.

Chapter 14

DERIVED TYPES

This chapter covers 'derived types', i.e. special non-standard types of data that may be set up by the Fortran programmer. A derived type is defined in a block headed by a TYPE statement, and subsequently data of that type can be declared by a variant of the type declaration statement (section 14.1). Functions and operators, and the meaning of assignment ('='), may be defined for use with a derived type (sections 14.5 and 14.6).

A derived type (often called a 'structure') is built up ultimately from components of intrinsic types. A 'derived type constructor' (analogous to an array constructor) is used to specify the values of all the components making up a particular structure (section 14.2). To extract an individual component from a structure, there is a special notation involving the % character (section 14.3).

There are two main ways in which derived types are useful. One is to let the programmer use unusual mathematical structures, e.g. geometrical figures, quaternions, sets, and groups. The other is to set up a shorthand to work with large or complex data sets, whether it be entries in a bibliography, pages of text, printer drivers, or radionuclide decay data.

14.1   DERIVED-TYPE DEFINITION

A block of nonexecutable code, headed by a derived-type definition statement, must be provided among the declaration statements at the start of any program unit where the new type is to be used. This block of code must declare the name of the type and specify how an item of this type is built up from items of intrinsic type. For example, if complex numbers were not already an intrinsic type in Fortran, they could be derived with the definition block

```
TYPE Complex
REAL :: x, y
END TYPE Complex
```

which simply declares that a new data type, 'Complex', is to consist of a pair of real numbers. The details of complex arithmetic would be a matter for function definitions and operator definitions subsequently.

Usually, the derived-type definition statement simply consists of the keyword TYPE followed by a name. This statement is followed by one or more statements declaring, in order, the components of the structure. These component declarations are very similar in syntax to ordinary type declaration statements, except that

(a)   the only attribute specifiers available are DIMENSION and POINTER,

(b)   character lengths must be constant expressions,

(c)   arrays must have explicit shape specifiers with constant expressions as the bounds (or, for pointer components as in chapter 15, deferred-shape specifiers), and

(d)   initial values cannot be appended.

Finally, the block is finished with an END TYPE statement optionally suffixed by the type-name.

Another example:

```
TYPE Mail
        CHARACTER(10) :: title
        CHARACTER :: initials (3)
        CHARACTER(30) :: surname
        CHARACTER(30) :: address (5)
        CHARACTER(10) :: postcode
        INTEGER :: telephone
        LOGICAL :: gender
        INTEGER :: refnumber, spouseref, entrydate
END TYPE Mail
```

This sets up a data structure which could form the basis of a mailing list. Note that components of different intrinsic types may be included among the components of a structure, and so can arrays.

Once a structure has been defined, variables of that type can be declared by type declaration statements such as

```
TYPE (Quaternion) :: rho, sigma, phi
TYPE (Mail) :: newentry, spouse
TYPE (Currency_rates) :: yesterday, today, forward1, forward2
```

It is essential to understand the distinction between a statement like

```
TYPE Mail
```

which introduces the definition block for the type itself, and

165

```
TYPE (Mail) :: dud
```

which declares that a particular variable will be of that type. Although both starting with the keyword TYPE, these two statements do quite different jobs. The type definition block must come first, and could be provided most conveniently by being written once and for all in a module accessible to the whole program. The type declaration statement is really just like any of the TDS's described in chapter 13, it may have all the possible attribute specifications just like an intrinsic type declaration statement, and it may declare arrays. For example,

```
TYPE (Mail) :: retirees (5000)
```

declares an array with 5000 elements, each being a structure of the type called 'Mail'. If 'Mail' is defined as above, then 'retirees' will actually contain a total of 55000 character strings, 20000 integers, and 5000 logical data items!

Here is a derived data type to represent a set of co-ordinates in three-dimensional space:

```
TYPE Coord3
REAL :: x(3)
END TYPE Coord3
```

and here are type declaration statements using that definition:

```
TYPE (Coord3) :: neworigin
TYPE (Coord3) :: redgiants(50)
```

Although Coord3 consists of an array, x(3), the type Coord3 is not of itself an array or a scalar, any more than the type REAL is of itself either an array or a scalar. The variable neworigin is of type Coord3, but is a scalar, even though the array x subsists in it. The variable redgiants is also of type Coord3, but is an array of size 50.

14.2   STRUCTURE CONSTRUCTORS

It has been explained above how a derived type is defined and how a variable of that type would be declared. But how are actual values given to the components of a derived-type structure? It can be done with a 'structure constructor' which takes the general form

```
Typename (component1, component2, component3,....)
```

i.e. the values of the components are simply listed in brackets after a reference to the type name. So, using some of the examples from the previous section, we could have assignment statements such as

```
retirees(1) = Mail ("Prof.", (/"H", "J", ""/), "Wallace",&
                    (/"", i=1, 5/), 0, .TRUE., 386740, 386741, 211090)
locus = Coord3 ((/56.923, 20.768, 91.004/))
```

Note that array constructors occur when the structure components are arrays. We can have more complicated expressions such as

```
locus = Coord3 ((/r*COS(theta)*COS(phi), r*SIN(theta)*COS(phi), r*SIN(phi)/))
```

The ordinary rules of assignment apply if there is any difference of detail between the list in the structure constructor and the list which originally defined the structure. So, for example,

```
locus = Coord3 (1)
```

would set all the elements of the array a(3), within locus, equal to 1.0.

Another example (which could define, for example, a plane in 3-dimensional space) is the type

```
TYPE Vtriplet
REAL :: v1(3), v2(3), v3(3)
END TYPE Vtriplet
```

with variables defined by, say,

```
TYPE (Vtriplet) :: pa, pb, floor
```

and with actual values being set by assignment statements such as

```
pa = Vtriplet (0.0,0.0,0.0)
pb = Vtriplet ((/0.34,0.81,0.08/),(/0.88,0.00,0.55/), (/0.60,0.28,0.31/))
floor = Vtriplet (a,b,(/c,d,e/))
```

where the variables a and b are 3-vectors and c, d and e are scalars.

A structure may be given an initial value, or it may be a named constant, e.g.

TYPE (Vtriplet), PARAMETER :: &
pb = Vtriplet ((/0.34,0.81,0.08/),(/0.88,0.00,0.55/), (/0.60,0.28,0.31/))

14.3   STRUCTURE COMPONENTS

Given a variable which is a structure whose components have defined values, how can the components' values be got at? This is done by giving the component name after the variable's name, separated by the % symbol. With the structure

```
TYPE Date
        INTEGER :: day, month, year
        CHARACTER(10) :: dayname
        LOGICAL :: holiday, public_holiday
END TYPE Date
```

and data

TYPE (Date) :: q = Date (25, 5, 1992, "Monday", .FALSE., .TRUE.)

then q%day is the integer 25, q%holiday is the logical item .FALSE., and so on. This also holds good for variable names, e.g. with

q = Date (n1, n2, n3, daystring, flaga, flagb)

then the expression

q%dayname

is equivalent to the name daystring. This kind of thing can be applied to arrays, e.g. going back to the earlier examples

retirees%telephone

is an array of 5000 integers, consisting of the component 'telephone' from each of the 5000 structures in the array 'retirees'. A similar thing can be done if the component itself is the array, e.g. neworigin%x is simply the array x which is within the structure 'neworigin' of type Coord3. And, with the type Vtriplet above, pb%v2 is the array (/0.88,0.00,0.55/). However, this notation is forbidden when both the structure itself and the component are both arrays, because an ambiguity would arise: it wouldn't be clear what sort of array

retirees%initials

is supposed to be, since there are 3 elements of 'initials' in each of 5000 elements of 'retirees'. So, in general, a%b

means the component called b within the derived-type variable called a, and it is an array if either a or b (but not both!) is an array. Notice that a may be an array element, so we could have

redgiants(1)%x

which would be the 3-vector of the co-ordinates of the first red giant. However, in a%b it is not permissible for b to be an array element, it must simply be the bare component-name from the structure definition block. This means that the expression

a%b(i)

is the ith element of a%b. It does not necessarily refer to the ith element of b. In fact a%b(i) refers to the ith element of b only if the structure a is scalar and the component b is an array.

EXERCISES 14A

14A1   (i) Write a derived-type definition block for a data type to be called 'Species' which is to describe a species of animal. The type is to be composed of a name (a 12-character string), the average weight, length and height of the animal (3 real numbers), how many legs it has (an integer), and whether or not it can swim (logical). Choose sensible names for the components.

    (ii) Write a type declaration statement for four scalar objects of type 'Species', calling them 'panda', 'shark', 'whale' and 'butterfly'.

    (iii) Write a type declaration statement for a rank=1 array of objects of type 'Species', having 15 elements and being named 'big_cats'.

    (iv) Write an assignment statement using a structure constructor to say that the 'whale', as in (ii) above, is called "cetus_____", on average has a weight of 4578.0 kg, a height of 2.86 m and a length of 12.71 m, has no legs, and can swim.

    (v) Write an assignment statement using a structure constructor to say that the fifth element of the 'big_cats' array, as in (iii) above, has the name "snow_leopard", average weight 46 kg, height 0.69 m and length 1.35 m, and has four legs and can swim.

    (vi) Write an assignment statement using a structure component to change the average weight of the 'whale', first set in (iv) above, to 4287 kg.

    (v) Write an assignment statement using a structure component to say that the "snow_leopard", in (v) above, cannot swim.

14A2   (i) Suppose that arrays did not exist in Fortran. Write a derived-type definition block for a data type called 'Vector' consisting of 20 real numbers (called 'x1', 'x2', 'x3', etc.) and an integer. The integer (called 'length') is to represent the number of significant elements in a vector.

(ii) Write a type declaration statement for an 'Array'-type variable called 'qwt' of 3 real numbers, initialising their values to zero.

(iii) Write an assignment statement using a structure component to set the second element of the 'Array' qwt to the value 4.12.

14.4   STRUCTURES OF STRUCTURES

If derived-type structures were composed only of data items of intrinsic types, life would be interesting but not fascinating. In fact, components of a structure may themselves be derived-type structures.   This example sets up a special type, Coord, to represent co-ordinate pairs in 2-dimensional space; and then a further type, Circle, is set up to represent circles; but the definition of Circle involves a data item of type Coord:

```
        TYPE Coord
                REAL :: x, y
        END TYPE Coord

        TYPE Circle
                TYPE (Coord) :: centre
                REAL :: radius
        END TYPE Circle
```

This means that structure constructors may be nested, e.g.

        ring = Circle (Coord(1.0,-1.0), SQRT(2))

and that we can have components of components:

        ring%centre%y

would be equal to -1.0. This can be extended over several levels, e.g. the type

170

```
TYPE Sixcircles
        TYPE (Circle) :: round(6)
END TYPE Sixcircles
```

consisting of a set of six circles, each based on a co-ordinate pair and a radius. Then, if hex is a scalar of type Sixcircles, there can be components

```
hex%round(5)
hex%round
hex%round(1:3)
hex%round%radius
hex%round%centre(1)
hex%round%centre%x(2)
hex%round%centre%y
```

These expressions represent respectively the fifth circle in hex, an array (of type Circle) of all six circles, an array formed with the first three circles, a real array of the circles' radii, the centre (type Coord) of the first circle, the x-component of the centre of the second circle, and a real array of the y-components of the centres of the six circles!

It is important to remember that a type definition may include other derived-type structures only if the latter have previously been defined. However, a structure may have a component which is of the same type as itself if that component has the POINTER attribute (see chapter 15).

EXERCISES 14B

14B1   Write derived-type definition blocks for

(i) a person, the components being a 40-character name and a 3-integer date of birth,

(ii) a married couple, the components being two persons (husband and wife) and a date of marriage, and

(iii) a family, the components being a married couple and an array with up to 8 children.

(iv) If 'robinson' is the name of a variable of the 'family' type, as in (iii) above, write expressions for the year of marriage of the couple who head this family, and for the value of the wife's name.

Like those of intrinsic type, data items of derived type may be used as the arguments of procedures. Functions of derived-type data may be used to define special operators. The following example shows data items representing points and circles in two dimensions, together with a function that will calculate the area of overlap between two circles.

```
MODULE Ringtypes
        TYPE Coord
        REAL :: x, y
        END TYPE Coord
        TYPE Circle
        TYPE (Coord) :: centre
        REAL :: radius
        END TYPE Circle
END MODULE Ringtypes


MODULE Ringover
        INTERFACE OPERATOR (.over.)
        REAL FUNCTION Overlap(c1,c2)
        USE Ringtypes
        TYPE (Circle) :: c1, c2
        END FUNCTION Overlap
        END INTERFACE
END MODULE Ringover


REAL FUNCTION Overlap(c1,c2)
        USE Ringtypes
        TYPE (Circle) :: c1, c2
        REAL x1, x2, y1, y2, d, r1, r2, ca1, ca2, s, a1, a2, trisq
        x1 = c1%centre%x    ;    x2 = c2%centre%x
        y1 = c1%centre%y    ;    y2 = c2%centre%y
        d  = SQRT((x1 - x2)**2 + (y1 - y2)**2)
        r1 = c1%radius      ;    r2 = c2%radius
        IF (d>(r1+r2)) THEN
                Overlap = 0.0   ;   RETURN
        ELSE IF (D<ABS(r1-r2)) THEN
                Overlap = MAX(r1,r2)**2*3.14159 ;   RETURN
        ELSE
                ca1 = (r1**2 + d**2 - r2**2)/(2.0*r1*d)
                ca2 = (r2**2 + d**2 - r1**2)/(2.0*r2*d)
                s = (r1+r2+d)/2
                a1 = ACOS(ca1) ;   a2 = ACOS(ca2)
```

```
                    trisq = s*(s-r1)*(s-r2)*(s-d)
                    Overlap = (a1*r1 + a2*r2 - SQRT(trisq))*2.0
            END IF
    END FUNCTION Overlap

    MODULE Rings
            USE Ringtypes
            USE Ringover
    END MODULE Rings
```

Here, the type definition blocks have been put into a module called Ringtypes. The function itself, Overlap, is an external function and is not therefore in any module. It is necessary to provide an interface for the function Overlap, because an operator is being defined, and this interface put into a module called Ringover. The function itself, Overlap, uses the derived types and therefore includes a USE Ringtypes statement. Finally, a combination module, Rings, brings together Ringtypes and Ringover so that any program unit using these need contain only the statement USE Rings.

Here is another example where a new type, Location, is defined and may be operated on with a function Distance:

```
    MODULE Locdef
            TYPE Location
            REAL :: dlatitude, dlongitude
            END TYPE Location
    END MODULE Locdef

    MODULE Interdistance
            INTERFACE OPERATOR (.to.)
            REAL FUNCTION Distance(a,b)
            USE Locdef
            TYPE (Location) :: a, b
            END INTERFACE
    END MODULE Interdistance

    REAL FUNCTION Distance(a,b)
    USE Locdef      ;       TYPE (Location) :: a, b
    REAL, PARAMETER :: rdn = 57.296, rds = 6330000.0
    REAL :: ta, tb, pa, pb, ra, rb, direct, aa(3), bb(3), absq(3)
    ta = a%dlongitude/rdn   ;       tb = b%dlongitude/rdn
    pa = a%dlatitude/rdn    ;       pb = b%dlatitude/rdn
    aa(1) = sin(ta)         ;       bb(1) = sin(tb)
    ra  = cos(ta)           ;       rb  = cos(tb)
    aa(2) = ra*sin(pa)      ;       bb(2) = rb*sin(pb)
    aa(3) = ra*cos(pa)      ;       bb(3) = rb*cos(pb)
```

173

```
absq = (aa - bb)**2
direct = sqrt(sum(absq))
Distance = 2.0*rds*asin(direct/2)
END FUNCTION Distance
```

This function would be invoked by any expression of the form

paris.to.moscow

from any program unit with access to the appropriate modules, if paris and moscow are defined data items of type Location.

In the above examples, derived type data occurs as arguments but the function values themselves are of an intrinsic (real) type. But in general a function result itself may be of derived type, as in

```
TYPE (Circle) FUNCTION Loop (c)
USE Ringtypes
TYPE (Coord) :: c(3)
REAL csq1, csq2, csq3, top, bot, xcent, ycent, radsq, rad
csq1 = c(1)%x**2 + c(1)%y**2
csq2 = c(2)%x**2 + c(2)%y**2
csq3 = c(3)%x**2 + c(3)%y**2
top = (c(2)%y - c(3)%y)*(csq1 - csq2) -(c(1)%y - c(2)%y)*(csq2 - csq3)
bot = (c(1)%x-c(2)%x)*(c(2)%y-c(3)%y) -(c(2)%x-c(3)%x)*(c(1)%y-c(2)%y)
xcent = 0.5 * top / bot
ycent = 0.5 * (csq1 - csq2- 2.0 * xcent * (c(1)%x-c(2)%x)) / (c(1)%y - c(2)%y)
radsq = (xcent - c(1)%x)**2 + (ycent - c(1)%y)**2
rad = SQRT(radsq)
Loop = Circle (Coord (xcent, ycent), rad)
END FUNCTION Loop
```

This function uses the types Coord and Circle that we met in previous examples, and forms the circle that passes through a set of three points c. It is not mandatory to have an interface for the function Loop because no operator is being defined.

14.6   DEFINED ASSIGNMENT

Defined operators were covered in section 12.6, and in some ways it would have been logical to deal with 'defined assignments' at the same time. Both are special types of procedure interface; a defined operator permits a function reference to be made through an operator, and a defined assignment permits a subroutine to be called through a form of assignment statement ('=').

However, defined assignment is especially useful in the context of derived types and so has been deferred until this chapter.

First of all, recall that the general form of the assignment statement is

variable = expression

and this simply gives the variable on the left the value of the expression on the right, as long as they are of the same types and (if arrays) have the same shapes. This applies also to objects of the same derived type: the components of the variable are set equal to the corresponding components of the expression. But we do not always have to have the same types and shapes on each side of an assignment statement. It is permissible for the expression to be a scalar and the variable an array, in which case all the array's elements will be set to the value of the expression. If the variable and the expression are of different numeric types, then the expression will be converted to the variable's type as if by the intrinsic function INT, REAL or CMPLX. If the variable and the expression are character strings of different lengths, the expression will be either truncated or padded to conform to the length of the variable. Those are the rules of 'intrinsic' assignment.

'Defined assignment' permits the assignment statement to be given a meaning when it would normally be undefined, i.e. in cases where the variable and the expression are of different types that would normally be incompatible. It also permits the rules of intrinsic assignment to be redefined, or 'overloaded', with something different from what was mentioned in the previous paragraph. Defined assignment is specified with a subroutine having exactly two dummy arguments and having an interface of the form

```
INTERFACE ASSIGNMENT(=)
    SUBROUTINE ....
            .
            .
            .
    END SUBROUTINE ....
END INTERFACE
```

the first line meaning that the subroutine can be invoked by a use of the '=' sign in an assignment statement. When this happens, the variable on the left hand side will be the first argument of the subroutine and the expression on the right will be the second.

As an example, suppose we want to define the assignment a=b when a is a real scalar variable and b is of the type Circle used in previous examples above. In this case, suppose we want the number a to be set equal to the area of the circle b. This could be done with

```
SUBROUTINE Discus (a, b)
USE Ringtypes
REAL, INTENT (OUT) :: a
```

```
        TYPE (Circle), INTENT (IN) :: b
        REAL, PARAMETER :: pi=3.14159265
        a = pi * b%radius**2
        END SUBROUTINE Discus
```

where, to define the type Circle, the module Ringtypes has been included (see previous section). It is necessary to have an interface whenever a subroutine is to be used to define an assignment, and in this case there would be

```
        INTERFACE ASSIGNMENT (=)
                SUBROUTINE Discus (a, b)
                USE Ringtypes
                REAL, INTENT (OUT) :: a
                TYPE (Circle), INTENT (IN) :: b
                END SUBROUTINE Discus
        END INTERFACE
```

There are a few things to notice about this example. The dummy arguments a and b are arbitrarily named, and need not even be the same between the subroutine and the interface. The first argument has INTENT (OUT) and the second has INTENT (IN), since the purpose of the subroutine is to give a value to the former based on the latter. In fact Fortran will assume INTENT (OUT) and INTENT (IN) in these circumstances, so it is not actually necessary to give the INTENT attributes at all in this example. However, it is conceivable that the value of the variable a might depend not only on the expression b but also on the initial value of a; so INTENT (INOUT) is possible for the first argument of a defined assignment.

A defined assignment will be invoked whenever the objects on either side of the '=' match the combination of types and/or shapes given for the arguments in the interface block. The interface block could contain interfaces to different subroutines, corresponding to different type/shape combinations of the arguments, and it would then be a 'generic' interface. Suppose that we wished to define assignments in either direction between integers and single characters: a suitable generic interface would be

```
        INTERFACE ASSIGNMENT (=)

                SUBROUTINE C_to_I (i, char)
                INTEGER :: i
                CHARACTER :: char
                END SUBROUTINE C_to_I
```

```
            SUBROUTINE I_to_C (char, i)
            CHARACTER :: char
            INTEGER :: i
            END SUBROUTINE I_to_C

        END INTERFACE
```

and the corresponding subroutines could be similar but including the executable statements

$$i = IACHAR(char) - 48$$

and

$$char = ACHAR(i + 48)$$

respectively.

Defined assignments can be great fun, and one more example won't go amiss:

```
        MODULE Get
            USE Gettype
            USE Getint
            TYPE (Grab) :: get
        END MODULE Get

        MODULE Gettype
            TYPE Grab
            CHARACTER :: c
            END TYPE Grab
        END MODULE Gettype

        MODULE Getint
            INTERFACE ASSIGNMENT (=)
                SUBROUTINE Smash (c, g)
                USE Gettype
                CHARACTER :: c
                TYPE (Grab) :: g
                END SUBROUTINE Smash
            END INTERFACE
        END MODULE Getint

        SUBROUTINE Smash (c, g)
        USE Gettype
        CHARACTER :: c
        TYPE (Grab) :: g
```

```
                    READ (*,*) c
                    END SUBROUTINE Smash
```

With this, in any program unit headed by

USE Get

a statement such as

qwerty = get

will lead to the character variable on the left (whatever its name) being evaluated by reading in one character from the keyboard.

EXERCISES 14C

14C1   Write a function to calculate the two points of intersection of two circles, following the example in section 14.5.

14C2   Write code to set up a special type ('Fuzzy') composed of two real numbers to represent an estimate of the value of something together with the statistical error on that estimate. Write functions with defined operators to add, subtract, multiply and divide Fuzzies together, combining the errors according to the correct statistical procedure for uncorrelated errors. Using generic interfaces, include other functions so that the proper results are given also when Fuzzies are combined with ordinary real numbers. (If you found that easy, write a square root function for a Fuzzy argument, working on the assumption that the quantity concerned must be positive whatever its statistical error.)

14C3   (i) Devise a derived type to represent sparse matrices, i.e. data equivalent to a real rank=2 array with extents that may be very large but with only a few elements having non-zero elements. Allow for a dimensionality up to 1024x1024, but with no more than 512 non-zero elements. The idea is to avoid storing all the zeros and thereby save space.

       (ii) Write a function to form the product of two sparse matrices.

14C4   Write a subroutine and an interface block defining assignment when a variable of integer type is set equal to one of character type. The integer is to be set equal to the ASCII code for the first character in the string, or to zero for a zero-length string.

14C5   In an array assignment statement it is normally necessary that the two arrays have the same shape. With an interface for defined assignment, write a subroutine using assumed-size arrays so that '=' will operate between any two real arrays, setting the elements of the left-hand-side array equal to the elements of the right-hand-side array taken in normal array element order. If necessary, it should pad out the left-hand-side array with zeros.

14C6   The game of 'Life' is based on a large two-dimensional rectangular array of cells, each of which is either 'alive' or 'dead'. Each cell has nine nearest neighbours, i.e. the cells immediately above, below, to either side, and in the four diagonal directions from it. The state of the array changes generation by generation, with cells dying or being born. Each time, the fate of each cell depends on the number of live neighbours it had in the passing generation. A live cell will die if it had fewer than 2 or more than 4 live neighbours, and will survive otherwise. A previously-dead cell will come to life if it had 2 or 3 neighbours. As parts of a program to model the game of life, devise a derived data type to represent the array of cells and write a function that takes the array from one generation to the next.

14C7   An interesting function of a positive integer (investigated by Dijkstra) is defined by

$$FUSC(1) = 1$$

$$FUSC(2*n) = FUSC(n)$$

$$FUSC(2*n + 1) = FUSC(n) + FUSC(n+1)$$

Write a function to yield FUSC(n) and use it to look into the function's properties. What is its average value for the values of n lying between 9900 and 10100?

N14.1   SEQUENCE

A derived-type definition block may include the statement

SEQUENCE

after the initial TYPE statement but before the statements defining the components. The effect is to make the derived type a 'sequenced' structure, which means that any object of this type will be ultimately resolved into individual numbers or characters in the same way wherever the object is declared. This is necessary if such an object is to appear in a COMMON (N11.2) or EQUIVALENCE (N16.4) statement.

Chapter 15

ARRAYS AND POINTERS

This chapter begins by presenting some further details about arrays and array constructors, including the idea of 'array element order' and the intrinsic function RESHAPE. After explaining vector subscripts (section 15.2), we move on to allocatable arrays (section 15.3), involving the statements ALLOCATE and DEALLOCATE and the function ALLOCATED. A few other intrinsic functions, namely LBOUND, UBOUND, SHAPE and SIZE, are dealt with in section 15.4.

The next major topic is that of pointers, taking up sections 15.5 to 15.8. As well as special attributes within the type declaration statement, we meet the pointer assignment statement, the NULLIFY statement, and the intrinsic function ASSOCIATED.

15.1   ARRAY ELEMENT ORDER; ARRAY CONSTRUCTORS; RESHAPE

It was explained in chapter 7 that a Fortran array is a set of scalar elements ordered in up to seven dimensions, forming what can be visualised as a hyper-rectangular array. The number of dimensions is the 'rank'; the number of elements spanned by a particular dimension is the 'extent' in that dimension; the total number of elements, the 'size', is equal to the product of the extents; and the set of extents is the 'shape' of the array. For example, a rank=3 array with an extent of 5 in each dimension has a size of 125 and a shape of (5,5,5).

Nevertheless, in a sense any array may be regarded as a continuous linear sequence of elements. Within the processor's memory, an array of any rank will usually be stored in an uninterrupted sequence of memory locations. Moreover, a statement such as

WRITE (*,*) table

where 'table' is an array of any shape, will output a series of values depending on the size, but not the detailed shape, of the array 'table'. In Fortran, all the elements of an array form a sequence in what is known as 'array element order'. In the trivial case of a rank=1 array, this is simply the order of increasing subscript, i.e. the array q(-3:3) gives the sequence

q(-3), q(-2), q(-1), q(0), q(1), q(2), q(3)

For a rank=2 array, the array element order is given by letting the first subscript run repeatedly, i.e. the array q(2,3) gives the sequence

q(1,1), q(2,1), q(1,2), q(2,2), q(1,3), q(2,3)

In general, whatever the rank, 'array element order' is given by letting earlier subscripts vary more quickly than later ones.

Array element order is relevant not only to READ and WRITE statements but also to assumed-size arrays (section 13.4) whereby a procedure's argument is passed as a sequence of elements rather than as an array of determinate shape.

It is sometimes convenient to rearrange the elements of an array into another array of different shape. This could be done by assignment statements, looping through all the elements, as in

```
DO j = 1, 32
        DO i = 1, 32
                v(32*(j-1)+i) = w(i, j)
        END DO
END DO
```

which forms a rank=1 array v(1024) from the elements of the rank=2 array w(32,32). Another example is

```
DO k = 1, 1024
        i = 1 + MOD(k,32)
        j = k/32
        w(i, j) = v(k)
END DO
```

which does the opposite. Another way of re-ordering the elements of an array would be to WRITE and READ 'internal files', which will be explained in chapter 17. Yet another approach would be to use array constructors with 'implied DO' loops, as in

$$v = (/((w(i,j), i= 1, 32), j= 1, 32)/)$$

or a mixture of techniques:

```
DO j = 1, 32
        w(1:32, j) = (/ v(32*j)-31 : v(32*j) /)
END DO
```

These last two examples do the same jobs as the earlier two above. Array constructors with implied-DO loops can be extremely powerful, although an array constructor can only be used to define a rank=1 array.

The general syntax for an array constructor is

$$(/ \text{ item, item, item, ... } /)$$

where each item is either an expression or is a controlled list taking the form

$$(\text{item, item, item, ..., ivar = istart, istop, istride})$$

where here again each item could be either a scalar expression or, nestwise, yet another controlled list. The control parameter 'ivar' must be the name of a scalar integer variable, and it may occur within the expressions defining the items which it controls. The other control parameters, 'istart', 'istop' and 'istride', are scalar integer expressions. The final parameter, 'istride', may be omitted, in which case it is taken to be unity. The parameter 'ivar' is an index running from the value 'start' to 'stop' in increments of 'stride'. This is analogous to the DO loop syntax

$$\text{DO ivar = istart, istop, istride}$$

(see section 8.3). An example of an array constructor with nested implied-DO loops is

$$\text{harlequin} = (/((\text{casque}(j,17-i).OR.(i==j), i= 1, 16), j= 1, 16)/)$$

which is a rank=1 logical array of size 256 whose elements depend on a rank=2 logical array called casque.

This discussion began with a consideration of how the elements of an array can be used to form another array of different shape. In fact, the most straightforward method in Fortran is to use RESHAPE, an array-valued intrinsic function provided specifically for reshaping arrays. RESHAPE can be referenced with the argument keywords

$$\text{RESHAPE (SHAPE, SOURCE, PAD, ORDER)}$$

and the last two arguments, PAD and ORDER, are optional. Let us suppose firstly that PAD and ORDER are absent. The argument SOURCE can be an array of any sort, and its elements are rearranged to form the result RESHAPE. The elements of RESHAPE are therefore of the same type as those of SOURCE. However, the shape of RESHAPE is given by the argument SHAPE, which is a rank=1 integer array specifying, as one would expect, the desired extents of the dimensions of RESHAPE. The rank of RESHAPE is therefore equal to the size of SHAPE. The effect of the function is to take the elements of SOURCE and place them into RESHAPE in normal array element order, RESHAPE having the shape specified by SHAPE. Using again our earlier examples,

$$v = \text{RESHAPE(SHAPE=(/1024/), SOURCE=w)}$$

and

$$w = \text{RESHAPE(SHAPE=(/32,32/), SOURCE=v)}$$

If SOURCE has more elements than RESHAPE, the unwanted elements will not be used. If RESHAPE has more elements than SOURCE, then the argument PAD must be present, and it must be an array of the same type as SOURCE. The elements of PAD are used, in array element order, to fill the remainder of RESULT, if necessary running through PAD more than once. So,

$$xout = RESHAPE(SHAPE=(/100/), SOURCE=xin, PAD=(/0.0/))$$

forms the rank=1 real array xout using the elements of xin, padding xout with zeros if xin has fewer than 100 elements.

The optional argument ORDER provides an opportunity of placing the elements of RESHAPE not in normal array element order but as if some of its dimensions were switched around. ORDER must be an integer array of the same size and rank (=1) as SHAPE, but containing the integers 1, 2, 3, ... in a permuted order. The array ORDER then tells the processor in what order it should run through the dimensions of RESHAPE when fixing its elements. If ORDER is omitted, it is like having ORDER=(/1,2,3,.../) and so on up to the rank of RESHAPE. This means that if 'twist' and 'metric' are 4x4 arrays, and

$$twist = RESHAPE(SHAPE=(/4,4/), SOURCE=metric, ORDER=(/2,1/))$$

then twist(i,j)=metric(j,i). In this example, RESHAPE is being used to do what the TRANSPOSE function does (section 10.2).

Using the RESHAPE function and array constructors, a multidimensional array can be compactly specified in one statement, as in

```
LOGICAL, PARAMETER :: oddcolumns(16,16) = &
        RESHAPE (SHAPE=(/16,16/), SOURCE=(/(.TRUE.,.FALSE.,i=1,128)/))
```

or

```
iternary = RESHAPE( SHAPE = (/3,3,3,3,3,3,3/) &
           SOURCE = (/(i, i=0, 2186)/) &
           ORDER = (/7, 6, 5, 4, 3, 2, 1/) )
```

15.2   VECTOR SUBSCRIPTS

Section 7.4 dealt with 'array sections', i.e. the notation for picking out a subset of the elements of an array. This was done with a colon notation, as in the simple rank=1 example

```
decade(10:1:-1)
```

The three integers, separated by colons, form what is known as a 'subscript triplet', specifying a starting index, a final index, and a 'stride' in a way very similar to the implied-DO notation mentioned for array constructors in the previous section. (The phrase 'subscript triplet' is used even when the stride is omitted.)

'Vector subscripts' are a further tool for forming array sections, permitting a set of indices to be specified in any order. The idea is that, instead of a subscript triplet, a rank=1 integer array is given which contains the desired indices in the desired order. Thus, if we have an array

$$\text{npick} = (/10, 9, 8, 7, 6, 5, 4, 3, 2, 1/)$$

then the array section mentioned above could be specified equally well by

$$\text{decade(npick)}$$

In other words, an array may have an index which is itself a rank=1 array. In decade(npick), if npick were a scalar integer then we would just have a single element of the array; but because npick is an array so is decade(npick). Another example: with the vector subscript

$$u = (/4,9,1,6/)$$

the array section $x(u)$ consists of the elements $x(4)$, $x(9)$, $x(1)$ and $x(6)$ in that order.

A vector subscript may be any integer expression of rank=1, as long as its elements are within the bounds of the array of which it is a subscript. With the arrays

$$\text{INTEGER :: matrices(4,4,200), triad(3), mum(3,3)}$$

and if, say,

$$\text{triad} = (/196,2,34/)$$

then

$$\text{mum} = \text{matrices(3:1:-1,2,triad)}$$

is the rank=2 array with elements

$$\text{mum(1,1)} = \text{matrices(3,2,196)}$$
$$\text{mum(2,1)} = \text{matrices(2,2,196)}$$
$$\text{mum(3,1)} = \text{matrices(1,2,196)}$$
$$\text{mum(1,2)} = \text{matrices(3,2,2)}$$
$$\text{mum(2,2)} = \text{matrices(2,2,2)}$$
$$\text{mum(3,2)} = \text{matrices(1,2,2)}$$
$$\text{mum(1,3)} = \text{matrices(3,2,34)}$$
$$\text{mum(2,3)} = \text{matrices(2,2,34)}$$
$$\text{mum(3,3)} = \text{matrices(1,2,34)}$$

185

As this example illustrates, it is possible to have an array section with different dimensions having different forms of subscript, i.e. we can have a mixture of single subscripts, subscript triplets, and vector subscripts.

A multidimensional array may have more than one vector subscript. For example, if

$$\text{isquare} = \text{RESHAPE(SHAPE}=(/8,8/), \text{SOURCE}=(/k**2, k=1, 64/))$$

and we have the vector subscript k3=(/1,2,3/), then

$$\text{knine} = \text{RESHAPE(SHAPE}=(/9/),\text{SOURCE}=\text{isquare(k3,k3))}$$

is the rank=1 array (/1,4,9,81,100,121,289,324,361/). Here, isquare is an 8x8 array of integers, and isquare(k3,k3) is an array section with two vector subscripts which happen to be equal.

A vector subscript may have more than one element of the same value, in which case it forms what is called a 'many-one' array section. For example, given the array of single characters

$$\text{chars} = (/(\text{"abcdefghijklmnopqrstuvwxyz\_"(i:i), i=1, 27)/})$$

and the vector subscript given by

$$\text{name} = \quad (/13,1,18,20,9,14,27,10,1,13,5,19,27,3,15,21,14,9,8,1,14/)$$

then chars(name) is a many-one array section consisting of 21 single-character elements such that

$$\text{WRITE (*,*) chars(name)}$$

spells out

$$\text{martin\_james\_counihan}$$

If a vector subscript has many repeated elements, the resulting array section could be much greater in size than the array of which it is a section.

There are just a few restrictions on the use of vector subscripts: in particular, a many-one array section may not appear as the variable on the left side of an assignment statement, and an array with a vector subscript may not be used as the argument of a procedure which will redefine it. Also, a pointer assignment statement (explained later in this chapter) may not have as its target an array section with a vector subscript.

There are other games we can play. An array may have itself as a vector subscript, so if, say,

$$z = (/1,3,4,2/)$$

then z(z) is (/1,4,2,3/) and z(z(z)) is (/1,2,3,4/).

15.3   ALLOCATABLE ARRAYS

'Allocatable arrays' are Fortran's most direct tool for dynamic memory management, in other words for letting arrays have variable bounds. Already, in connection with procedures, we have come across other forms of arrays with non-constant shape (section 13.4), namely automatic arrays, assumed-shape arrays and assumed-size arrays; but these all involve fixing an array's shape when a procedure is entered. Allocatable arrays have nothing directly to do with procedures.

An allocatable array, which is sometimes called a 'deferred-shape' array, is initially declared with a certain rank, i.e. a certain number of dimensions, but the extent of each dimension (the 'bounds') can be set and may be changed during the running of the program. This can be very valuable whenever a processor is limited in memory, and it means that a program may expand and contract its memory requirements during running to minimise the demands made on the processor. For example, a program may need a large amount of memory to read a database, but may then carry out an analysis using just a small fraction of the input information: using allocatable arrays, most of the memory needed at input could be released by the program when it proceeds to the analysis stage.

An allocatable array is declared in a type declaration statement by specifying the attribute ALLOCATABLE, and at that point its rank is specified by giving an array specifier with a series of colons, one colon for each dimension. This is a 'deferred-shape' specification (see section 13.4). The following are examples of allocatable arrays of ranks 1, 2, 3 and 4:


```
INTEGER, ALLOCATABLE, SAVE :: bitstream(:)
REAL, ALLOCATABLE :: matrix1(:,:), matrix2(:,:)
CHARACTER, ALLOCATABLE, DIMENSION(:,:,:) :: pages
LOGICAL, ALLOCATABLE :: truthtable(:,:,:,:)
```


An allocatable array may not be a function-name or a procedure's dummy argument.

The bounds of allocatable arrays are set by a special statement, ALLOCATE, which simply lists the arrays' names and shapes. The ALLOCATE statement causes the required amount of memory space to be allocated to the arrays named. Examples are


```
ALLOCATE (bitstream(4097))
ALLOCATE (matrix1(45,90), matrix2(45,180), pages(65,30,1))
```

Following the usual notation for array shapes (e.g. section 13.4), lower and upper bounds may be specified:

ALLOCATE (truthtable(0:1,0:1,0:7,14)

In an ALLOCATE statement the bounds may be expressions. Moreover, they are not restricted to the 'specification expressions' allowed for automatic arrays (section 13.4) but may be scalar integer expressions of more or less any kind, as long as they have definite values when the ALLOCATE statement is executed. So, we could have an arrangement such as

REAL, ALLOCATABLE :: rmem(:)
.
.
.
READ (*,*) n
ALLOCATE (rmem(2*n))
.
.
.

Statements such as the following would also be possible:

ALLOCATE (workspace(120*nrecords, 15))
ALLOCATE (bytes(npersons, LEN(names))
ALLOCATE (scratchpads(dataset(1:1),3,SIZE(dataset))

but not

ALLOCATE (results(npoints), display(SIZE(results))

because a bound of one array may not depend on an array inquiry function whose argument is another array which is being allocated within the same ALLOCATE statement. (For SIZE, see section 15.4.) But it would be quite possible to have the sequence of two statements

ALLOCATE (results(npoints))
ALLOCATE (display(SIZE(results))

The ALLOCATE statement may have, after the list of arrays, a status variable for the purposes of error-checking. It is given with the keyword STAT as in

ALLOCATE (display(SIZE(results)), STAT=k)

or

$$\text{ALLOCATE (a(2), b(3), c(55,4), STAT=icheck)}$$

The name after STAT= is arbitrary, but it must be a scalar integer variable. After execution of the ALLOCATE statement, the status variable will be zero if the allocation was successful, but will be positive if there was an error. (If STAT=... is not included in the statement, then an error in executing it will cause the program to terminate.)

The ALLOCATE statement gives space to an array, but the space can be later released with a DEALLOCATE statement. The syntax is just like that for ALLOCATE except that the arrays' names are not followed by their shapes:

$$\text{DEALLOCATE (bitstream, matrix1, matrix2, pages, STAT=iflag)}$$
$$\text{DEALLOCATE (truthtable, workspace, bytes)}$$

DEALLOCATE may only be used on allocatable arrays which have actually been allocated, and ALLOCATE may only be used on a previously-allocated array if it is deallocated first.

It can be useful to have a way of checking, during program execution, whether or not space has been allocated to an array. To do this there is an intrinsic function ALLOCATED. The ALLOCATED function has one argument, which must be the name of an allocatable array, and it has the logical value .TRUE. or .FALSE. according to whether the array is currently allocated. So, it is possible to have statements like

$$\text{IF (ALLOCATED(scratchpads)) DEALLOCATE(scratchpads)}$$

and

$$\text{IF (.NOT.ALLOCATED(results)) ALLOCATE(results(4,100))}$$

When using allocatable arrays, a problem may arise if an array is allocated within a procedure and then the program returns back to the program unit that invoked the procedure. Under these circumstances the array will in effect be lost, even if the procedure is entered again later. In fact, it won't even be possible to deallocate the array later because its allocation status will have become undefined. There are two ways around this problem: one is to give allocatable arrays the SAVE attribute, in which case they are not lost on returning from the procedure, and the other way is to put allocatable arrays into modules. With modules, the arrays are preserved as long as the modules are being used by whichever program units are executing.

EXERCISES 15A

15A1 Use RESHAPE in an assignment statement setting the first 48 elements of an 8x8 matrix, in normal array element order, equal to the elements of size=48 vector. The matrix is called 'chessboard' and the vector is called 'six_rows'. They are to be of logical type. The 16 elements of 'chessboard' which are not filled by 'six_rows' are to be filled with alternating .TRUE. and .FALSE. values.

15A2 If vowels = (/"a","e","i","o","u"/), khard = (/1,4,5/) and ksoft = (/2,3/) what are the values of

(i) vowels(khard) (ii) vowels(ksoft) (iii) khard(ksoft)
(iv) vowels((/4,2/)) (v) vowels(khard)//vowels(2)

15A3 (i) Write type declaration statements for an allocatable rank=2 array of complex numbers, to be called 'cmatrix', and an allocatable rank=1 array of length=12 character strings, to be called 'rivernames'.

(ii) Write statements to allocate the shape (4,4) to 'cmatrix' and allocate 200 elements to 'rivernames'.

(iii) Write code that will deallocate 'rivernames' if it has already been allocated, and will then allocate 150 elements to it.

15A4 Write code that will take a character string, of whatever length, and produce a vector of that size containing the individual characters that formed the string.

15.4 LBOUND, UBOUND, SHAPE AND SIZE

There are intrinsic functions LBOUND and UBOUND which yield the lower and upper bounds on the subscripts of whatever array is given as the argument. If arrays were declared by

REAL :: a(21:30), b(10)

then LBOUND(a) is 21, UBOUND(a) is 30, LBOUND(b) is 1, and UBOUND(b) is 10. The values of LBOUND and UBOUND are, obviously, integers, whatever the types of the arguments. With multidimensional arrays, LBOUND and UBOUND are rank=1 integer arrays containing the sets of lower and upper bounds: so with

LOGICAL :: c(0:2,0:2,0:2,0:3)

190

LBOUND(c) is equal to (/0,0,0,0/) and UBOUND(c) is (/2,2,2,3/).

In fact LBOUND and UBOUND may have an optional second argument, the keywords being LBOUND(ARRAY, DIM) and UBOUND(ARRAY, DIM). If DIM is present it must be a scalar integer no greater than the rank of the argument ARRAY, and then the function yields the subscript bound relevant to the dimension indicated by DIM. Using the previous example, UBOUND(ARRAY=c, DIM=4) is equal to 3. If the argument ARRAY is an array expression or section, rather than just the name of an array variable, then LBOUND will be given equal to 1 and UBOUND will be the extent of the appropriate dimension.

SHAPE is a very straightforward intrinsic function, having a single argument which may be any array. Its value is a rank=1 integer array specifying the argument's shape, i.e. with the series of dimensional extents. So, the expression SHAPE(RESHAPE(SHAPE=a,SOURCE=b)) is just the array a.

The intrinsic function SIZE is also very simple. With a single argument, which must be an array, SIZE is the total number of elements in it. There is an optional second argument, the keywords being SIZE(ARRAY, DIM), in which case SIZE is the extent of ARRAY along the dimension labelled by the integer DIM. So, if SHAPE(a) is (/4,5,100/), SIZE(a) is equal to 2000 and SIZE(ARRAY=a,DIM=2) is 5.

EXERCISES 15B

15B1   With the array declared by

INTEGER :: spreadsheets (1:12,1901:2050,1:20,0:199)

what are the values of

(i)   LBOUND (spreadsheets)
(ii)   SHAPE (spreadsheets)
(iii)   SHAPE (spreadsheets(1:1,:,:,:))
(iv)   UBOUND (spreadsheets(1:1,:,:,:))
(v)   SHAPE (spreadsheets(1,:,:,:))
(vi)   UBOUND (spreadsheets(1,:,:,:))
(vii)   LBOUND (ARRAY=spreadsheets(:,1967,:,:),DIM=2)
(viii)   SIZE (spreadsheets(1:10,1967,:,:))
(ix)   UBOUND(LBOUND(spreadsheets(1:10,1967,:,:))
(x)   SIZE(SHAPE(spreadsheets(2,:,1967,:)))

15.5   SIMPLE POINTERS

'Pointers' are a powerful and elegant feature of Fortran and of some other modern programming languages such as C. Unfortunately pointers are notoriously difficult to understand when you first meet them, mainly because it is not immediately clear what sort of problem they are there to solve. In this section we will explain the use of pointers in the simplest of circumstances, in relation to ordinary scalar data of intrinsic type. This is straightforward but will not seem terribly useful. Later sections will extend the idea to derived-type structures (section 15.6), function results and dummy arguments (section 15.7), and arrays (section 15.8), and it is in these contexts that most powerful practical applications of pointers arise.

Normally, there are two aspects to any data object in Fortran. Firstly there are the various attributes that describe what sort of object it is: its type, its name, its rank if it is an array, its length if it is a character string, and the other attributes that can be set by a type declaration statement. This set of details is sometimes known as the 'descriptor' of the data. Secondly, there is the actual value of the object. When a data object is first declared, the data descriptor is fixed and memory space is set aside to hold the value of the data. If the type declaration statement includes data initialisation, that memory space will be filled with the initial data values immediately.

It is very important to distinguish clearly between the data descriptor, which is unaffected by the value of the data, and the value itself. The value may occupy a large amount of memory, especially if the object is a long character string, an array, or a derived-type structure. The descriptor will occupy relatively little space, but is essential for making sense of the data's value, because the content of an area of memory is meaningless unless the processor knows whether it is to be interpreted as a real number, a character, or whatever.

A type declaration statement, then, normally sets up a data descriptor (name, type, etc) and reserves memory to hold its value, and it may fill that memory with an initial value. A 'pointer', however, is a data object that does not have its own reserved area of memory. In other words, a pointer is a data descriptor without its own space for a value. A pointer, as its name suggests, 'points' to memory space occupied by the value of some other variable, the 'target'. At its simplest, a pointer can be regarded as a name which can be associated and disassociated dynamically with memory space occupied by other data. A pointer-name can therefore be used as an 'alias'.

A particular pointer can only point to data of a particular type. A pointer must be declared with a type declaration statement giving its name, type, etc., and the attribute specification list must include the keyword POINTER. The effect is to establish a data descriptor, including the pointer's name, but without memory of its own to hold a value. It follows that there can be no initial value given when a pointer is declared. When the program is executing, the pointer may be associated with a variable of the appropriate type by means of a special statement, a 'pointer assignment' statement. Variables to which a pointer may be associated need to be declared initially with a special attribute, TARGET. The type declaration statements

        REAL, TARGET :: a, b, c, d, e, f
        REAL, POINTER :: p

set up the pointer p and the six real variables a,...,f which can be targetted. A pointer assignment statement has a form such as

```
p => a
```

which would mean that the name p will henceforth refer to the memory space occupied by the value of the target variable a. After such a statement, p could be used as an alternative name for a, either in statements like

```
b = p**2/2.0
WRITE (*,*) p, b
```

or in

```
p =  c + SQRT(d)
```

which, since p 'points' to a, actually changes the value of a.

The pointer assignment statement ('=>') by itself doesn't change the value of anything: it simply connects the named pointer to the named target. The general syntax of the pointer assignment statement is

```
pname => tname
```

where pname is the name of a pointer (i.e. a variable previously declared with the POINTER attribute) and tname is the name of a target. As far as we are concerned for the time being, tname must be the name of a variable previously declared with the TARGET attribute, but some exceptions to this will be mentioned later. The pointer and the target must be of the same type. Once a pointer assignment statement has been executed, the pointer is said to be 'associated' with the target, but if the same pointer subsequently appears on the left of another pointer assignment statement, the first association is broken and the second takes effect.

There is an intrinsic inquiry function, ASSOCIATED, which can be used to determine whether or not a pointer is associated with a target. ASSOCIATED(pname) is logical and has the value .TRUE. if pname points to any target and .FALSE. if it does not. This function has an optional second argument which may specify a particular target: the argument keywords are POINTER and TARGET, and ASSOCIATED(POINTER=pname, TARGET=tname) is .TRUE. if and only if pname is associated with tname.

As a simple example, this code fragment finds the value of the largest of six numbers:

```
REAL, TARGET :: a, b, c, d, e, f
REAL, POINTER :: p
        .
        .
        .
p => a
IF (b>p) p => b
IF (c>p) p => c
IF (d>p) p => d
IF (e>p) p => e
IF (f>p) p => f
WRITE (*,*) p
        .
        .
```

This is a rather artificial example, since it does no more than

$$\text{WRITE } (*,*) \text{ MAX}(a,b,c,d,e,f)$$

but the principle should be clear. The name p is being used to point to one of the six numbers a,...,f. The value of p does not, itself, occupy any additional memory space, because p doesn't have a 'value' in its own right. The above code could be written with p being an ordinary non-pointer variable, and with ordinary assignments ('=') instead of the pointer assignment statements, but a little more memory would be taken up. In the above example, using a pointer has saved a trivial amount of memory space, but later we will come across array pointers that can in principle save a good deal of memory.

Any variable with the POINTER attribute may also be used as a target, and it is not necessary to declare the TARGET attribute as well as POINTER. If we have

```
REAL, POINTER :: p, q, r
REAL, TARGET :: a, b, c
```

then the statements

```
r => b
p => r
```

associate r with b and then p with r. Because r is a pointer, the effect of the second statement is actually to associate p with the target currently pointed to by r, i.e. to b. In other words, targetting is 'transitive'. The statements

```
                    r => a
                    q => r
                    p => q
```

associate p directly with the value of a, and the processor does not 'remember' that this happened via q and r. If q or r is subsequently disassociated from a, p still points to a. Note that a target may be pointed to by more than one pointer: the code above leaves the target a pointed to by the three pointers p, q and r.

If a statement like

```
                    p => r
```

is executed at a time when r is not associated with a target, the effect is not to link p and r in any way but to leave p 'hanging', and if p was previously associated with something else it will become disassociated.

There is a special statement, NULLIFY, which can be used to disassociate a pointer. The keyword NULLIFY is followed by a bracketed list of pointer names. Examples are

```
            NULLIFY (p)
            NULLIFY (q, r)
            IF (ASSOCIATED(POINTER=p, TARGET=r)) NULLIFY (p)
```

Like allocatable arrays, a pointer declared within a procedure could be left with undefined status on return from that procedure to another program unit, so it is usually wise to declare pointers with the SAVE attribute.

Pointers can be of character type, and may point either to a complete character string or to a substring as long as the pointer was declared with a length matching that of the target. If the target is a substring, it must be part of a string declared with the TARGET attribute. The following code indicates how pointers could be used to work on a long character string while keeping memory utilisation to a minimum.

```
        !       Delete the beginning of chapter 5

        CHARACTER(*), TARGET             :: document
        CHARACTER(9), POINTER            :: word
        CHARACTER(2000), POINTER         :: startchapter
        CHARACTER(9), PARAMETER          :: heading = "Chapter 5"
        CHARACTER, PARAMETER             :: blank = " "
                    .
                    .
```

```
DO index = 1, LEN(document)-1999
        word => document(index:index+9)
        IF (word/=heading) CYCLE
        startchapter => document(index:index+1999)
        startchapter = REPEAT(blank,2000)  ;  EXIT
END DO
```

It was explained earlier that a pointer has a name and specifies the attributes of a particular type of data, but does not have its own memory space to hold a value. The pointer assignment statement, however, associates a pointer with memory space containing the value of an ordinary data object, the 'target', and the pointer name can then be used as an alias for that target. Besides that, there is another way of associating a pointer with memory space without using a pointer assignment statement. It can be done by using the ALLOCATE statement, which we met in section 15.3 in connection with allocatable ('deferred-shape') arrays. The ALLOCATE statement can be used with the names of pointers, in which case the effect is simply to associate the pointer with an area of memory for data storage. So, if we have the statements

```
REAL, POINTER :: x
ALLOCATE (x)
```

the first establishes x as the name of a real scalar data object and the second allocates space to hold the value of x. Unlike the situation when a pointer is associated with an object previously declared as a target, there is no other name for the piece of data. In fact, the above two statements have much the same effect as

```
REAL :: x
```

ALLOCATE is an executable statement and it allocates memory space during the running of the program. Moreover, memory so allocated may be deallocated by the DEALLOCATE statement, just as for arrays in section 15.2. This might seem rather pointless in the case of a single real variable, but it could be useful for efficient memory management if, say, a long character string were involved. For example,

```
CHARACTER(2**20), POINTER :: megabyte
        .
        .
        .
ALLOCATE (megabyte)
        .
        .
        .
DEALLOCATE (megabyte)
```

sets up a 1-megabyte character string and later allocates and deallocates the memory space dynamically. (But note that the inquiry function ALLOCATED must have an allocatable array as its argument and cannot be used to check the allocation status of a pointer!)

15.6   POINTERS AS STRUCTURES AND AS STRUCTURE COMPONENTS

Pointers are not restricted to being of intrinsic data types such as REAL or CHARACTER. A pointer may also be of derived type, as in

        TYPE (Partnumbers), POINTER :: assembly1, assembly2

and this could point to any variable of that type as long as it has the TARGET attribute, such as those declared by

        TYPE (Partnumbers), TARGET :: UKspec, USAspec, Pilotspec

The type 'Partnumbers' could have been defined by the block

            TYPE Partnumbers
                CHARACTER(24)   :: shortname
                INTEGER   :: nbits, idbit(30), nbit(30)
                LOGICAL   :: stockflags(30)
            END TYPE Partnumbers

and there is no need for POINTER or TARGET specifications to be included within the type definition block. Just as for intrinsic-type data, derived types may be used in pointer assignment statements and as arguments of the functions ASSOCIATED and NULLIFY:

            NULLIFY(assembly2)
            IF (ASSOCIATED(assembly1)) assembly2 => USAspec

The name of an associated pointer may be used in structure components, e.g.

            item = assembly1%shortname
            assembly1%stockflags = stockstatus

The second of these statements is an array assignment statement, because the component 'stockflags' is an array, although the complete objects declared to be of type 'Partnumbers' are scalars. The idea that a pointer may itself be an array will not be discussed until section 15.8.

A derived-type pointer, like one of intrinsic type, can have memory space allocated to it dynamically by ALLOCATE and DEALLOCATE statements, as in

```
        TYPE (Errormatrix), POINTER :: pmeasured, temp, pfitted
             .
             .
             .
        ALLOCATE (pmeasured) ! Space for data input
             .
                            (read in data 'pmeasured')
             .
        ALLOCATE (temp, pfitted) ! Space for calculation
             .
                            (using 'temp' for temporary workspace,
             .               calculate 'pfitted' from 'pmeasured')
             .
        DEALLOCATE (pmeasured, temp) ! Space no longer needed
             .
                            (write out data 'pfitted')
             .
        DEALLOCATE (pfitted) ! Space no longer needed
             .
             .
             .
```

Here, the objects called pmeasured, temp and pfitted are derived-type structures and they could occupy a great deal of memory space; their components could include large arrays. The ALLOCATE and DEALLOCATE statements are being used to keep the program's memory requirements to a minimum during program execution.

So far in this section we have been considering pointers to structures of derived type. In addition, it is possible for a structure to have a component that is a pointer. For example,

```
        TYPE Employee
                CHARACTER(30) :: name, jobtitle
                CHARACTER(10) :: idcode
                INTEGER :: ntelephone, idepartment, igrade
                CHARACTER(50), POINTER :: salarydatum
        END TYPE Employee
```

The pointer 'salarydatum' could be associated with data stored separately, e.g. in the array 'salaries' as below:

```
TYPE (Employee) :: staff(3500)
CHARACTER(50), TARGET :: salaries(3500)
CHARACTER(10) :: code
INTEGER :: iselect
        .
        .
        .
code = staff%idcode(iselect)
DO i = 1, 3500
        IF (code==salaries(i)(1:10)) THEN
                staff%salarydatum(iselect) => salaries(i)
                EXIT
        END IF
END DO
```

For an element of the array 'staff', the pointer 'salarydatum' is associated with a corresponding element of the array ('salaries').

Using pointers like this, cross-references can be created between different arrays of data. As another example, we could have a bibliography with data objects of the structure given by

```
TYPE Book
        CHARACTER(50) :: title, author, publisher
        INTEGER :: iyear, isbn1, isbn2
        LOGICAL :: statusflags(6)
        CHARACTER(200) :: notes
END TYPE Book
```

and a title index with elements of the type

```
TYPE Booktitle
        CHARACTER(50) :: title
        TYPE (Book), POINTER :: ref
END TYPE Booktitle
```

and an author index with elements

```
TYPE Bookauthor
        CHARACTER(50) :: author
        TYPE (Book), POINTER :: ref
END TYPE Bookauthor
```

Type declaration statements might be

```
TYPE (Book), TARGET :: bibliography(400)
TYPE (Bookauthor) :: authorindex(400)
TYPE (Booktitle) :: titleindex(400)
```

and there could be procedures to read the bibliography from a disk file, create author and title indices, use the indices to interrogate the bibliography, make changes to the bibliography, and write the modified bibliography back onto disk. The important thing is that the bulk of the information is kept in a single array, 'bibliography', while the author index and title index are relatively short and can be scanned through relatively quickly. A similar job could be done without pointers, using a system of reference numbers, but the system would then be more complex, probably less memory-efficient, and possibly more error-prone.

It is possible for a structure to have, as a component, a pointer to a data object of the same type as the structure itself. The best-known example of this sort of thing is a 'linked list', i.e. a set of data items each of which 'points' to another member of the set, thereby linking them all together into an ordered sequence. Consider first the type

```
TYPE Link
        REAL :: x
        TYPE (Link), POINTER :: nextlink
END TYPE Link
```

and suppose that there are several objects of this type:

```
TYPE (Link), TARGET :: alpha, beta1, beta2, beta3, gamma, ....
```

then we could have a situation where, say,

```
alpha%x = 0.34
alpha%nextlink => beta2
beta2%x = 0.79
beta2%nextlink => gamma
```

```
gamma%x = 0.04
gamma%nextlink => beta1
```

and so on. Each 'Link' in the chain contains a real number and a pointer to the next link. We have created a sort of pseudoarray, i.e. a set of data items ordered into a particular sequence. In that example, each link in the chain had its own name (alpha, beta2, etc.). By using ALLOCATE statements, however, it is possible to be much more clever and to create a chain of arbitrary length while giving a name only to the first item. Using the same type 'Link' as above, we could have

```
TYPE (Link), TARGET :: alpha
TYPE (Link), POINTER :: beta, gamma
READ (*,*) alpha%x
beta => alpha
DO i, i = 1,100
        ALLOCATE (gamma)
        beta%nextlink => gamma
        gamma%x = SQRT(ABS(1.0 - beta%x**2))
        NULLIFY (gamma%nextlink)
        beta => gamma
END DO
```

It is worth working through the meaning of this in some detail. First there is a statement declaring alpha to be a targettable object of type Link. We will see shortly why it is given the TARGET attribute. The second type declaration statement sets up names (beta and gamma) for two pointers of type Link. Being pointers, they have no memory space associated with them at this stage, and both of them are going to be used dynamically to represent different data objects at different times as the program runs.

We then start the executable part with the READ statement, which simply allows a value to be given to the first component of alpha.

The DO loop is going to create a linked list of data items of the type Link, starting from alpha, and on each occasion the name beta will be used for the previously-created member of the list and gamma will be used for a newly-created member. So, before entering the DO loop, we have to start things off by pointing beta to the initial item, alpha. (That's why alpha was given the TARGET attribute.)

The first statement within the DO loop is ALLOCATE(gamma). This has the effect of allocating memory space to hold data under the name of the pointer gamma. This is, as declared earlier, of the type Link.

Next is a pointer assignment statement, and this points the second component of beta to the newly-allocated memory space of the object gamma. In other words, the previous member of the list points to the new one that is being created.

Next, a value is given to gamma%x, the first component of gamma: in this example, it is a simple algebraic function of the preceding value beta%x.

The next statement, the NULLIFY statement, defines the association status of the second component of gamma, i.e. the pointer gamma%nextlink. When the statement ALLOCATE(gamma) was executed earlier, the pointer gamma%nextlink was created but its association status was undefined. In fact, the association status of any pointer is initially undefined. The NULLIFY statement ensures that gamma%nextlink is for the time being disassociated, in the sense that the result .FALSE. would be given for it by the intrinsic function ASSOCIATED. (Without the NULLIFY statement, a reference ASSOCIATED(gamma%nextlink) would give an error.) To summarise: at this point in the DO loop, memory space has been allocated for a new object called gamma, the second component of the previous object (beta) points to gamma, the first component of gamma has been given a value, and the second component of gamma has 'disassociated' status.

The final statement within the loop points beta to gamma; this means that beta no longer represents the previous object in the chain, but now represents the new object that has just been set up. The first time we go through the loop, this statement switches beta from pointing to the first object in the chain, alpha, and points it instead to the second object. The second time we go through the loop, this statement stops beta from pointing to the second link and points it to the third: this is interesting because the second link is then left with no name at all, although it consists of actual data occupying actual memory space. Subsequently, it will be possible to get access to this data only through the pointer alpha%nextlink.

When the program goes through the DO loop on the second and subsequent times, the statement ALLOCATE(gamma) causes additional new memory space to be associated with the pointer gamma, and the previous association of gamma is broken off. Incidentally, this situation is different from the case with allocatable arrays: to ALLOCATE a currently-allocated array is an error, but to ALLOCATE a currently-allocated pointer is not.

In our example, when the DO loop has been executed 100 times there will be 101 objects in memory, each containing a real value and a pointer to the next one. The first in the chain has the name alpha, and the last is still pointed to by beta and gamma, but the other 99 are not directly accessible. To look through the chain of data we would need code such as

```
beta => alpha
DO
        WRITE (*,*) beta%x
        IF (.NOT.ASSOCIATED(beta%nextlink)) EXIT
        beta => beta%nextlink
END DO
```

which uses the pointer beta to run from one link to the next. You know you're at the end of the list when a link is reached whose forward pointer has 'disassociated' status.

This example has been explained in detail because it teaches some very important facts about the effect of the ALLOCATE and NULLIFY statements on pointers, because of the interesting concept of nameless data, and because it shows how pointers within derived types could be used to invent pseudo-arrays if ordinary arrays did not already exist in Fortran!

The type called 'Link', above, included a pointer component so that one object could point to another. However, if a type were constructed with two pointer components, then each object could point to two others. For example, a family tree could in principle be constructed on the basis of the type

```
TYPE Person
        CHARACTER(30) :: name
        INTEGER :: nyearofbirth
        TYPE (Person), POINTER :: mother, father
END TYPE Person
```

While on the subject of derived-type structures, there is a question that arises about the meaning of assignment statements between structures that have pointer components. Taking the example of the type 'Person' immediately above, and having

```
TYPE (Person) :: candidate, brother
        .
        .
        .
candidate = brother
```

the assignment statement is equivalent to

```
candidate%name = brother%name
candidate%nyearofbirth = brother%nyearofbirth
candidate%father => brother%father
candidate%mother => brother%mother
```

the last two being pointer assignments and not ordinary assignments. In other words, an ordinary assignment statement between structures is equivalent to ordinary assignments between their non-pointer components and to pointer assignments between their pointer components. Of course, the programmer is at liberty to change this by providing a defined-assignment subroutine as in section 14.6!

203

In section 15.5 it was mentioned in passing that a pointer may be used as an argument of a procedure. When a procedure has an argument which is normally an ordinary variable or expression, the argument may be a pointer as long as it has a definite target at the time. This is true of intrinsic procedures as well as external procedures or module procedures. Using a pointer in this context is just like using it on the right hand side of an ordinary assignment statement, and the pointer is no more than an alias for its target.

A slightly more complicated situation arises if a dummy argument is declared with the POINTER attribute within a procedure. In that case, the corresponding actual argument must also be a pointer, and an explicit interface to the procedure must be provided so that the processor always 'knows' that a pointer argument is expected. When the procedure is referenced, what happens is that the dummy argument pointer is associated with the target of the actual argument. On return from the procedure, the actual argument is associated with the target of the dummy argument, but if the latter target is local to the procedure and is not saved then the actual argument will be left with undefined association status. Incidentally, a dummy argument which is a pointer is not allowed to be declared with the INTENT attribute. Here is an example of a procedure with pointer dummy arguments:

```
SUBROUTINE Switchpoint (a, b)
CHARACTER(*), POINTER :: a
CHARACTER(*), POINTER :: b
CHARACTER(LEN(a)), POINTER :: c
IF (LEN(a)/=LEN(b)) THEN
        NULLIFY (a, b)
        RETURN
END IF
c => a                  ! Point c to the target of a
a => b                  ! Point a to the target of b
b => c                  ! Point b to the target of c
END SUBROUTINE Switchpoint
```

It is also possible for a dummy argument to have the TARGET attribute, but here again it is necessary to provide an explicit interface to the procedure. The following procedure has both TARGET and POINTER arguments:

```
SUBROUTINE Randomfork (from, toleft, toright)
USE Typedefs
TYPE (Structure), POINTER :: from
TYPE (Structure), TARGET :: toleft, toright
REAL :: x
CALL RANDOM (x)
```

```
                    IF (x>0.5) THEN
                            from => toleft
                    ELSE
                            from => toright
                    END IF
                    END SUBROUTINE Randomfork
```

To round off this section, it remains to consider the case where a function result is a pointer. This is allowed in Fortran, but (as for pointer and target arguments) an explicit interface is then needed. The next example has as its argument a character string object which itself is a pointer, and the function result is a pointer to one individual character within that string:

```
                    FUNCTION Pickstar (string)
                    CHARACTER, POINTER :: Pickstar
                    CHARACTER(*), POINTER :: string
                    k = SCAN (string,"*")
                    IF (k=0) THEN
                            NULLIFY (Pickstar)
                    ELSE
                            Pickstar => string(k:k)
                    END IF
                    END FUNCTION Pickstar
```

By the way, if a pointer-valued function appears in a type declaration statement at the start of the calling procedure, it can be specified with the POINTER attribute but not the EXTERNAL attribute.

15.8   ARRAY POINTERS

Towards the end of section 15.5 it was shown that pointers can be used to economise on memory space if they are associated with long character strings. Likewise, pointers can be associated with derived-type structures (section 15.6). In both these cases the pointers themselves were scalar, although pointing to large or complex structures. But pointers do not necessarily have to be scalar: Fortran allows for pointers to be arrays, in which case they have properties similar in many ways to the 'allocatable arrays' explained in section 15.3.

Array pointers are declared with the POINTER attribute and with a special kind of array specification known as a 'deferred-shape' specification (section 13.4), as in the type declaration statements

```
COMPLEX, POINTER, DIMENSION(:) :: coefficients, roots
REAL, POINTER :: rates(:,:)
CHARACTER(2048), POINTER :: k2(:)
CHARACTER, POINTER :: tiestring(:,:,:)
TYPE (Person), POINTER :: family(:)
```

These statements fix the ranks of the arrays by the numbers of colons after each name, but the shapes are not fully determined at this stage. Deferred-shape arrays are always either pointers or 'allocatable' arrays.

Array pointers may point to array targets, or to sections of them, which would therefore need to be declared with the TARGET attribute as in

```
INTEGER, TARGET :: jobcodes(180)
```

Array pointers cannot be given the ALLOCATABLE attribute, because in a sense they are allocatable anyway. However, array targets may be allocatable:

```
INTEGER, TARGET, ALLOCATABLE :: jobcodes(:)
```

Array pointers, like scalar pointers, may be used in pointer assignment statements. The targets need not be complete arrays: array sections are allowed (but not with vector subscripts). If a target is an allocatable array, it needs to have been allocated before the pointer assignment statement is executed.

One effect of an array pointer assignment statement is to determine the shape of the pointer: the pointer's extent in each dimension, and the bounds of its subscripts, are taken from the target array. Once an array pointer is associated with a target, it may be used in an ordinary assignment statement, representing its target's value. The inquiry function ASSOCIATED may be used with an array pointer just as with a scalar pointer (see section 15.5).

It is possible to make use of array pointers without having named targets at all, with the statements ALLOCATE, NULLIFY and DEALLOCATE. Although these statements have been met previously in this chapter, it is worth reviewing here what they will do with array pointers as arguments.

ALLOCATE can be used to fix the shape of an array pointer and at the same time to create memory space to which it will point. The syntax is just like that for allocatable arrays, and in fact the same statement could allocate a mixture of pointers and allocatable arrays, e.g.

```
ALLOCATE (rates(0:3,0:3), family(nlinked), jobcodes(143), STAT=mtest)
```

NULLIFY disassociates target space previously associated with its arguments, but does not deallocate it, i.e. the memory space still exists and may hold data, but is no longer pointed to by this pointer. It is important to remember that the ALLOCATE statement, with a pointer argument, allocates new space but like NULLIFY does not deallocate the old. ALLOCATE can therefore be used repeatedly with the same pointer argument to create an unlimited amount of 'hidden' memory.

To disassociate a pointer and also to deallocate the memory space it is necessary to use the DEALLOCATE statement, but this is not applicable if the pointer was associated with a named target by means of a pointer assignment statement. In fact, to avoid confusion, it is best to distinguish sharply between two styles of pointer array usage, firstly

(a) with named targets, which could be allocatable arrays, using pointer assignment statements and if necessary NULLIFY, and secondly

(b) without named targets, without using pointer assignment statements, using only ALLOCATE, NULLIFY and DEALLOCATE.

Case (b) is very similar to the straightforward use of allocatable arrays described in section 15.3, but with the crucial difference that an array pointer may be allocated several times, creating a set of nameless objects in memory: but there is obviously no point in doing this unless the 'hidden' objects are accessible as the targets of other pointers.

EXERCISES 15C

15C1   Based on the type 'Link' in section 15.6, write a program that will read in an indefinitely long sequence of real numbers from the keyboard. The input of the number 9999999 is to be used to indicate that the sequence has ended. After input, the program should calculate and write the average of the numbers.

15C2   (i) Write a function whose argument is an assumed-size real array and which converts the array into a linked list of the type 'Link' in section 15.6. The function's result is therefore to be a scalar pointer of derived type.

15C3   The derived type

```
TYPE Character_Chain
    CHARACTER :: q
    TYPE (Character_Chain), POINTER :: qnext
END TYPE Character_Chain
```

could be used for variable-length chains of characters. This could offer some advantage over ordinary character strings because the latter cannot vary in length during program execution. Write a subroutine and interface to define the concatenation operator ('//') for these character chains (but not for arrays of them!), and a function like the intrinsic LEN function, and a subroutine which will write out a Character_Chain.

N15.1 POINTER and TARGET

As an alternative to including POINTER or TARGET as an attribute in type declaration statements, it is possible to use separate 'attribute specification statements' such as

TARGET :: x, y, z(12,12), jswitch
POINTER :: sheet(:,:)

These are declarative statements and must appear near the beginning of a program unit following the type declaration statements.

Chapter 16

INPUT AND OUTPUT; DATA FORMAT SPECIFICATIONS

In chapter 3 the READ(*,*) and WRITE(*,*) statements were introduced so that programs could be written which would read and write data from/to the processor's default input/output devices. It has often been assumed in this book that these default devices are a keyboard and a screen. It is now time to consider READ and WRITE statements in much more detail. The NAMELIST statement and the function TRANSFER are also explained in this chapter.

16.1   DATA TRANSFER STATEMENTS

The READ and WRITE statements are essential for any program that is to communicate with the outside world. READ and WRITE are the Fortran 'data transfer statements', by which information is transferred from or to any external medium (keyboard, screen, disk files, printers, magnetic tapes, etc.).

The information is usually expected to take the form of a sequence of characters (possibly including special control characters), and in this case the data is said to be in 'formatted' i/o records. So far we have always used formatted i/o, and most of this chapter will be devoted to formatted data. However, there is such a thing as 'unformatted' i/o which will be explained in section 16.9.

As we shall see, reading and writing data can be a complex and sophisticated task for the programmer. As a general rule it is advisable for those parts of a program that deal with i/o statements to be organised into dedicated subroutines, and they could be kept in a special module. It is usually bad programming practice to scatter data transfer statements across subroutines whose primary functions are otherwise. Grouping i/o statements together also simplifies matters if the program ever needs to be modified for use on a processor with a different set of i/o devices.

The general forms of the data transfer statement are

> READ (UNIT=..., FMT=..., ...) input-item-list

and

> WRITE (UNIT=..., FMT=..., ...) output-item-list

except that FMT may be replaced by NML in the special case of 'namelist' formatting which will be described in section 16.8.

READ or **WRITE** indicates, obviously, the direction of data transfer. **UNIT**= is normally followed by a unit number which is an integer (or a scalar integer-valued expression) indicating which i/o unit is to be used. The idea is that different numbers will point to different devices. The available devices will be system-dependent. More details about i/o units are given in chapter 17. Fortunately, to simplify matters the default i/o devices can be selected by inserting an asterisk in place of the unit number.

The **FMT** keyword gives a 'format specifier' which will normally be a character expression or character variable as described in 16.5 below. However, there is a simple kind of default formatting, 'list-directed' formatting, which is invoked by putting an asterisk as the format specifier. List-directed formatting, which in fact we have used so far in this book, is described in more detail in sections 16.3 and 16.4.

Between the brackets following READ or WRITE there may in fact be a fairly lengthy list of control specifications in addition to UNIT= and FMT=. The additional control specifications are optional, and will arise mostly in connection with reading and writing magnetic disk files and tapes (chapter 17). The control specifications in the brackets can appear in any order, being identified by the keywords UNIT, FMT, and others. However, the keyword UNIT is unnecessary if this specification comes first, and the FMT keyword is unnecessary if this specification follows second; hence READ(*,*) is equivalent to READ(UNIT=*,FMT=*).

16.2   THE I/O ITEM LIST

The data transfer statement, after the bracketed set of control specifications, has a list of input items or output items. Items for input, in a READ statement, must be represented by the names of variables, and if the statement is successful those variables will thereby be assigned values. In principle the items may be of any type or dimension, with just one or two technical exceptions mentioned below. Examples of input lists are:

```
namestring
x, y, z
bstring(1:5), bstring(7:7)
address % postcode
address
kounts, (milliamps(j), j = 1, kounts)
```

Here, 'namestring' could be one string of characters or could be an array of strings, as long as it has been previously declared as such. When an i/o list contains an array or an array section, it is as though the elements were specified one after another in array element order (see section 15.1). However, it is not possible to input data into an assumed-size array.

In the second example above, x, y and z could be three real numbers, but if they have been declared as (say) complex numbers then the equivalent of six real numbers will be input. The third example illustrates that input characters may be assigned to sections of strings. Also, a single derived-type structure-component can be read (address%postcode), as can a complete data structure (address), but input and output statements are not allowed with derived-type structures containing pointer components. The final example shows how the 'implicit-DO' notation can be used to control an i/o list: here we have one integer (kounts) followed by that number of further integers, namely milliamps(1), milliamps(2), ..., up to milliamps(kounts). The integer variable j is an arbitrarily-named dummy index. This example is equivalent to

kounts, milliamps(1:kounts)

Any of the above could equally well appear as output item lists in a WRITE statement as long as the variables have previously-assigned values. An output item list may also contain constants and expressions, such as:

"There is no further data available to you"
"Date: ",nday," ",months(nmonth)," ", nyear+2000-100*INT(nyear/50)
"Sines: ", (SIN(theta(i)), i = 1, 99, 2)
((rmass(i), Prob(rmass(i), errbar(i), rm(i), nalgo), i = 1, 22), nalgo = 1, 3)

The second of these consists of a character string constant, an integer variable, another character constant (the blank), an element of a character string array, another blank, and an integer expression which depends on the integer variable nyear and invokes the function INT. The third example outputs the values of the sines of alternate members of the array 'theta'. Implied 'DO' loops in i/o may be nested, as illustrated in the final example, and in a WRITE statement there is no reason why an external function (e.g. 'Prob' above) should not appear.

By using arrays or derived types, very large amounts of data can be handled by short and elegant statements. For example, the statement

WRITE (UNIT=laserprinter, FMT=memo) document

could do a great deal of work, all the complications being expressed elsewhere in the definitions of 'memo' and 'document'.

16.3   LIST-DIRECTED INPUT

The FMT control specification will be explained in more detail in section 16.5 below, but it is often sufficient to use what is called 'list-directed' formatting, invoked by inserting an asterisk (FMT=*). With list-directed formatting, the input or output format is determined by the nature of the i/o item list alone.

Bear in mind that list-directed formatting (like all forms of i/o formatting in Fortran) amounts to a conversion between internal Fortran data and a sequence of characters used by an external device. On input, a sequence of characters is converted into Fortran data objects (real, logical, character or whatever) and on output the conversion goes the other way.

List-directed input is really much more straightforward than the length of this section will suggest!

If a single integer number is to be input, then the input format will be simply the number expressed in ordinary decimal form, e.g.

     365

and this is also a valid input format for a real number which happens to have no fractional part. Remember that here we are not talking about Fortran statements but about the form of data input (e.g. through a keyboard) to the processor as it runs the program. For a real number having a fractional part, a decimal point may be used:

     365.242

For convenience with numbers of very large or very small magnitude, a multiplying power of ten may be indicated by putting the exponent after the letter E immediately following the number: examples are

          2.997925E8
          2.997925E+8
          6.626176E-34
          365242E-3

of which the first two are equivalent to one another and the last is exactly equivalent to the example in the previous paragraph. If a complex number is to be input, then its real and imaginary parts are enclosed together in brackets; valid forms of complex numbers are:

          (0,1)
          (-0.5, 1.73205)
          (41975.9 , 3.7E6)

212

If a series of numbers are input, their types must match the names listed in the READ statement and the numbers can be separated by commas. For example, the Fortran code

```
INTEGER :: k   ;   REAL :: days, root3
COMPLEX :: omega, zero
        .
        .
READ (UNIT=*, FMT=*) k, days, root3, omega, zero
```

will be satisfied by the input data

```
365, 365242E-3, 1.73205, (-0.5, 1.73205), (0,0)
```

Blanks alongside a comma are not significant and may be omitted, as in the data

```
365,365242E-3,1.73205,(-0.5,1.73205),(0,0)
```

but one or more blanks may be used (outside a complex number) as separators by themselves instead of commas:

```
365   365242E-3 1.73205 (-0.5,1.73205) (0,0)
```

An 'end of record' (i.e. the 'enter' or 'return' key on a keyboard) normally has the effect of a blank and so this may be used as a separator or a terminator: so all the above examples should be understood as having the 'return' key pressed after the final character of the line. It is possible for every item to appear on a separate line:

```
365
365242E-3
1.73205
(-0.5, 1.73205)
(0,0)
```

Arrays of numbers, or derived data types formed out of numbers, may be input in the same way. If we have

```
INTEGER :: nwars(6)
        .
        .
READ (UNIT=*, FMT=*) nwars
```

then the data may be put in as

1914, 1918, 1939, 1945, 1998, 2007

If the input data is of type logical, it is sufficient if it consists of letters T (for TRUE) and/or F (for FALSE) separated like numbers by blanks or commas, e.g. for seven logical items we may have

T,F,F,F,T,T,F

or

T F F F T T F

but the T or F may be immediately preceded by a decimal point, and other arbitrary characters may follow it before the next separator, so

TRUE FALSE FALSE FALSE TRUE TRUE FALSE

and

.T .F .F .F .T .T .F

and also

.TRUE. .FALSE. .FALSE. .FALSE. .TRUE. .TRUE. .FALSE.

are all equivalent valid input formats.

Things can be a little more complicated if character constants are to be input. A pair of statements like

CHARACTER(20) :: title, forename, surname
.
.
.
READ (UNIT=*, FMT=*) title, forename, surname

will be satisfied by the input

Vice-President Dan Quayle

because the blanks (which could equally well be commas) will act as separators between the three character strings. However, ambiguities could arise if the strings themselves are supposed to contain blanks or commas (or slashes). To get over this, it is possible to use apostrophes or quotes when a character string is input, just as we do when specifying a character constant in Fortran itself. In other words,

"Vice-President" "Dan" "Quayle"

will have exactly the same effect as the previous example, and

"Air Vice-Marshall" "Howard" "Tudor Jones"

will correctly include the spaces in the first and third items. The usual rules for character string constants apply: a quote may appear as part of a string delimited by apostrophes, an apostrophe may occur as part of a string delimited by quotes, a doubled quote can be used to represent a single quote within a quote-delimited string, and a doubled apostrophe can be used to represent a single apostrophe within an apostrophe-delimited string. A quote- or apostrophe-delimited string may run from one record (i.e. one line) to the next, as long as the end-of-record does not appear between doubled quotes or doubled apostrophes within the string.

If this seems complicated, remember that when character input is contained within one line, does not involve any blanks, slashes, or commas, and does not start with a quote or apostrophe, then there is no need for it to be enclosed in quotes or apostrophes at all.

It remains to be said that, with list-directed character string input, an input string longer than that declared for the list item will be truncated from the right; while if it is shorter, the list item will be padded out with blanks to the right. This is just the same as happens in character assignment statements when strings of different length are equated.

Whatever the type of the input data, null values can be input by having no characters between successive commas, e.g. for six integers of which only the first four are actually input

1914, 1918, 1939, 1945, , ,

or, if the line is ended by pressing enter/return, we can have

1914, 1918, 1939, 1945, ,

Remember that a blank is purely cosmetic when it is next to a comma. In the above example, the first four integers are specified but the last two are not altered within the program: a null value does not change anything, and an undefined value will remain undefined. A null value is not equivalent to a zero or (for character data) a blank. If items in an input list have been preset to certain values by assignment statements before the READ statement, null inputs will leave the preset values unchanged.

It is sometimes convenient to input a series of identical values. This can be done by a 'multiplier', or 'repeat specification', as in

3*0 3*1 3 5 5*T 3*F 7*Yes

215

which is equivalent to the collection of integer, logical and character string inputs

0 0 0 1 1 1 3 5 T T T T T F F F Yes Yes Yes Yes Yes Yes Yes

In general, if the form r* (where r is an unsigned positive integer) immediately precedes any input value, the value is regarded as having been input r times. (For this reason, a character string being input naked, i.e. not enclosed in quotes or parentheses, may not begin with numeric digits followed by an asterisk.) If the r* is immediately followed by a blank, then a series of r null values is understood, e.g.

1914 1918 1939 1945 2*

or

1914,1918,1939,1945,2*

are equivalent to the example given earlier. At the end of a list, another way of inputting null values is with a slash as in

1914 1918 1939 1945/

The slash always terminates the execution of a list-directed input statement, with null values for any remaining items, unless of course the slash is part of a character string delimited by quotes or apostrophes.

16.4   LIST-DIRECTED OUTPUT

A statement such as

WRITE (UNIT=*, FMT=*) o/p item list

will output the values of the listed items according to a simple convention similar to what we have seen for list-directed input. Integer numbers appear in the obvious format, and logical items appear as T or as F. Real numbers appear in decimal form, if necessary with an exponent (i.e. an E suffix and power of ten) if they are very large or very small: the number of decimal places given, and the exact criterion for using the exponent notation, are processor-dependent. Complex numbers will be in parentheses, with a comma between the real and imaginary parts. Integer, real and complex data items will be separated by commas and/or blanks, but character strings will normally appear without separators or surrounding quotes or apostrophes.

So far we have only considered data transfer statements in which the format of the data is determined by default conventions according to the nature of the data, i.e. 'list-directed' formatting with FMT=*. However, for complete flexibility the programmer can control the format through the FMT specifier. The FMT specifier should take the form of a character expression. Below, most of our examples will refer to WRITE statements, but the same rules generally apply to READ.

Suppose there is just one object in the i/o item list, and we are writing its value onto the standard output device:

WRITE (UNIT=*, FMT=format1) datum

Before the execution of this statement, format1 (which is, of course, an arbitrary name) must have been assigned a character value, e.g. by

format1 = "(I10)"

Here, quotes are present because the variable format1 is being set to the character constant

(I10)

and this character constant is known as the 'format specification'. The parentheses are a feature of the syntax needed for any format specification. Inside the parentheses we have in this example the single 'edit descriptor'

I10

and this means that the output item is an integer and can occupy up to ten spaces, i.e. the specification allows for an integer of up to ten digits to be printed or displayed, or nine digits with a minus sign. In other words, datum should be an integer not greater than 9999999999 and not less than -999999999. If datum were going to be a real number, we would need something like

format1 = "(F10.4)"

The edit descriptor F10.4 means that datum is real (the F stands for 'floating point'), that a total of ten spaces are allowed, and that the value will be shown rounded to four decimal places. For example, if datum is equal to 22.0/7 then the above will display four blanks followed by

3.1429

In general a format specification takes the form of a bracketed list of edit descriptors, where the total number of edit descriptors should normally match the number of data items in the i/o item list. For example, for a series of three real numbers and one integer we could have the format specification

(F10.4, F10.4, F10.4, I10)

(the blanks between the edit descriptors are not significant). To abbreviate things, there is a simple notation for repeating identical edit descriptors: the number of them is put immediately before the letter F or I, so the above example is equivalent to

(3F10.4, I10)

Repetitions may be nested using brackets, i.e. we could have something like

(3(2I10,F10.4))

which is an abbreviation for

(I10, I10, F10.4, I10, I10, F10.4, I10, I10, F10.4)

and this would present the nine numbers side by side over ninety spaces.

If a format specification is a character array rather than a single string, it is interpreted as if its elements were taken in order and concatenated.

Here is a more complete example:

```
REAL ::  volume(3), weight(3)
INTEGER :: number(3)
       .
       .
       .
format99 = "(3I6,6F8.3)"
       .
       .
       .
WRITE (*, FMT=format99) number, weight, volume
```

So far only the simplest edit descriptors have been mentioned for integer and real-number data (I and F editing). There are in addition many other types of edit descriptor in Fortran. In practice, format specifications often consist of long lists of edit descriptors of different sorts. They fall into three classes, namely (a) data edit descriptors, (b) character string edit descriptors, and (c) control edit descriptors. These will be explained in turn in the sections following.

In addition we could say that there is a fourth class (d) consisting only of the null edit descriptor where there is nothing between the brackets, as in

WRITE(*, FMT="()")

which has the effect of writing an empty record (or, on input, skipping over a record). So the statement

    READ (*, FMT="()")

should just pause the execution of the program until the 'return' key is pressed.

EXERCISES 16A

16A1 Which of the following are valid format specifications? And which are valid edit descriptors?

(i) "(F10.4)"	(ii) (F10.4)	(iii) F10.4
(iv) 8(F10.4)	(v) 8F10.4	(vi) (8F10.4)
(vii) ((F10.4))	(viii) (F10.6,I8)	(ix) ( )
(x) "3()"		

16A2 Write a format specification to output a four-digit integer, followed by three real numbers, all neatly spaced out over an 80-column line. Assume that the real numbers do not exceed a value of 1000.0 and must be specified to two decimal places.

16.6 DATA EDIT DESCRIPTORS AND CHARACTER EDIT DESCRIPTORS

Data edit descriptors guide the input or output of the data items listed at the end of the READ or WRITE statement. Each edit descriptor starts with a letter depending on the nature of the data and how it is to be edited. The possible initial letters are listed below.

I	Integer data (decimal form)
B	Integer data (binary form)
O	Integer data (octal form)
Z	Integer data (hexadecimal form)
F	Real or complex data (simple decimal form)
E	Real or complex data (exponential notation)
L	Logical data
A	Character data
G	Generalised editing (for data of any type)

For I editing, as we have seen, the letter I is followed immediately by an integer specifying the total number of character positions used to display the data item. For example, on input, I6 will read a decimal integer from a field of six characters, i.e. with up to six digits or five digits and a sign. On output, I6 will display an integer in a field six characters wide, if necessary with leading blanks. B, O and Z editing is very similar to I editing except that the integer is displayed or stored in binary, octal or hexadecimal form. For example, B10 will edit an integer in binary form up to a maximum value of 1111111111, i.e. (in decimal) up to 1023.

Note that binary, octal and hexadecimal editing has nothing to do with how the integers are stored within the processor's memory. The descriptors I, B, O and Z would all apply to data of the same Fortran integer type. The editing simply determines the external display or storage format.

For output with I, B, O and Z editing it is possible to display leading zeros so that each data item has a certain specified minimum number (m) of digits. This is done by adding the integer m after a decimal point, e.g. the descriptor 4I10.8 might display

$$00079451 \quad 00175600 \quad 10905502 \quad 00000000$$

given the data 79451, 175600, 10905502, and 0. So, the general forms of integer edit descriptors are Iw, Iw.m, Bw, Bw.m, Ow, Ow.m, Zw, and Zw.m, where w is the total field width and m is used to arrange leading zeros. Obviously m, if present, cannot exceed w.

The integers w and m, and similar elements of the other edit descriptors mentioned below, must appear in Fortran as actual integers and not as variables or expressions.

An F edit descriptor is used for real-number data (or two of them could be used for a complex number). The general form is Fw.d, where w is an integer giving the total field width. On output, there will be a decimal point in the appropriate position followed by d places of decimals. On input, if there is a decimal point, d could mean that the final d digits are interpreted as the fractional part of the number, but if a decimal point appears explicitly in the input stream then the value of d is irrelevant. Also on input (but not output) the actual data item may include an exponent as described under E editing below.

E editing has exactly the same effect as F editing for input. E7.0 and F7.0 will both take a real number from a field seven characters wide. On output, however, E editing writes the data in exponential notation, i.e. with a power of ten so that very large or very small numbers can be represented compactly. This is best illustrated by examples: the edit descriptor E10.4 could display numbers in the form

-.5000+009	(meaning -500 million)
-.3408-015	(-0.34×10^{-15})
.1000+129	(10^{128})
.1000+000	(0.1)
.0000+000	(0)

So, the number appears as an optional sign followed by a decimal fraction less than 1 but not less than 0.1, followed after a + or - sign by a power of ten (exponent) which determines the magnitude of the number. In these examples up to three digits are allowed for the exponent, but if necessary more can be allowed by an extension to the edit descriptor: the general form is Ew.dEe, and e gives the maximum number of digits in the exponent (default 3). The above examples are therefore equivalent to E10.4E3.

There is a further elaboration of E editing, relevant for output, known as EN ('engineering') editing. The general form ENw.d will display a real number across a field of w characters in exponent notation but with the exponent being always a multiple of three. To do this the number appears first in the range from 1 to 999 with a fractional part specified to d places of decimals. With EN12.4 the number of seconds in a year would appear as 31.5360+006, and half a millionth would appear as 500.0000-009. The extended form ENw.dEe extends the possible magnitude of the exponent as mentioned in the previous paragraph.

Finally, there is a another variation known as ES editing (general forms ESw.d and ESw.dEe) which is like E editing but displays one significant figure before the decimal point. With ES12.4, therefore, the last example would appear as 5.0000-007.

L editing is for transmitting data of logical type. The letter L is followed by an integer giving the number of character positions taken up by the data item. The item is represented, on output, by a right-justified letter T or F representing the values .TRUE. or .FALSE. respectively. The edit descriptor 8L4 could produce the ouput

            T   T   F   T   F   F   F   F

On input, the T (or F) may be preceded by a decimal point and may be followed by other characters, as in the case of list-directed input. Thus, forms like .T, .T., TRUE and .TRUE. would all be acceptable inputs as long as the field width is adequate.

For data of character type the A edit descriptor is used. (This is not quite the same thing as a 'character edit descriptor' which will be explained at the end of this section.) The letter A can be followed by an (integer) field width, and that number of characters are directly transferred in or out.

Character editing is particularly simple because we are, in effect, doing the trivial job of converting a character string into a character string, whereas all the other data edit descriptors have to carry out a conversion between a character string and some other data type. The letter A need not be followed by a field width: if it is not, the length of the string is taken to be the length of the corresponding data item as listed in the READ or WRITE statement. If a field width is specified and is not equal to the length of the corresponding list item, then characters may be lost or padding blanks may be inserted, so it is generally best just to use the descriptor A by itself to transfer a character string of any length.

As an alternative to all the data edit descriptors mentioned so far in this section, G ('generalised') editing can be used for data of any type. A descriptor of the form Gw.d or Gw.dEe will output a real number in exactly the same way as Ew.d or Ew.dEe. If the data is of integer, logical or character type, the d and e parameters are ignored, and Gw.d (or Gw.dEe) is equivalent to an Iw, Lw or Aw descriptor.

A 'character string edit descriptor' is a kind of descriptor which, technically, is not a data edit descriptor because it does not correspond to an item in an i/o item list and therefore does not transfer a data object. A character string edit descriptor is simply a character constant, specified explicitly between quotes or apostrophes, and is used only with a WRITE statement to output a fixed set of characters. For example,

"The result is "

is a character string edit descriptor, and could be included within a format specification such as

presentation = "('The result is ', F10.4, ' ', A)"

to guide the output statement

WRITE(*, FMT=presentation) result, units

In fact this format specification actually has two character string edit descriptors, the second containing only a blank character to write a space between the number 'result' and the word 'units'.

It is always possible to use character data instead of a character string edit descriptor. Instead of

f = "('Execution terminating.')"
WRITE(*, FMT=f)

we could have

f = "(A)"
signoff = "Execution terminating."
WRITE(*, FMT=f) signoff

Bear in mind that character variables must be declared and must have defined lengths, so in the above examples f and signoff must have previously appeared in CHARACTER type declaration statements. This could of course be avoided by having simply

WRITE(*, FMT="('Execution terminating')")

and remember that the need to count characters can be avoided by statements like

222

```
CHARACTER(*) :: f = "('Execution terminating.')"
                  .
                  .
                  .
WRITE(*, FMT=f)
```

16.7 CONTROL EDIT DESCRIPTORS

Control edit descriptors, as their name suggests, are useful to control i/o devices but they do not themselves refer to individual i/o data items. Fortran's control edit descriptors are listed below.

Tn	Tabulate to character position n in the i/o record
TLn	Tabulate n characters to the left
TRn	Tabulate n characters to the right
nX	Skip forward n characters
/	Skip to start of next record
:	Stops i/o immediately if the i/o list is finished
S	Plus signs optional (numeric o/p only)
SP	Plus signs written (numeric o/p only)
SS	Plus signs omitted (numeric o/p only)
BN	Ignore blanks (numeric i/p only)
BZ	Treat blanks as zeros (numeric i/p only)
kP	Scale numbers by 10^k

With the first four of these, n is a positive integer which must be specified explicitly. For example, T1 will move to the first character of the current record. With printed output,

WRITE (UNIT=iprint, FMT="(3(T1, A))") word, word, word

will write the word 'word' in bold (3 times superimposed) at the beginning of the line. Note that TL (leftward tabulation) cannot move further left than the beginning of the record. TRn and nX are equivalent to one another. On output, TR1 and 1X are both equivalent to the character string edit descriptor containing one blank (" ").

The slash (/) skips to the start of the next record, and may be preceded by an integer greater than one if it is to be repeated. So,

WRITE (UNIT=iprint, FMT="(6/)")

leaves six blank lines. Slash editing (or format reversion, mentioned below) is used whenever one i/o statement is to transfer more than one record. For example,

WRITE (UNIT=mtape, FMT="(50(A,/))") strings

writes 50 records (followed by a final empty record) if there are 50 elements in the array 'strings'.

The colon (:) is useful if it is not known in advance how long the i/o item list will be. So if keynumbers is an array of any size, but not greater than 100,

WRITE (*, FMT="(:,"keynumbers ",/,T10,100(I6,:,/,T10))") keynumbers

will output all the elements of keynumbers but will not execute the / and T10 after the final element. The first colon means that nothing at all is written if keynumbers is a size-zero array. The same effect could be achieved with

WRITE (*, FMT="(:,"keynumbers ",100(/,T10,I6))") keynumbers

Usually, if a format specification allows for more data items than are actually present in the i/o list, the statement terminates only when an unfulfillable data edit descriptor is encountered, and this may mean that some unnecessary control or character string edit descriptors are executed.

Incidentally, if a format specification allows for fewer data items than are present in the i/o list, then a process known as 'reversion' occurs and the processor runs through the format specification (or the last bracketed section of it) again as often as necessary. So in fact,

WRITE (*, FMT="(:,"keynumbers ",/,(T10,I6))") keynumbers

would work just like the example above, irrespective of the size of the array keynumbers. When a format specification involves nested brackets, format reversion only goes back over the edit descriptors within the current level brackets, so in the above example it is (T10,I6) that is repeated, not the whole format specification. Reversion always involves moving forward to the next i/o record, so we have (T10,I6) and not (/,T10,I6) in the above example. Simpler examples of format reversion are

WRITE (UNIT=mtape, FMT="(A)") strings
READ (UNIT= mtape, FMT="(A)") strings

both of which will transfer as many records (each interpreted as a single character string) as there are elements in the character array 'strings'.

When numbers are output, positive numbers may or may not be preceded by plus signs. The S, SP and SS descriptors control this. SP means that subsequent positive numbers written by the WRITE statement will have plus signs, SS means that the plusses will be omitted, and S lets the processor decide. BN and BZ refer to the interpretation of non-leading blanks in numeric input. BN means that they will be ignored, i.e. it doesn't matter if the digits of a number are interspersed with blanks or followed by blanks. BZ means that blanks in or after a number are treated like zeros.

The kP descriptor is a rather irritating feature of Fortran which is more trouble than it's worth. It is for use in conjunction with F editing. The number k must be an integer, interpreted as a power of ten, and with subsequent F editing (without exponent) real and complex data items are scaled up (for o/p) or down (for i/p) by that factor. When the exponent notation is being used, the kP descriptor can change the presentation but not the values of the data items.

EXERCISES 16B

16B1   Write a WRITE statement, incorporating the format specification, to output an integer variable called 'n' in decimal, binary and octal form on one line, the three forms suitably separated with blanks. Assume that n does not exceed (in decimal) 99.

16B2   What is the output from

    (i)   WRITE (*, "(2L2,2X)") (/.TRUE.,.FALSE.,k=1,3/)

    (ii)   WRITE (*, "(A4,:,TR1)") "Cause", "of", "death"

    (iii)   WRITE (*, "(2F7.4)") SQRT(2.0), SQRT(3.0)

    (iv)   WRITE (*, "(B6,1X,I6.6)") 40, 40*40

    (v)   WRITE (*, "(2E12.4)") SQRT(2.0), 40.0*40.0

    (vi)   WRITE (*, "('FA',L1,'E')") 2+2<5

16B3   Write a WRITE statement to produce the output

    T E R M I N A T I O N

(i.e. underlined and with spaces between the letters) given a character string called 'caption' such that

    caption = "TERMINATION"

16.8 NAMELISTS

A data transfer statement such as

READ (UNIT=..., NML=..., ...)

provides a concise method of reading (or writing, in the case of a WRITE statement) a set of data the structure of which is defined elsewhere in a special kind of statement, a NAMELIST statement. Because the NAMELIST statement gathers data together under a collective group name, there is no need to specify an i/o list in this data transfer statement. Neither is it necessary to have a format specifier. When namelists are used for input or output, the data is given in the input or output records in a standard annotated form described below. Namelist output is especially convenient as a way of dumping out data when a program is being debugged.

The NAMELIST statement is a specification statement with the syntax

NAMELIST / group-name / group-object-list

where 'group-name' is a name constructed according to the usual Fortran rules. The 'group-object-list' is simply a list of the names of variables. These variables can be of a mixture of types, including arrays and derived types, but they must have been declared (or be implicitly defined) previous to the NAMELIST statement. Examples are

        NAMELIST /Years/ nwars, nfloods, nfamines
        NAMELIST /Person/ title, forename, surname
        NAMELIST /Coordinates/ x, y, z

A single NAMELIST statement can include more than one group, as in

        NAMELIST /Months/ birthmonths, deathmonths &
                /Years / nbirthyears, ndeathyears

and one group can be continued later on a second or successive NAMELIST statement, e.g.

        NAMELIST /Person/ bmonth, dmonth, nbyears, ndyears

would append four more items to the group /Person/ defined in the earlier example. There is no reason why the same item of data should not crop up in two or more different namelist groups.

The sets of data in the above examples could be input or output by statements like

        READ (UNIT=*, NML=Years)

WRITE (UNIT=*, NML=Person)

or

READ (UNIT=*, NML=Coordinates)

but note that group names cannot be manipulated or switched about by assignment statements: group names can only occur in NAMELIST, READ or WRITE statements, and they cannot be passed as arguments of procedures. In some respects a namelist group is similar to a derived-type data structure, but derived types can be manipulated and assigned with much more flexibility.

Returning to the example above, the statement

READ (UNIT=*, NML=Coordinates)

will invoke the input of three real numbers, thereby assigning values to the variables x, y and z. The input must take a form like

&Coordinates x=3.8, y=-6.6, z=0 /

i.e. on a keyboard the user must type an ampersand followed by the group name, then a blank (or a number of blanks), then a series of values. Each value must be specified by the name of a group member followed by an equals sign followed by the value itself. The group members need not all be specified, nor need they be in the original order; so we could input

&Coordinates y = 0.332, x = 4.9 /

in which case the value of z would not be changed. The value specifications are separated from one another by commas and/or one or more blanks, and the set must be terminated with a slash. The values themselves must be specified according to the same rules as for list-directed input, described earlier in this chapter, except that character input must always be enclosed in quotes or apostrophes, as in

&Security Keyword="Carthaginian" /

Array elements may be specified. We could have, for example,

```
LOGICAL :: leaps(2000)
NAMELIST /Calendrical/ leaps
leaps = false
READ (UNIT=*, NML=Calendrical)
```

with the actual input

&Calendrical leaps(4:2000:4) = 500*T /

so the program presets as false all members of a logical array called 'leaps', and at execution time the user sets every fourth member to be true. The great advantage of namelist input is that the program user can decide at execution time to change any selection of variables as long as their names have been included in the namelist group.

It is much more straightforward to use namelists for output rather than input, since with output the program user does not need to remember any names or syntax. A statement like

WRITE (UNIT=*, NML=Coordinates)

could output the following data:

&COORDINATES X=4.9, Y=0.332, Z=0.0 /

16.9   UNFORMATTED I/O

Formatted i/o, in Fortran, involves some sort of transformation between data as it is stored internally in the processor and data as it is stored or displayed externally. Whatever the internal form, the external form can always be regarded as a sequence of characters divided into records. The 'records' may simply be lines, as on a printed page, and the characters will almost always be separate bytes coded according to a convention such as ASCII.

Unformatted i/o, by contrast, involves no conversion of the structure of the data: it is transferred to or from the external medium in the same form that it has within the processor. The internal form is a technical matter, and Fortran does not care about the details of it. In general, unformatted records can only be read by the same processor (or the same type of processor) that wrote them: portability between processors cannot be assumed.

The advantage of unformatted i/o is that it is likely to be faster and more efficient than formatted i/o, and it is easier for the programmer because no format specification or namelist specification is needed.

In practice, unformatted i/o does not arise in Fortran with data coming from a keyboard or going to a display device such as a screen or printer. It can arise if, say, data is being dumped onto a tape for periodic backup purposes, or if data needs to be transferred between disk files.

Unformatted i/o is achieved simply by omitting the FMT specifier in an i/o statement.

To be on the safe side, especially where derived-type data structures are concerned, unformatted data should be written and read with similar data item lists. If Decay_Modes is a data structure (not involving pointers), and if disk99 is the number of a disk unit, then we could have

WRITE (UNIT=disk99,REC=1) Decay_Modes

.

.

.

READ (UNIT=disk99,REC=1) Decay_Modes

These statements could be used to store the data temporarily outside the processor's memory, or perhaps to put it into chip memory if disk99 refers to a 'RAM disk'. (The meaning of REC will be mentioned in section 17.4.)

16.10   THE TRANSFER FUNCTION

When data is input to a Fortran program (say, by reading a magnetic tape) it cannot normally be interpreted properly unless each data item is of a type known within the program. The data types that are read must correspond to the variables named in the input list. This can lead to difficulties when, as sometimes happens, the contents of a file are not known in advance. Suppose 'intin' is a size-100 array and we have

READ(UNIT=7, FMT="(100I10)") intin

then what happens if in fact the file contains 100 real numbers? Or an unpredictable mixture of integer and real numbers? Fortunately Fortran provides an intrinsic function, TRANSFER(SOURCE,MOLD,SIZE), which can be used to change the type interpretation of a piece of data within the processor, i.e. when it has already been read in. For example, the above statement could be followed by

realin = TRANSFER(SOURCE = intin, MOLD = 0.0, SIZE = 100)

and this would put values into the real-valued array realin by reinterpreting the source data. It is very important to understand that TRANSFER does not convert data between types: the functions REAL, INTEGER, etc. do that. TRANSFER leaves unchanged the bit-patterns within the processor's memory, but simply interprets them in a different way. TRANSFER alters not the value of a data object, but its 'descriptor', in the terminology of section 15.5.

TRANSFER(SOURCE,MOLD,SIZE) gives a result whose internal representation is exactly the same as SOURCE but whose type is that of MOLD. SOURCE may be an array. SIZE is an optional argument discussed below. TRANSFER works for any data type, including a derived type.

Normally if MOLD is scalar the result is a scalar, whereas if MOLD is an array the result will be a rank=1 array of sufficient size to hold the contents of SOURCE. The result of TRANSFER is never an array of rank greater than 1.

For example,

$$\text{TRANSFER(SOURCE=(1.0,2.0), MOLD=(/0.0/))}$$

produces a size=2 rank=1 real array whose elements are the real and imaginary parts of the complex number (1.0,2.0).

The SIZE argument, if it is present, must be a scalar integer. Its effect is to ensure that the result is an array and to fix its size. If SIZE is specified and does not match the size of SOURCE, then in forming the function result it is possible that the trailing part of SOURCE may be lost or that the trailing part of the result may be left undefined. So,

$$\text{TRANSFER(SOURCE=(/1.0,2.0,3.0,4.0/), MOLD=(0.0,0.0), SIZE=2)}$$

produces a size=2 complex array whose members are (1.0,2.0) and (3.0,4.0). The expression

$$\text{TRANSFER((/-7.0,5.1,6.4/),(0.0,0.0),1)}$$

has the value (/(-7.0,5.1)/), while

$$\text{TRANSFER((/-7.0,5.1,6.4/),(0.0,0.0))}$$

is a scalar with the value (-7.0,5.1).

If the argument ch is of character type, TRANSFER(SOURCE=ch, MOLD=1) will give an integer-type result of processor-dependent value preserving the bit-pattern of ch; this could be used in conjunction with the bit manipulation functions described in chapter 18.

Incidentally, TRANSFER(SOURCE=array, MOLD=array) provides a neat way of replacing an array of any shape by the corresponding rank-one array containing the same elements. This could otherwise be done using the RESHAPE function (chapter 15).

The TRANSFER function means that a formatted READ statement can be made very flexible and the data unravelled later, e.g.

```
READ (UNIT=in, FMT="(A)") chararray
       .
       .
       .
header = TRANSFER(SOURCE=chararray(1:5), MOLD="", SIZE=5)
length = TRANSFER(SOURCE=chararray(6:10), MOLD=1)
IF (length>0.AND.length<(recmax-7)) THEN
        rdata  = TRANSFER(SOURCE=chararray(11:), &
                        MOLD=/0.0/, SIZE=length)
       .
       .
       .
```

where header, length and rdata are of character, integer and real types respectively. A long program which reads records of different sorts from different tapes could in this way be written with a single generalised READ statement.

16.11   SUMMARY

This has been a long chapter, and it contains a lot of material that the average Fortran programmer will need to use only very occasionally. We have really been dealing with just two types of statement, i.e.

$$READ\ (UNIT=..., FMT=..., ...)\ ....$$

and

$$WRITE\ (UNIT=..., FMT=..., ...)\ ....$$

There are four possibilities for the FMT/NML specifier, namely

(a)   FMT = character expression (explicit format)

(b)   FMT=* (list-directed i/o)

(c)   NML = namelist group name (namelist formatting, with no i/o list)

(d)   FMT and NML absent (unformatted i/o)

When FMT is a character expression giving an edit descriptor list, the format of the data can be specified in very fine detail. This power can be extremely valuable but at other times it can be very tedious. The edit descriptor list may involve syntax for repeating and nesting edit descriptors, but basically it comes down to a list of descriptors which are either

(a)   Data edit descriptors: I, B, O, Z, F, E, EN, ES, L, A, G

(b)   Character string edit descriptors: "...."

(c)   Control edit descriptors: T, TL, TR, nX, /, :, SP, SS, BN, BZ, kP

In principle you could almost get away with using only the G edit descriptor (generalised editing) for data, but the A descriptor is useful for characters when the string length cannot be fixed in the format specification. Most of the different edit descriptors are relevant principally for displaying data on a screen or a printer. It should be remembered that, with formatted i/o, the data edit descriptors are to transform information between Fortran's various data types and the character strings of external records.

Nowadays the widespread use of general-purpose Fortran-callable graphics packages and other interfaces means that programmers can sometimes avoid READ and WRITE statements altogether.

N16.1   THE PRINT STATEMENT

A statement PRINT f, ... (where f is any format specifier) can be used as an alternative to WRITE (UNIT=*, FMT=f) ....   Also, it is possible to replace the statement READ (UNIT=*,FMT=f) .... by READ f, ...

N16.2   THE FORMAT STATEMENT

The format specifier in an i/o statement need not only be a character expression or an asterisk. It may alternatively be a statement label (chapter 10). In that case the labelled statement must be of a special kind, a FORMAT statement, which gives the format specifier. For example,

          101   FORMAT (3(8X,F12.4))
          WRITE (UNIT=3, 101) a, b, c

is equivalent to

          CHARACTER(*) :: f101 = "(3(8X,F12.4))"
          WRITE (UNIT=3, FMT=f101) a, b, c

It is also possible to have the name of an integer variable as a format specifier, but the variable must be assigned (by an ASSIGN statement, see N10.3) to the label of a FORMAT statement.

N16.3   HOLLERITH DATA

For formatted output there is another type of edit descriptor, nH, for writing a specific string of characters. Such a string is sometimes called 'Hollerith' data. The descriptor nH... causes the ouput of a string of n characters immediately following the letter H. So, 8HOVERFLOW is equivalent to 'OVERFLOW' and 8HMartin's is equivalent to 'Martin''s'.

N16.4   THE EQUIVALENCE STATEMENT

There exists an EQUIVALENCE statement used to perform a task similar to that of the TRANSFER function. EQUIVALENCE lets data have two or more different names and therefore be interpreted as of different types. So, the statement EQUIVALENCE(integer_in, real_in) permits the same bit-patterns in the processor's memory to be interpreted either as integers or as real numbers. This equivalence statement should follow the variables' type declaration statements.

Chapter 17

FILE HANDLING

The previous chapter dealt with the data transfer statements READ and WRITE, and explained in detail the formatting of Fortran data, but little was said about the nature of the input and output devices. This chapter covers a number of ways in which it is possible to control i/o devices and files. The statements concerned are OPEN, CLOSE, BACKSPACE, ENDFILE, REWIND and INQUIRE. Also, we will mention here with a number of special control specifications that can be used with the READ and WRITE statements but were not discussed in chapter 16. Finally, section 17.6 explains 'internal' files.

17.1   UNITS, FILES AND RECORDS

Terms such as 'unit', 'file' and 'record', although often used loosely, have precise technical meanings. A 'record' is to be understood simply as a sequence of data items, usually in the form of characters. A record may have any length, and if it is a sequence of characters then the 'length' is defined simply as the number of characters in it.

For example, a single line of printed characters is usually regarded as a 'record'. A sequence of characters from a keyboard would usually constitute a single input record. In general a record does not have to end with any particular kind of character, even though the end of a record may be indicated to Fortran by pressing the 'enter' or 'return' key (keyboard input) or by the slash (/) edit descriptor.

There are two types of 'file', external and internal. The latter will be explained in section 17.6. An 'external' file is a set of data having a physical existence external to the program. It is rarely necessary to work with internal files, and so the word 'file' is usually used by itself to refer to an external file. For example, you might say that a magnetic tape contains a 'file' of data.

A file may consist of any number of records (including zero!) and may have, as its final record, a special 'endfile record'. The word 'file' is usually used to refer to a durable set of machine-readable data, as opposed to something ephemeral like a screen display or the tapping of a keyboard. As we shall see, a file can have a name in Fortran. Most commonly, files are stored on magnetic media, disks or tapes. Some processors may store files on other media such as optical disks or in special areas of memory ('RAM disks').

An important distinction must be made between 'sequential access' and 'direct access' files. A sequential-access file has a beginning and an end, and the data items must be must be read or written in sequence. When such a file is first opened it will be positioned at the beginning. As a general rule, sequential-access files consist of 'formatted' records, i.e. each record consists of a sequence of characters. 'Unformatted' records (section 16.9), on the other hand, are most often of direct-access type.

Historically, the concept of sequential access arose from the use of magnetic tapes: obviously a magnetic tape has to be wound from one end to the other, although backspacing and rewinding are possible. By contrast, a direct-access file corresponds to something like a magnetic disk where any part of the file can be reached very quickly.

It is assumed that a direct-access file is divided into records, and that any record can be read or written independently of the others. However, it is not possible to dive into the middle of a record: each record must be read or written from the first character. For reference purposes, the records of a direct-access file are numbered, but the numbering need not correspond to physical positions on the surface of the disk. The physical layout of data on a disk is a matter for the operating system, not for Fortran, and a sophisticated system may switch records about in complicated ways to optimise the utilisation of space on the disk. In a direct-access file the records must all have the same length and they must be numbered: otherwise the operating system would have to be inordinately complicated. The record numbers must be positive integers. In the case of a direct-access file there is no such thing as an 'endfile record'.

A sequential-access file, such as a file on a magnetic tape, can have records of varying lengths. Unless otherwise specified (and we shall see soon how these things are specified) all files are assumed by Fortran to be sequential-access files. The keyboard, for example, is treated like a sequential-access file, since the records must be input in a particular order - the real-time order - and the records may vary in length. It is possible for a sequential-access file to have zero length.

A possible feature of a sequential-access file is 'nonadvancing' i/o, as opposed to the usual 'advancing' i/o. Usually, a WRITE or READ statement will transfer data to or from an exact number of records. Even if a READ statement only looks at the data in the first part of a record, nevertheless the unit will have physically passed over the whole of the record. So, between two i/o statements a file will always be positioned between two records. If you want to examine two parts of a record separately, you must either read the record twice (using BACKSPACE, section 17.3) or you must read the whole thing once and store in memory the information that you're not ready to analyse. 'Nonadvancing' i/o offers an alternative: you can read or write a record on a character-by-character basis, executing i/o statements several times as you move through one record. This is called 'nonadvancing' because the file does not advance automatically to the end of the record after a READ or WRITE, which is the usual procedure.

In Fortran, external files are associated with 'units'. A 'unit' is an i/o device, such as a printer, a tape drive, a barcode reader, or whatever. The definition of a unit is quite independent of the particular data that happens to be flowing through it. A processor will have access to a range of different units, usually numbered by different non-negative integers, except that a standard input device and a standard output device may be referred to by asterisks.

It must be remembered that a 'unit' is not the same thing as a 'file'. A unit is a channel by which the processor may access a file.

In the earlier part of this book, READ and WRITE were the only types of i/o statement mentioned. It could be imagined that the input device was the keyboard and the output device was a VDU or perhaps a printer. There was no need to do any more than READ or WRITE to transfer the data, and distinctions between, say, direct-access and sequential-access files did not arise. In general, however, it is not possible to READ or WRITE a file without first executing a special setting-up statement, OPEN. The OPEN statement is used to connect a file to a numbered unit and to decide certain options. It is most commonly used with magnetic tape or disk files. The syntax is simply

OPEN (connection specification list)

where 'connection specification list' is a selection of specifications, separated by commas, of the sort

UNIT = ...	the unit number (compulsory!)
IOSTAT = ...	for error-checking
FILE = ...	to specify the file's name
STATUS = ...	new file or old?
ACCESS = ...	SEQUENTIAL or DIRECT
FORM = ...	FORMATTED or UNFORMATTED
RECL = ...	record length
BLANK = ...	NULL or ZERO
POSITION = ...	ASIS, REWIND or APPEND
ACTION = ...	READ, WRITE or READWRITE
DELIM = ...	APOSTROPHE, QUOTE or NONE
PAD = ...	YES or NO

None of these may appear more than once in the same OPEN statement. They need not all be present, but there must be a UNIT specifier. In many cases an OPEN statement will only involve a small number of the possible options. A typical OPEN statement might be

```
OPEN (UNIT=6, IOSTAT=ncheck, FILE="april.dat",     &
      STATUS="NEW", ACCESS="DIRECT",               &
      FORM="FORMATTED", RECL=512)
```

What do the specifiers mean? Taking them in the order listed above, each is discussed at more length below.

UNIT

This specifier must be set to an integer expression. It would be quite possible to have, say,

OPEN (UNIT= ndisk1, ...)

with ndisk1 being an integer to be specified as a parameter at the start of the program. The particular meanings of the unit numbers will be processor-dependent. It is not possible to have UNIT=* in an OPEN statement, i.e. opening the processor's default i/o units.

IOSTAT

This supplies the name of a scalar integer variable which, on execution of the statement, will be given either

(a) a positive value if an error condition is encountered, or

(b) negative values if an end-of-file or an end-of-record condition is encountered, or

(c) the value zero otherwise.

In fact only case (a) or (c) may occur as a result of the OPEN statement, but it will be seen that the IOSTAT specifier can also be used with other statements such as READ and WRITE and then case (b) may arise.

In case (b) above, the end-of-file condition can only be relevant to a sequential-access file, and the end-of-record condition can only be relevant to a sequential-access file with nonadvancing i/o. With a direct-access file, case (b) is never relevant.

FILE

This specifier lets the programmer state a name for the file as a scalar character expression. It is not always needed: for example, magnetic tape files or printers do not usually have names. However, processors usually require disk files to be named. To read an existing file from a disk, it will be necessary to know its name, and to write a new file, a name must be supplied. The convention for constructing names will depend on the processor. It is possible to specify the filename either as a constant expression (like "april.dat") or through the name of a variable.

STATUS

This is a character string (or a character expression) which must be either "OLD", "NEW", "SCRATCH", "REPLACE", or "UNKNOWN". OLD means that a named file already exists, NEW means that it does not yet exist, and REPLACE creates a fresh file and deletes any old file of the same name. SCRATCH is used for a file that has not been given a name, creating a 'scratch' file for temporary use as the program executes: a scratch file is deleted when the program terminates or when a CLOSE statement (below) is executed for the unit. The UNKNOWN option, which is the default if STATUS is omitted, simply means that the status is processor-dependent.

For STATUS, and for the other specifiers below which call for character expressions, there is no distinction between upper and lower case and any trailing blanks will be ignored.

ACCESS

This is a character expression string equivalent to either "SEQUENTIAL" or "DIRECT", specifying whether this is a sequential-access or direct-access file. The default is SEQUENTIAL.

FORM

This specifier determines whether the file is formatted or unformatted, and it must be a character expression equal to "FORMATTED" or to "UNFORMATTED". The default is FORMATTED for a sequential-access file, or UNFORMATTED in the case of direct access.

RECL

This specifier, which is set to an integer expression, gives the record length. For formatted records this means the number of characters in a record. In the direct-access case, RECL is the length of every record, and must be specified. In the sequential-access case records may be of variable length and RECL is taken to be the maximum record length: it may be omitted, in which case a processor-dependent default value takes effect. (See also the comment on RECL in section 17.5.)

BLANK

BLANK, a specifier applicable to formatted input files, is set to a character expression equal to either "NULL" or "ZERO", the former being the default. NULL means that blanks are ignored in numeric data (except that a whole field of blanks is treated as a zero) and ZERO means that blanks are treated as zeros.

POSITION

POSITION is a character expression equal to "REWIND", "APPEND" or "ASIS", and it can be specified in the case of an existing sequential-access file. It determines whether the file will be positioned at its start or at its end. REWIND positions it at the start, and APPEND at the end. The ASIS option, which is the default, leaves the file positioned wherever it was.

ACTION

This permits the file to be restricted to read-only or write-only use. ACTION may have the character values "READ", "WRITE" or "READWRITE". The first two are self-explanatory. READWRITE, the default, permits both reading and writing to take place on this file.

DELIM

This may have one of the character values "APOSTROPHE", "QUOTE" or "NONE", and it has a significance in relation to list-directed or namelist character-string data output. It specifies whether character strings will be displayed between apostrophes, between quotes, or without any delimiters.

PAD

PAD is a character expression equal to "YES" or "NO". It determines whether or not a formatted input record should be padded out with blanks if it is shorter than expected. If NO, the record's length must match what the READ statement demands. The default is YES.

The list of specifiers above seems long and confusing at first sight, but in practice the OPEN statement is not difficult to use. A simple procedure is:

(a) Specify the UNIT number. This will depend on the particular configuration of the processor being used.

(b) Does the unit refer to a sequential-access file, such as a printer or a tape drive? Or is it a direct-access file such as a disk file? If the latter, skip to (e) below. For sequential access, continue with (c) below. If you don't know, there is an intrinsic function INQUIRE which can tell you (section 17.5)

(c) If direct access is not specified, files are taken by default to be sequential-access. And, unless otherwise specified, sequential-access files are taken by default to be formatted. Formatted sequential-access records may vary in length, but there will be a processor-dependent maximum record length. The INQUIRE function (17.5) can tell you the processor's maximum record length.

(d) The specifiers BLANK, DELIM and PAD, which are for formatted records, are not of great interest. They can almost always be omitted. The optional POSITION specifier, for a sequential file, is an opportunity to position the file at its starting point ("REWIND", equivalent to the REWIND statement of section 17.3) or at its end ("APPEND").

Skip to (f) below.

(e) For direct access, specify ACCESS="DIRECT". A direct-access file is taken by default to be unformatted. For direct access, it is necessary to specify the record length using the RECL specifier.

(f) A file-name may be given using the FILE specifier, but a file name is usually only needed in the case of direct-access disk files. The specifiers STATUS and ACCESS may be useful for protecting files from being inadvertently overwritten. Remember that when STATUS="SCRATCH", the file should not have a name.

(g) The IOSTAT specifier is not compulsory but should be included if the code is to be watertight.

Here are a few examples of OPEN statements:

```
OPEN (UNIT=7, ACCESS="DIRECT", RECL=128, &
        FILE='studentgrades.dat', ACTION=READ)
OPEN (UNIT=14, POSITION="APPEND", &
        IOSTAT=k_error_unit_14)
OPEN (UNIT=ndiskb, ACCESS="DIRECT", &
        RECL=nrecs, FILE=fstring)
OPEN (UNIT=4, ACCESS="DIRECT", &
        RECL=idata_unit(4), STATUS="SCRATCH")
```

After opening a file, records may be written or read and other operations may be performed as in section 17.3 below. Finally, the CLOSE statement may be used to disconnect the file from a unit. The syntax is similar to that for OPEN:

CLOSE (specification list)

but the specification list for CLOSE is taken from

UNIT = ...	the unit number (compulsory!)
IOSTAT = ...	for error-checking, as for OPEN
STATUS = ...	keep or delete?

The optional STATUS specifier may be set either to "KEEP" or "DELETE". In the latter case, the file will be deleted when CLOSE is executed. Note that a file opened with STATUS="SCRATCH" is always deleted on closure anyway. The default STATUS is "KEEP".

Some examples of CLOSE statements are

```
CLOSE(UNIT=6, IOSTAT=ncheck)
DO k=1,6 : CLOSE(k) : END DO
CLOSE(UNIT=14, IOSTAT=k_error_unit_14)
CLOSE(UNIT=ndiskb, STATUS="DELETE")
```

17.3   BACKSPACE, ENDFILE AND REWIND

These are the 'file positioning statements' and their functions should be clear from their names. They are applicable only to sequential-access files, and in particular magnetic tapes. The syntax can be illustrated by the BACKSPACE statement, which takes the form

BACKSPACE (UNIT=..., IOSTAT=...)

where the UNIT specifier is compulsory and IOSTAT is as usual optional. UNIT and IOSTAT have the same meanings as for the OPEN statement. BACKSPACE moves the file back to the start of the previous record if there is one. The REWIND statement moves the file back to the start of the first record. ENDFILE writes an 'endfile' record. However, an endfile record will be written automatically after a CLOSE statement or simply if a program terminates normally after writing on the file has taken place.

17.4   CONTROL SPECIFICATIONS FOR I/O

So far READ and WRITE statements have been considered of the form

READ (UNIT=..., FMT=..., ...) input-item-list

and

WRITE (UNIT=..., FMT=..., ...) output-item-list

and for namelist groups NML has been explained as an alternative to FMT. If the data is unformatted, neither FMT nor NML will be present. The following additional specifiers may be included:

IOSTAT = ...	as for OPEN
REC = ...	record number
ADVANCE = ...	advancing or nonadvancing i/o
SIZE = ...	number of characters to be read

If IOSTAT is present it allows the program to detect an i/o error or the end of a record or of a file as was described for the OPEN statement earlier.

REC

If REC is present the file must be of direct-access type and REC specifies the number of the record which is to be written or read. Records in a direct access file do not have to be written or read in any particular order (that's what direct-access means, of course) and so the i/o statement has to include the record number. If REC is not present the file is of sequential-access type.

ADVANCE

This is an option available when formatted sequential files are being written or read. The default option, ADVANCE="YES", the most common situation, simply means that the i/o statement will read or write one record, moving the file from the start of one record to the start of the next: it is not possible to read or write a fraction of a record and stop partway through. The option ADVANCE="NO" means that 'nonadvancing' i/o will take place, i.e. the file does not automatically advance to the start of the subsequent record. The effect of this is to make it possible to read or write a record piece by piece. Individual characters can be transferred, the exact number of them depending on the format specification and the i/o item list.

SIZE

In the case of a READ statement, with formatted sequential non-advancing input, the SIZE specifier may be used to give the name of an integer variable which will yield, after the statement has been executed, the number of characters transferred.

Some examples of i/o statements are:

```
WRITE (UNIT=*, FMT=format, IOSTAT=icheck) (title(k), data(:,k), k=1,6)
READ (UNIT=4, REC=1) dump
READ (UNIT=11, FMT=f4, ADVANCE="NO", SIZE=nchars) string
READ (*, FMT="(A1)", ADVANCE="NO") char
```

The last of these reads a single character from the keyboard. Because ADVANCE="NO" the statement is not expecting to input a complete record, and therefore the data is transferred without any need for the 'return' or 'enter' key to be pressed.

17.5   THE 'INQUIRE' STATEMENT

Some of the statements mentioned above, especially OPEN, may require a knowledge of the detailed properties of the i/o unit being referred to. But the Fortran programmer doesn't have to look up all these details in the processor's user guide: there is a statement called INQUIRE which permits the program, at execution time, to find out most of the necessary information automatically. In fact INQUIRE can yield a bewilderingly large array of information. The statement's syntax is simple enough:

> INQUIRE (specification list)

In many respects the specification list is similar to what we have already seen for OPEN and other statements above. The specification list for INQUIRE must include either UNIT=... or FILE=..., but not both, specifying either a unit number or a filename. If a unit is specified, we have what is said to be the 'inquire by unit' form of the statement. If a filename is given, it is 'inquire by file'. (There is a third possibility, 'inquire by output list', mentioned at the end of this section.)

With 'inquire by unit', the keyword UNIT= may be omitted if the unit specifier is the first in the list, i.e.

> INQUIRE (3, EXIST=being_3)

is a permissible statement to check the existence of unit 3. In any INQUIRE statement the unit number must be specified by an integer expression, not by an asterisk, and consequently the default i/o devices cannot be referred to.

After UNIT or FILE, other items in the specification list are of the usual form

> SPECIFIER = variable-name

and depending on the specifier the variable may be of integer, character or logical type. The possible specifiers are listed below, and they are all optional, but none of them may appear more than once in the statement. The variables named must all be scalars. They will be given values when the statement is executed.

IOSTAT = ...	as for OPEN
EXIST = ...	does the unit/file exist?
OPENED = ...	file and unit connected?
NUMBER = ...	what is the unit number?
NAMED = ...	does the file have a name?
ACCESS = ...	as for OPEN
SEQUENTIAL = ...	can this be sequentially accessed?
DIRECT = ...	can this be directly accessed?
FORM = ...	as for OPEN
FORMATTED = ...	is formatted i/o possible?

UNFORMATTED = ...	is unformatted i/o possible?
RECL = ...	maximum record length
NEXTREC = ...	number of next record
BLANK = ...	as for OPEN
POSITION = ...	as for OPEN
ACTION = ...	as for OPEN
READ = ...	can the file be read?
WRITE = ...	can the file be written?
READWRITE = ...	are reading and writing both allowed?
DELIM =- ...	as for OPEN
PAD = ...	as for OPEN

It should be stressed that all the specifiers in the above list are for the program to obtain information from the processor, not to supply information to it. For example, the ACCESS specifier here is working in the opposite direction from that in the OPEN statement.

Except for those already explained in section 17.2, more details of the above specifiers are given below.

EXIST

This specifies a logical variable which will be true if the file, or unit, exists, and false otherwise.

OPENED

This is also a logical variable. In an 'inquire by file' statement it is true if the named file is connected to a unit. In 'inquire by unit' it is true if the unit has got a file attached.

NUMBER

In an 'inquire by file' statement, this is an integer equal to the file's unit number. If the file cannot be found it is set to -1.

NAMED

In 'inquire by unit', this logical variable says whether or not there is a named file at this unit.

SEQUENTIAL

This will be a character string equal to "YES" if the file/unit can be used in sequential-access mode, and "NO" if it can only be used in direct access. The processor may answer "UNKNOWN"!

DIRECT

This is similar to SEQUENTIAL. A character string is set to "YES" if the file/unit may be used in direct-access mode, and to "NO" if it may not.

FORMATTED

This is a character string equal to "YES" if formatted records are possible, and "NO" if it is restricted to unformatted use.

UNFORMATTED

The opposite of FORMATTED: "YES" means that unformatted i/o is possible, "NO" means that i/o must be formatted.

RECL

This specifies an integer, the processor's maximum record length for this file/unit. This cannot be exceeded by the RECL specified for the same unit in an OPEN statement.

NEXTREC

When a direct-access file is being written or read, it can be useful to know the number of the next record. The integer specified by NEXTREC is one greater than the number of the last record, or is equal to 1 if none have yet been written or read.

READ

This is a character string set to "YES" if the file/unit may be read from, and "NO" otherwise.

WRITE

This is equal to "YES" if writing is possible, and "NO" if it is not. For example, this specifier will give "NO" if the unit is a keyboard, because a keyboard is an input device. You can't write onto a keyboard!

READWRITE

"YES" is given if, and only if, the file/unit can be used both for reading and writing.

INQUIRE is an extremely useful statement because it can be used to interrogate a processor and yield information on the basis of which other i/o statements can be constructed to make the best use of the facilities available to the processor. INQUIRE is the key to writing good, portable and crashproof i/o code. A few examples of INQUIRE statements are

```
INQUIRE (UNIT=laser_printer, RECL=linelength)
INQUIRE (UNIT=3, IOSTAT=j, FORM=sform)
INQUIRE (FILE=scratch_disk_output, NEXTREC=k)
```

The following subroutine could be used to set up and read a named disk file:

```
SUBROUTINE Read (filename, nrec)
USE Data, ONLY : input => stringbank
CHARACTER(*) :: filename
INTEGER :: nrec, n_unit, icheck,
LOGICAL :: q
INQUIRE (FILE=filename, IOSTAT=icheck, EXIST=q, NUMBER=n_unit)
IF (icheck/=0) THEN ; filename="FAULTY" ; RETURN ; ENDIF
IF (.NOT.q) THEN ;  filename="NOTFOUND" ; RETURN ; ENDIF
OPEN (UNIT=n_unit, IOSTAT=icheck, FILE=filename, ACCESS="DIRECT")
IF (icheck/=0) THEN ; filename="ERROR1" ; RETURN ; ENDIF
READ (UNIT=n_unit, REC=nrec, IOSTAT=icheck) input
IF (icheck/=0) filename="ERROR2"
END SUBROUTINE Read
```

So far two forms of the INQUIRE statement have been described: 'inquire by unit' and 'inquire by file'. A third form uses the syntax

```
INQUIRE (IOLENGTH=integer) output-list
```

where 'integer' is the name of a scalar integer variable and 'output-list' is a list of data such as could appear in a WRITE statement. The purpose of this statement is to ascertain the record length that the processor would require to output the data with an unformatted WRITE statement. The integer variable specified by IOLENGTH will be set to the necessary record length, and could then be used to open an output file with records of sufficient length, as in

```
INQUIRE (IOLENGTH=n) stringbank
OPEN (UNIT=k, ACCESS="DIRECT", RECL=n, STATUS="SCRATCH")
WRITE (UNIT=k, REC=1, IOSTAT=nasty) stringbank
```

'Internal' files are not really files at all: they are simply areas of the processor's memory being treated as if they were sequential-access formatted files. Data can be written to or read from internal files using WRITE and READ statements, but there is no transfer of information outside the processor. Internal files can be useful for changing the type interpretation of data: you can write to an internal file in one format, then read from it in another format.

Internal files can only be used with the READ and WRITE statements. All the other i/o statements are inapplicable to them, and 'nonadvancing' i/o is not possible. An internal file is not only internal to the processor, it is internal to the program, and cannot be used to transfer information between different programs or to save data from one program run to another. In fact, an internal file is a local entity which cannot even be used to transfer data between program units unless it is declared in a module.

An internal file is no more than a character variable. To read or write an internal file, the unit number is replaced by the name of the character variable. An example should make the principle clear:

WRITE (UNIT=digit_string, FMT="(I6)") nref

This statement requires 'digit_string' to have been previously declared in the usual way as a character variable of length 6 or more. The integer 'nref' is written into the string 'digit_string', taking up 6 character positions. If the length of 'digit_string' is greater than 6 it will be padded out with trailing blanks. Subsequently,

READ (digit_string, "(5X,I1)") junits

would yield the last digit of the number. The statement

READ (digit_string, "(F6.0)") ref

will yield the original number but now as a variable of real type. If the integer nref had been, say, 524288, then digit_string would be given the value "524288", junits would be the integer 8, and ref would be the real number 524288.0. Within the processor's memory, the internal representations of nref, digit_string and ref would be quite different since they are variables of different types.

The next example shows how an internal file WRITE statement can be used for concatenation:

```
CHARACTER(10) :: title
CHARACTER(30) :: forename, midname, surname
CHARACTER(100) :: name
  .
  .
WRITE (name, "(A,1X,A,1X,A,1X,A)") title, forename, midname, surname
```

This is equivalent to

name = title//" "//forename//" "//midname//" "//surname

In the above examples, the internal files called 'digit_string' and 'name' were scalar variables regarded as having one record. If the internal file is an array, then each element of the array is regarded as a 'record' of the internal file, taken in normal array element order. An internal file may be an array section, but not with a vector subscript.

If 'names' is a character array, the statement

READ (names(1:2),"(A12)") forename, surname

reads a file of two records, each being a length=12 string. This statement involves format reversion (section 16.7) and is equivalent to

forename = names(1) ; surname = names(2)

except that the READ statement, unlike the assignment statements, will ignore leading blanks in the elements of 'names'. Moreover,

WRITE (names(1:2),"(2A12)") forename, surname

is equivalent to

names(1:2) = (/forename, surname/)

but the WRITE statement would give an error if the elements of 'names' have lengths less than 12. Notice that, in our previous examples, it would be possible for digit_string, nref, junits, ref, title, forename etc. to be arrays as long as they are declared as such and as long as the internal files conform in shape with the data.

EXERCISES 17A

17A1   Write OPEN statements

(i) To open a magnetic tape scratch file on unit 7

(ii) To open a magnetic tape file on unit 3, positioning it at the end of the file so that more data can be appended.

(iii) To open a direct-access disk file called "s_sheet_45" on unit 2, the record length being 256. Then write a CLOSE statement to close the file and discard it.

17A2   Write statements to

(i) Write the 20 elements of an array called 'datasave' as 20 records in an unformatted file on unit 5. (Use a DO loop.)

(ii) Read the first 10 characters of a record on unit 1, without advancing further through the record. The 10 characters are to be interpreted as two five-digit integers.

(iii) Inquire which of the units 1 to 10 exist on the processor, and which may be used for unformatted i/o. (Use a DO loop.)

(iv) Inquire whether a file called 'tempora' is attached to a unit, and what the number of the unit is.

17A3   Imagine that the concatenation operator for character strings (//) does not exist. Write a function that would do the same job by writing an internal file.

N17.1 THE ERR, END AND EOR SPECIFIERS

In the OPEN, CLOSE, READ, WRITE, BACKSPACE, ENDFILE, REWIND and INQUIRE i/o statements the list of specifications may include ERR=... with the number of a statement label (section 10.4) being given. The effect is to transfer control to a statement with that label if there is an error as the i/o statement executes.

Similarly, in a READ statement there can be an END=... specification giving the label of a statement to which control passes if the end of the file is encountered.

There can also be an EOR=... specification in a READ or WRITE statement being used for nonadvancing i/o. Control then passes to the labelled statement if the end of the record is reached.

N17.2 INCLUDE

A Fortran program may include a line of the form

        INCLUDE "filename"

if "filename" is a character-string constant specifying a file which contains additional Fortran statements. Technically, an INCLUDE line is not itself a Fortran statement: it is just a way of including, at this point in a program, lines of Fortran that have been stored elsewhere. A file included in this way may itself include other files!

Chapter 18

BITS

Fortran's intrinsic data types are INTEGER, REAL, COMPLEX, CHARACTER and LOGICAL, but in addition it is possible to manipulate data in the form of individual binary bits. Bits are similar in some ways to LOGICAL data, in that both are restricted to two possible values, called .FALSE. or .TRUE. for LOGICAL and 0 or 1 for a bit. However, lengthy sequences of binary data can be handled much more naturally and flexibly as bits than in LOGICAL form. Bits are packed within data of integer type, and stored in memory much more economically than LOGICAL data.

To handle bits, Fortran provides the intrinsic functions BIT_SIZE, IBSET, IBCLR, IBITS, ISHFT, NOT, IAND, IOR, and IEOR, and the subroutine MVBITS. These procedures manipulate sets of bits which have to be declared as data of integer type.

18.1   INSIDE INTEGERS

A non-negative integer i may be regarded as a sequence of 'bits' or binary digits w_k as in

$$i = \sum_k w_k.2^k \tag{18.1}$$

with the sum running from k=0 to a value s-1, where s is the number of bits. This formula is taken in Fortran to relate an integer i to the sequence of bits $w_0, w_1, ..., w_{s-1}$.

It is important to know how many bits can be contained in each integer, i.e. what is the processor's value of s, and this is given by a special inquiry function BIT_SIZE(I). The argument I is any integer. The statement numbits=BIT_SIZE(1) will therefore tell the program the number of bits per integer on the processor being used. Typically this might be 32 or 64.

The function BTEST(I,POS) looks into the integer I and tests whether the bit in position POS is 0 or 1. The argument POS corresponds to the index k in equation 18.1 above, and so it must be an integer in the range from 0 to s-1. BTEST itself has logical value, i.e. BTEST(I=64, POS=k) has the value .TRUE. if and only if k=6.

BTEST is an elemental intrinsic function, as are the other bit functions mentioned below, and may therefore have an array as argument and result. Taking POS as an array, on a 32-bit processor, we could have

$$\text{INTEGER :: ibitstring} \quad ; \quad \text{LOGICAL :: bdigits(32)}$$

.
.

$$\text{bdigits} = \text{BTEST}(I=\text{ibitstring}, POS=(/(i, i=0,31)/))$$

converting ibitstring (an integer corresponding to a sequence of 32 bits) into the logical array bdigits.

The functions IBSET(I,POS) and IBCLR(I,POS) are used to reset individual bits within the integer I, the result being the modified version of I. IBSET sets the bit in position POS equal to 1 (if that is not already its value) and IBCLR clears the bit to 0. If POS were an array spanning the whole of the integer I, as in the previous example, then IBCLR would clear all the bits in I to zero.

There is a function IBITS(I,IPOS,LEN) which forms a new integer by picking out a subset of the bits within I, i.e. a number LEN of bits starting at position POS. The result IBITS is obtained by right-justifying the chosen bits and setting the others to 0. So, for example, IBITS(I=munch,POS=0,LEN=8) picks out the first byte from munch, and IBITS(I=munch,POS=8,LEN=8) picks out the second byte. When using IBITS, the sum of POS and LEN cannot exceed the total number of bits in I that would be given by the function BIT_SIZE.

18.2   BIT LOGIC

To carry out logical operations on bits we have the intrinsic functions NOT(I), IAND(I,J), IOR(I,J), and IEOR(I,J). The first of these simply yields the complement of I, i.e. NOT(17)=238 on an 8-bit machine. The other functions have two arguments and form the logical 'and', 'or', and 'exclusive or' combinations on a bit-by-bit basis. So, if

$$i \; = \; \sum_k w_k.2^k$$

and

$$j \; = \; \sum_k y_k.2^k \qquad\qquad (18.2)$$

the w's and y's being binary digits, then

$$\text{NOT}(i) \;\; = \;\; \sum_k (1-w_k).2^k \qquad\qquad (18.3)$$

$$\text{AND}(i,j) \;\; = \;\; \sum_k w_k.y_k.2^k \qquad\qquad (18.4)$$

$$\text{IOR}(i,j) \;\; = \;\; \sum_k (w_k+y_k-w_k.y_k).2^k \qquad\qquad (18.5)$$

and

$$\text{IEOR}(i,j) \;=\; \Sigma_k \;(w_k + y_k - 2.w_k.y_k).2^k \qquad\qquad (18.6)$$

There are two intrinsic functions to shift the bits around within an integer. ISHFT(I,SHIFT) shifts the bits within I by a number of places given by SHIFT. They go left if SHIFT is positive, and right if SHIFT is negative, and bits which fall off the end are lost, while places vacated at the other end are filled with zeros. Another function, ISHFTC(I,SHIFT) does a circular shift so that bits pushed off one end of I appear at the other end. In fact ISHFTC may have a third argument, SIZE, in which case the circular shift occurs only among the SIZE bits at the right. So, SHFTC(I=90,SHIFT=-2,SIZE=8) just operates on the first byte of I and has the value 150.

Finally, there is an intrinsic elemental subroutine called MVBITS (FROM, FROMPOS, LEN, TO, TOPOS) which will do the job of taking a sequence of bits (of length LEN) from the integer FROM (starting with bit position FROMPOS) and copying it into the integer TO (starting at position TOPOS). The statement

CALL MVBITS(FROM=source, FROMPOS=0, LEN=16, TO=dest, TOPOS=16)

uses the first two bytes of 'source' to replace the third and fourth bytes of 'dest'.

18.3   A WARNING

In Fortran, when we use the intrinsic procedures described above, bits are assumed to be packed into non-negative integers according to the equation at the beginning of section 18.1. That equation is fundamental to the working of the procedures. However, variables of integer type in Fortran are not normally represented according to that equation but according to another, processor-dependent, scheme which must of course allow for negative as well as positive numbers.

In other words, eqn. 18.1 is valid only in the context of the bit manipulation procedures. If a bit-pattern is set up according to eqn. 18.1, the value of the integer i will not necessarily be the same as the value we would get if the same bit-pattern were interpreted for the purposes of ordinary Fortran integer arithmetic. In fact if ibitstring defines a string of bits by eqn. 18.1, then its value when regarded as a 32-digit binary number is given by

```
intval = SUM (MERGE ( &
         TSOURCE=(/(2**k, k=0,31)/), &
         FSOURCE =(/(0, k=0,31)/), &
         MASK=BTEST(I=ibitstring, POS=(/(i,i=0,31)/))))
```

and this is not necessarily equal to ibitstring's value when regarded as being of Fortran's integer type.

The following subroutine is an example of how a 'nonadvancing' input statement could be used to read a stream of bits. Since there is no requirement for format conversion, character-type editing is used, and one character at a time is input. It is assumed that one character represents one byte (8 bits) and that four characters (32 bits) can be stored in the 'integer' ibitstring. The subroutine reads 32 bits, but with null bytes if there is an end-of-file, an end-of-record or an input error.

```
SUBROUTINE Instream (ibitstring, n_unit, icheck)
INTEGER :: ibitstring, n_unit, icheck=0
CHARACTER :: char(4), cnull=ACHAR(0)
DO k = 1, 4
        READ (UNIT=n_unit, FMT="(A)", &
        ADVANCE="NO", IOSTAT=icheck) char(k)
        IF (icheck==0) CYCLE
        char(k) = cnull
        EXIT
END DO
ibitstring = TRANSFER(SOURCE= char(1)//char(2)//char(3)//char(4), MOLD=1)
END SUBROUTINE Instream
```

The TRANSFER function here is taking a concatenation of 4 characters (32 bits) and designating it as the 'integer' ibitstring so that it could subsequently be used in the context of the intrinsic bit manipulation functions. The arithmetical value of ibitstring is irrelevant.

EXERCISES 18A

18A1   Write a function which will convert a length=32 logical array into the corresponding stream of 32 bits, assuming that BIT_SIZE(1)=32.

18A2   Write a function to convert a string of 32 bits (represented as an integer-type variable according to eqn. 18.1) into a hexadecimal number (in the form of a length=8 character string representing 8 hexadecimal digits).

18A3   Pretend that the intrinsic function IACHAR does not exist, and write a functions to do the same job for 8-bit characters, i.e. taking a single character as argument and returning a code in the range 0 to 255.

Chapter 19

PROGRAMMING CONVENTIONS AND PROGRAM ARCHITECTURE; PUTTING IT ALL TOGETHER

This chapter contains no new parts of the Fortran language that have not already been mentioned earlier in this book, but it summarises some ways in which programmers can improve their work by accepting conventions or constraints to regulate how they use Fortran. Sets of statement keywords and intrinsic procedures are listed which can be regarded as forming a recommended 'core' Fortran 90. Then, section 19.3 summarises the rules governing the ordering of statements within any program unit, and section 19.4 deals with the overall structure of a program.

19.1   CODING CONVENTIONS

It has been said before that, because of the language's history, Fortran contains a number of obsolescent or inessential features that a new programmer would be well advised to avoid. These features are not functionally necessary, i.e. there's nothing you can do with them that you can't do without them. Some of them (listed in note N2.1) are officially designated as 'obsolescent'. There are other old features whose usage is a matter of taste and personal opinion, but it would be reasonable to avoid all those which in this book have been mentioned only in the end-of-chapter notes. Some other good rules are:

(1) Stick to the capitalisation convention given in section 3.4, or one like it. In Fortran the difference between upper- and lower-case letters is not syntactically functional, so it is natural to use it for the programmer's benefit as a way of distinguishing as clearly as possible between different categories of lexical token.

(2) Avoid IMPLICIT and stick to the default initial-letter convention for naming real and integer variables. Ideally all variables should be specified in type declaration statements except for the integers that are used as DO-loop indices, etc.

(3) If a word already has a meaning in Fortran, e.g. as a keyword or intrinsic procedure, don't use it as name for something else.

(4) Use only apostrophes, not quotes, to delimit character strings.

(5) In expressions and assignment statements with mixed data types, type conversions should be explicit except in the most trivial of cases (e.g. avoid expressions like x+(1/2) and x==0 where x is real).

(6) Use parentheses freely rather than depending on the rules for the order of operations (e.g. don't use expressions such as x/2**y/2).

19.2   TOWARDS 'CORE' FORTRAN 90

Some more controversial suggestions are the following:

(1) Avoid GO TO and statement labels (section 10.4). They are very tempting, and there are seasoned programmers who imagine them to be essential, but they can easily result in an unreadable 'spaghetti' style of coding. It is always possible to avoid the inelegance of statement labels and the bad habits that GO TO encourages. Anyway, the code

```
      999 CONTINUE
            .
            .
      GO TO 999
```

can always be replaced by

```
      Jumpback999: DO
            .
            .
      END DO Jumpback999
```

(2) Chapter 18 gave details of 'bitstream' integers and associated intrinsic procedures. But errors can easily arise if these integers are treated arithmetically like ordinary integers. If you want to use bitstream data it could be safer and more elegant to define a special derived type (see chapter 14).

(3) Use <, ==, etc rather than .LT., .EQ., etc.

(4) Try to use only the statement types listed overleaf. This avoids many inessentials. For example, the standard form of the type declaration statement can always be used in place of attribute specification statements (see note N13.1). The numbers given are the chapters in which they are discussed in this book.

FORTRAN 90 RECOMMENDED STATEMENTS

Assignment Statement: = (3, 7)

Comment Statement: ! (3)

Code-Editing Statement: INCLUDE (17)

Data Type Declaration Statements:

CHARACTER (4, 6, 13) LOGICAL (4,13)
COMPLEX (4, 13) REAL (3, 4, 13)
END TYPE (14) TYPE declaration (14)
INTEGER (4, 13) TYPE definition (14)

Input/Output (i/o) Statements:

BACKSPACE (17) OPEN (17)
CLOSE (17) READ (3,16)
ENDFILE (17) REWIND (17)
INQUIRE (17) WRITE (3, 16)

Execution Control Statements:

CASE (8) ELSEWHERE (7) GO TO (10)
CONTINUE (10) END DO (8) IF (4, 8)
CYCLE (8) END IF (3, 8) IF...THEN (3, 8)
DO (8) END SELECT (8) SELECT CASE (8)
ELSE (3, 8) END WHERE (7) STOP (8)
ELSE IF (8) EXIT (8) WHERE (7)

Memory-Management Statements: (15)

ALLOCATE NULLIFY
DEALLOCATE Pointer Assignment =>

Program Unit Statements:

CALL (9) INTEGER FUNCTION (9)
CHARACTER FUNCTION (9) INTERFACE (12)
COMPLEX FUNCTION (9) LOGICAL FUNCTION (9)
CONTAINS (11) MODULE (11)
END (9) MODULE PROCEDURE (12)
END FUNCTION (9) PROGRAM (3)
END INTERFACE (12) REAL FUNCTION (9)
END MODULE (11) RECURSIVE FUNCTION (12)
END PROGRAM (3) RECURSIVE SUBROUTINE (12)
END SUBROUTINE (9) SUBROUTINE (9)
EXTERNAL (12) TYPE...FUNCTION (14)
FUNCTION (9) USE (11)

(5) Use only these intrinsic functions, avoiding 'specific' names:

Numeric Functions:

ABS	ANINT	CONJG	MAX	MODULO
AIMAG	CEILING	FLOOR	MIN	NINT
AINT	CMPLX	INT	MOD	REAL

Mathematical Functions:

ACOS	ATAN2	EXP	SIN	TAN
ASIN	COS	LOG	SINH	TANH
ATAN	COSH	LOG10	SQRT	

Character Functions:

ACHAR	IACHAR	LEN_TRIM	LLE	SCAN
ADJUSTL	INDEX	LGE	LLT	TRIM
ADJUSTR	LEN	LGT	REPEAT	VERIFY

Numeric Inquiry Functions:

DIGITS	HUGE	MINEXPONENT	RADIX	TINY
EPSILON	PRECISION	MAXEXPONENT	RANGE	

Bit Functions:

BIT_SIZE	IAND	IBITS	IEOR	ISHFT
BTEST	IBCLR	IBSET	IOR	ISHFTC
				NOT

Real Data Manipulation Functions:

EXPONENT	KIND	RRSPACING	SELECTED_REAL_KIND	
FRACTION	NEAREST	SCALE	SPACING	SETEXPONENT

Array Functions:

ALL	DOTPRODUCT	MAXVAL	PRODUCT	SUM
ANY	EOSHIFT	MINLOC	RESHAPE	TRANSPOSE
ALLOCATED	LBOUND	MINVAL	SIZE	UBOUND
COUNT	MATMUL	MERGE	SHAPE	UNPACK
CSHIFT	MAXLOC	PACK	SPREAD	

Other Special Functions: PRESENT   TRANSFER   ASSOCIATED

Intrinsic Subroutines: MVBITS   RANDOM   RANDOMSEED
DATE_AND_TIME   SYSTEM_CLOCK

19.3 PROGRAM UNIT STRUCTURE

There are rules governing the general ordering of statements of different types within each program unit. Note that a 'program unit' may be either a main program, an external subprogram, a module or a block data unit (N12.1). An 'external subprogram' is either a function or a subroutine. 'Internal procedures' (N9.3) and block data are not considered here.

Statements should be ordered according to the following schemes:

(a)   Main Program, Subroutines and Functions:

> PROGRAM, SUBROUTINE or FUNCTION statement (or variant)
>
> USE statements
>
> IMPLICIT statements (not recommended)
>
> Derived-Type Definition blocks (see below)
>
> Interface blocks (see below)
>
> Type Declaration statements
>
> Executable statements
>
> END

Here, the USE statements can give access to modules to share data with other program units, or to use module procedures, or to give type definitions, or to give interfaces to procedures. Any IMPLICIT statements must follow the USE statements. For simplicity, IMPLICIT statements are disregarded below.

There may then follow derived-type definition blocks and interface blocks, if any. However, it is generally a better idea to encapsulate such blocks in modules if a derived type is used in several different program units or if a subprogram requiring an interface is called from several different program units. It is obviously most elegant, and less error-prone, for a block to be specified in detail only once and then to be accessed with USE statements wherever it is needed.

Type declaration statements can generally be in any order, but there are sometimes cases where the order is important. For example, it could be that an array dimension in one statement is given in the form of a named constant specified in a different statement which must therefore come first.

After the type declaration statements come the executable statements. The executable statements are the essence of the program: they are the only statements that make things happen and which take up time when the program executes. The executable statements are assignment statements, i/o statements, execution control statements, and memory-management statements (these categories refer to the table of statement types given in section 19.2 above).

(b)   Modules (to contain data or module subprograms)

>   MODULE statement
>
>   USE statements
>
>   Type Declaration statements
>
>   CONTAINS
>
>   Module Subprograms
>
>   END MODULE

It is imagined that any necessary type definition blocks or interface blocks are themselves modularised, as in examples (c) - (f) below, and are therefore summoned by the USE statements in this example.

If the module only specifies data there will be no module subprograms and no need for the CONTAINS statement. If there are module subprograms, then each must be a subroutine or function with a complete structure just as in (a) above. The order of the module subprograms, if there is more than one, is immaterial.

(c)   Module containing a type definition block:

>   MODULE statement
>
>   USE statements
>
> >   TYPE Definition statement
> >
> >   Type Declaration statements
> >
> >   END TYPE statement
>
>   END MODULE

Here, the indented code is the type definition block itself. A module may contain more than one type definition block. Note that a type definition block may, in principle, include within it a type declaration referring to another derived type. In other words, a structure component may itself be a data item of some other derived type. Since that other derived type would have to be accessible, a USE statement may be required.

(d)   Module containing an interface block for one external procedure:

MODULE

INTERFACE statement

    SUBROUTINE or FUNCTION statement

    Non-Executable statements

    END

END INTERFACE

END MODULE

Here, the non-executable statements should correspond exactly with the set specified within the corresponding subroutine or function, as in the list under (a) above. To avoid direct repetition, this set of statements could be given in yet another module by itself, invoked by a USE statement both in the interface block and in the subroutine or function. However, the programmer should be aware of the danger of creating a program like a maze of 'chinese boxes' if there is a large number of very small modules, and modules within modules through several generations!

(e)   Module containing a generic interface to several external procedures:

MODULE statement

INTERFACE statement with generic name

For each procedure, a block such as that indented in (d) above

END INTERFACE

END MODULE

(6) Module containing a generic interface to several module procedures:

> MODULE statement
>
> USE statements (giving access to the module procedures)
>
> INTERFACE statement (with generic name)
>
> MODULE PROCEDURE statements
>
> END INTERFACE
>
> END MODULE

19.4   PROGRAM STRUCTURE

The preceding section was about the internal structure of each program unit, and leads immediately to the question of designing the overall structure of a program as a whole. This is a very large subject that cannot be dealt with adequately here, but the following hints may be useful:

(1) Keep the main program fairly short, with a simple structure that makes the overall working of the program as clear as possible. Use subroutines freely, but avoid excessively long argument lists.

(2) Use functions to carry out self-contained tasks depending on limited sets of arguments. It is not a good idea for functions to change the values of their arguments or of any other data that they might access through modules.

(3) Use different subprograms to do different sorts of job. For example, try to do all i/o in dedicated subroutines. Any processor-dependent code, e.g. something depending on an extended character set, should also be segregated.

(4) Use modules whenever complicated sets of data need to be shared between different program units, and to contain type definition blocks, and to avoid repeating code for interface blocks. Don't use module procedures unless there is a clear advantage in so doing.

(5) When designing a large program it is beneficial to think initially about the data objects that are being dealt with. Derived-type data structures and arrays can be defined and put into modules. Functions and subroutines can be written to carry out standard tasks with that data, e.g. reading it or displaying it. The job of programming becomes primarily one of data structure design. The actual flow of program execution will then be much easier

to devise. In other words, program design should be oriented towards the data objects rather than the sequence of execution.

19.5 FINAL REMARKS

On beginning to learn Fortran 90 the immediate problems may appear to be with things like the character set, the types of data, and the technical terminology. At a later stage, the sheer size of the language can be daunting, for example if you try to remember all the intrinsic procedures and what they do. In fact very few Fortran programmers carry around in their heads the meanings of all the statements and procedures listed above in section 19.2. If you forget whether SQRT can have a complex argument, or what the arguments of VERIFY are, you are in good company, and these things can easily be looked up when you need them. The real skill of programming is rather deeper: it is a matter of understanding the power of the language, of developing a feeling for what can be achieved using powerful tools such as derived-type data structures, allocatable arrays, and a well-planned 'tree' of subroutines and functions. Programming, like politics, is the art of the possible. And, ultimately, anything is possible.

ANSWERS TO SELECTED EXERCISES

3A1   A, $, %, :, ;, and > are in the Fortran character set.

3A2   (i)   6561
       (ii)   6/12 is evaluated first, and because it is an integer expression it is truncated to zero. Answer: 4
       (iii)   2**(-1) is evaluated first, and being an integer it is truncated to zero. Since you can't divide by zero the expression is illegal.
       (iv)   Exponentiations go right-to-left. Answer: 512
       (v)   Because divisions of integers give results that are truncated to integers, the answer is 1
       (vi)   32   (vii)   3
       (viii) 2048.0   (ix)   1.0
       (x)   1.0

3A3   (i)   (a+b+c+d+e)/5.0
       (ii)   ((a**2 + b**2 + c**2)/3.0)**0.5
       (iii)   100.0*b/(a+b+c+d+e)
       (iv)   (a*b)**0.5

3A5   PROGRAM Larger
               WRITE (*,*) "Input two numbers: "
               READ (*,*) a, b
               x=a
               IF (a<b) THEN
                       x=b
               END IF
               WRITE (*,*) "The larger number is ", x
               END PROGRAM Larger

       Using a function introduced later, five lines of the above could be abbreviated to

               WRITE (*,*) "The larger number is ", MAX(a,b)

3B1   The valid names are aramaic, zhq5, p998530, top_mark, and (having no more than 31 characters) state_population_estimate_1997. Others are invalid because the currency symbol, the apostrophe and the blank space are not allowed as parts of names, and although a name may include digits it may not start with one.

```
3B3         PROGRAM Quad
            WRITE (*,*) "Input the coefficients of the quadratic: "
            READ (*,*) a, b, c
            d = b**2 - 4.0*a*c
            IF (d<0) THEN  ; WRITE (*,*) "Solutions are unreal"
              ELSE         ; d=SQRT(d)
              e=(-b+d)/(2.0*a)      ;          f=(-b-d)/(2.0*a)
              WRITE (*,*) "The solutions are: " e, f"
            END IF
            END PROGRAM Quad
```

4A1   (i)   62   (ii)   -2   (iii)   0
       (iv)   -2   (v)   520   (vi)   0

4A2   (i)   0.666   (ii)   24000.0   (iii)   10.0
       (iv)   27E8   (v)   101E-7   (vi)   1E-16

4A3   (i)   -2.6   (ii)   95.8   (iii)   5.8
       (iv)   -9.0   (v)   5.8   (vi)   -7.111
       (vii) 0.25

4A4   PROGRAM Lsd
            REAL :: x, bob,
            INTEGER :: ipounds, ishillings, ioldpence
            WRITE (*,*) "Input a sum in pounds and pence, expressed as a decimal number"
            READ (*,*) x   ;   ipounds = INT(x)
            bob = 20.0*(x-ipounds) ;   ishillings = INT(bob)
            ioldpence = NINT(12.0*(bob-ishillings))
            WRITE (*,*) "The equivalent in pounds, shillings and old pence is £",&
                    ipounds," ",ishillings,"s ",ioldpence,"d"
            END PROGRAM Lsd

4B1   (i)   Illegal (a number must include a digit)
       (ii)   Real   (iii)   Real   (iv)   Integer
       (v)   Real   (vi)   Integer
       (vii) Illegal (a real number must have a digit in the 'significand' preceding the
              exponent letter)
       (viii) Character (with no relationship to the ACHAR function!)
       (ix)   Illegal (embedded blank not allowed)
       (x)   Illegal (commas not allowed within numbers)
       (xi)   Character
       (xii) This is a legal expression but not a legal constant
       (xiii) Real   (xiv)   Real   (xv)   Character
       (xvi) Real, of kind BIG
```
```

(xvii) Complex   (xviii) Integer

(xix)   Illegal (There must be an 'exponent' after the E)

(xx)   Integer (Fortran specifies no maximum number of digits)

4B2   (i)   REAL :: power1, power2, creeper

       (ii)   INTEGER :: kappa, kappa_prime

       (iii)   REAL(KIND=3) :: finetune

       (iv)   CHARACTER(4) :: v, w

4B3   COMPLEX :: c1, c2, c3, z = (-2, 0), power = (1/3, 0)

                c1 = z**power

                c2 = (-ABS(c1), 0)

                c3 = CONJG(c1)

When a complex number is raised to a complex power, say x**y, the result is equivalent to EXP(y*LOG(x)). The LOG of a complex number is the principal value with imaginary part in the range $\pm\pi$. In the above example LOG(z), i.e. LOG (-2, 0), has the value (LOG(2), π) and so c1 is set approximately equal to (1.09, 0.63), i.e. with magnitude 1.26 and argument $\pi/3$ radians. Then, c2 is set to (-1.26, 0) and finally c3 is set to (1.09, -0.63).

4B5   (i)   The order of operator precedence is such that .NOT. is evaluated first, and then .NEQV. and .EQV. are evaluated left-to-right. The answer is .TRUE.

       (ii)   This expression is equivalent to that in (i) above, whatever the values of the variables. Answer: .TRUE.

       (iii)   .FALSE.

       (iv)   .TRUE.

4B6   (ABS(n1-n2)-ABS(m1-m2))>=ABS(k)

4B7   PROGRAM Stringy

            CHARACTER(12) :: first, second, check = "satisfactory"

            WRITE (*,*) "Type in two strings each of 12 characters"

            READ (*,*) first, second

            IF (second==check) THEN

                 WRITE (*,*) first

            ELSE

                 WRITE (*,*) second, " is unsatisfactory"

            END IF

            END PROGRAM Stringy

4B8   PROGRAM Trapezium

            REAL :: a, b, c, d

            REAL :: area1=0.0, area2=0.0, areasq1=0.0, areasq2=0.0

            WRITE (*,*) "Input the lengths of the sides of a trapezium in cyclic order"

            READ (*,*) a, b, c, d

            IF (a==c.AND.b==d) THEN

```
                      WRITE (*,*) "That is a parallelogram"
            ELSE
                      ! We don't know which pair of sides are parallel
                      IF (d/=b) areasq1 = ((a**2-c**2)**2/(d-b)**2 &
                              + a**2 + c**2 -(d-b)**2) * (b+d)**2/16.0
                      IF (a/=c) areasq2 = ((b**2-d**2)**2/(a-c)**2 &
                              + b**2 + d**2 -(a-c)**2) * (a+c)**2/16.0
                      IF (areasq1>0.0) area1 = SQRT(areasq1)
                      IF (areasq2>0.0) area2 = SQRT(areasq2)
                      IF (area1==0.0.AND.area2==0.0) WRITE (*,*) &
                              "That is not a real trapezium"
                      IF (area1==0.0.NEQV.area2==0.0) WRITE (*,*) &
                              "The area is ", area1+area2
                      IF (area1/=0.0.AND.area2/=0.0) WRITE (*,*) &
                      "Possible values for the area are ", area1, " and ", area2
            END IF
            END PROGRAM Trapezium


4B10        PROGRAM Average
            REAL :: addin, totin=0.0, endmark=9999999
            INTEGER :: numin=0
            WRITE (*,*) "Input a series of numbers, and &
                    &show when you have finished by giving 9999999"
            READ (*,*) addin
            IF (addin/=endmark) THEN
            totin = totin + addin      ;        numin = numin + 1
            END IF
            WRITE (*,*) "The average is ", totin/numin



5A1   (i)   PROGRAM Secant
            REAL :: angle, radians, cosine, secant, c = 57.29577951
            WRITE (*,*) "Input the value of an angle in degrees: "
            READ (*,*) angle
            radians = degrees / c
            cosine = COS(radians)
            IF (cosine==0.0) THEN   ;        secant = HUGE(0.0)
            ELSE                    ;        secant = 1.0/cosine
            END IF
            WRITE (*,*) "The secant of the angle is ", secant
            END PROGRAM Secant

      (ii)  .
            arcsinh = LOG(x + SQRT(x**2 + 1))

            .
```

```
                  .
            REAL :: log16, ..., ratio = LOG(16.0)
                  .
                  .
            log16 = LOG(x) / ratio
                  .
```

5A2
```
            PROGRAM Interest
            REAL :: p, r, t, permonth, factor, total
            INTEGER :: months
            WRITE (*,*) "Principal: "      ;      READ (*,*) p
            WRITE (*,*) "Rate: "           ;      READ (*,*) r
            WRITE (*,*)    "Time: "             ;        READ (*,*) t
            !       If r is the annual interest rate then
            !       the annual growth factor is 1+r
            !       So, the monthly growth factor is
            permonth = EXP(LOG(1.0+r)/12.0)
            !       The number of months is
            months = INT(12*t)
            !       So the principal grows by a factor
            factor = permonth ** months
            !       giving a total sum to the nearest penny
            total = NINT(p * factor * 100)/100.0
            WRITE (*,*) "Final sum: ", total
            END PROGRAM Interest
```

5A4
```
            CHARACTER(9) :: mname
                  .
                  .
            CALL DATE_AND_TIME (MONTH=m)
            IF (m=1 ) mname = "January"
            IF (m=2 ) mname = "February"
            IF (m=3 ) mname = "March"
            IF (m=4 ) mname = "April"
            IF (m=5 ) mname = "May"
            IF (m=6 ) mname = "June"
            IF (m=7 ) mname = "July"
            IF (m=8 ) mname = "August"
            IF (m=9 ) mname = "September"
            IF (m=10) mname = "October"
            IF (m=11) mname = "November"
            IF (m=12) mname = "December"
            WRITE (*,*) "The month is ",TRIM(mname)
```

This can be done much more elegantly using an array of character strings (chapter 7).

5A5
```
            result = LOG((COSH(x),SINH(x)))
```

267

```
5A8         PROGRAM Smalls
            REAL :: eps, thoutimes, ntens, epssq,
            eps = EPSILON(0.0)
            thoutimes = 1000.0 * eps
            ntens = 3 - NINT(LOG10(thoutimes))
            !       thoutimes is used only to make sure that the
            !       argument of LOG10 is not too small
            WRITE (*,*) "EPSILON has the order of magnitude"
            WRITE (*,*)     "10**(-",ntens,")"
            epssq = eps ** 2
            IF (epssq>TINY(0.0)) THEN
                    WRITE (*,*) "Its square is distinct from zero"
            ELSE
                    WRITE (*,*) "Its square is, in effect, zero"
            END IF
            END PROGRAM Smalls

5A9         IF (a*b<0.0) a=-a
```

6A1   (i)   11   (ii)   ""   (iii)   o
      (iv) 32   (v)   .FALSE.
      (vi) This has a processor-dependent value since the character α is not in the ASCII
            character set.
      (vii) .FALSE.   (viii) .TRUE.

6A2   (i)   "at"   (ii)   "mull"   (iii)   "g"
      (iv) "wat"

6A3
```
            initialcode = IACHAR(x(1:1))
            IF (initial code>47.AND.initialcode<58) THEN
                    x = x(2:LEN(x))
            END IF
```

Alternatively, the SCAN function does the job in one line:

```
            IF (SCAN(x(1:1),"0123456789")==1) x=x(2:LEN(x))
```

6A4   (i)   CHARACTER(0) :: null
      (ii) CHARACTER(24) :: s1, s2, s3
      (iii) CHARACTER(*) :: me = "Eisenstein"
      (iv) CHARACTER, PARAMETER :: bs = ACHAR(92)

6A5
```
            ntrailers = LEN(x) - LEN(TRIM(x))
            WRITE (*,*) TRIM(ADJUSTL(x))//REPEAT(" ",ntrailers)
```

7A1   (i)   INTEGER :: n(60) = (/(-1, i=1,30),(1, j=1,30)/)

    (ii)   CHARACTER :: c(11) = (/("abracadabra"(1:k), k=1,11)/)

    (iii)   REAL :: powers(10) = (/(3.14159265358**m, m=1,10)/)

7A2   REAL :: p1(10), p2(10), greatness(10)
            COMPLEX :: z(10)
            READ (*,*) p1
            READ (*,*) p2
            z = CMPLX(p1,p2)
            greatness = abs(z)
            WRITE (*,*) z(MAXLOC(greatness))

7A4   (i)   (/"light", "trick"/)   (ii)   (/"beach", "shore"/)
    (iii)   (/"hazel", "witch"/)   (iv)   (/"gh", "ic"/)
    (v)   (/"hi"/)
    (vi)   (/"erohs","hcaeb","lezah","hctiw","kcirt","thgil"/)

7A7   .
           .
           REAL :: x(n), y(n), z(n), r(n), theta(n), phi(n)
           .
           .
           r = SQRT(x**2 + y**2 + z**2)
           theta = ACOS(z/r)
           phi = ATAN2(y, x)
           max = MAXLOC(r)
           WRITE(*,*) "The point nearest to the origin is at:"
           WRITE(*,*) "   r = ", r(max)
           WRITE(*,*) "   theta = ", theta(max)
           WRITE(*,*) "   phi = ", phi(max)
           .
           .

7A8   WHERE (MOD(n,2)==0) n = n/2

7A9   PROGRAM Stringpull
            CHARACTER(20) :: string
            CHARACTER :: blank = " ", asterisk = "*"
            LOGICAL :: trailers= .TRUE.
            READ (*,*) string
            DO k=20,1,-1
                   IF (string(k:k) /= blank) trailers = .FALSE.

```
                    IF (string(k:k) == blank . AND .. NOT . trailers) string(k:k) = asterisk
        END DO
        WRITE (*,*) TRIM(string)
        END PROGRAM Stringpull




8A2     SELECT CASE (IACHAR(string(1:1)))
                CASE(97:121)
                        string(1:1) = ACHAR(IACHAR(string(1:1)) - 32)
                CASE(65:90)
                        CONTINUE
                CASE(32)
                        string = string(2:)
                CASE DEFAULT
                        string(1:1) = "X"
        END SELECT

8A3     initialcode = IACHAR(string(1:1))
        IF (initialcode >= 97 . AND . initialcode <= 121) THEN
                string(1:1) = ACHAR(initialcode - 32)
        ELSE IF (initialcode >= 65 . AND . initialcode <= 90) THEN
                CONTINUE
        ELSE IF (initialcode == 32) THEN
                string = string(2:)
        ELSE
                string(1:1) = "X"
        END IF

8A4     INTEGER :: n, nsr, ncr
        REAL :: en, ensr, encr, eps = EPSILON(1.0)
        LOGICAL :: square = .FALSE., cube = .FALSE.
                .
                .

        en = REAL(n)   ;   ensr = SQRT(en)   ;   encr = en**(1.0/3.0)
        IF (ensr-INT(ensr) < eps) square = .TRUE.
        IF (encr-INT(encr) < eps) cube = .TRUE.
        IF (square . AND .. NOT . cube) THEN
                WRITE (*,*) "The number is a perfect square but not a perfect cube"
        ELSE IF (cube . AND .. NOT . square) THEN
                WRITE (*,*) "The number is a perfect cube but not a perfect square"
        END IF
```

```
8B1          nfac = 1
             DO j = 1, n
             nfac = nfac * j
             END DO

8B3          n = LEN(string)   ;   int = 0
             DO j = n, 1, -1
             int = int + (IACHAR(string(j:j) - 48) * 10**(n-j)
             END DO

8B6          PROGRAM Vowels
             CHARACTER(30) :: word
             CHARACTER :: v(5) = (/"a", "e", "i", "o", "u"/)
             READ (*,*) word
             DO k = 1, LEN_TRIM(word)
                    DO m = 1, 5
                          IF (word(k:k) == v(m)) THEN
                                  WRITE (*,*) v(m)
                                  EXIT
                          END IF
                    END DO
             END DO
             END PROGRAM Vowels



9A1          REAL FUNCTION Sphere (radius)
             REAL :: radius, fourthirdspi = 3.14159265358 * 4.0 / 3.0
             Sphere = fourthirdspi * radius * radius * radius
             END FUNCTION Sphere

9A2          COMPLEX FUNCTION Arcsine (z)
             COMPLEX :: z, eye = (0.0, 1.0)
             Arcsine = -eye * LOG(eye*z + SQRT(1.0 - z*z))
             END FUNCTION Arcsine

9B2          SUBROUTINE Order (r1, r2, r3)
             REAL :: r1, r2, r3, r(3), ar(3)
             r = (/r1, r2, r3/)
             ar = ABS(r)
             r1 = r(MAXLOC(ar))
             r3 = r(MINLOC(ar))
             r2 = SUM(r) - r1 - r3
             END SUBROUTINE Order
```

```
9B3        SUBROUTINE Rescale (average, array)
           REAL :: average, factor, array(*)
           factor = average / SUM(array)
           array = array * factor
           END SUBROUTINE Rescale


9B4        REAL FUNCTION Scalarise (x)
           REAL :: x(*)
           Scalarise = x(1)
           END FUNCTION Scalarise


9B5        CHARACTER FUNCTION Pick (string)
           CHARACTER(*) :: string
           INTEGER :: n, k   ;   REAL :: x
           n = LEN(string)  ;   CALL RANDOM (x)  ;    k = 1 + INT(x*REAL(n))
           Pick = string(k:k)
           END FUNCTION Pick




10A1       INTEGER FUNCTION Luck (i)
           REAL :: x
           INTEGER :: n1, n2
           Luck = 0
           DO
           CALL RANDOM(x)   ;   n1 = 1 + INT(6.0 * x)
           CALL RANDOM(x)   ;   n2 = 1 + INT(6.0 * x)
           Luck = Luck + n1 + n2  ;        IF (n1 /= n2) EXIT
           END DO
           END FUNCTION Luck

10A2       MERGE(TSOURCE=.TRUE., FSOURCE=.FALSE., MASK=(n==1))




11A1       MODULE Year
           CHARACTER(9) :: daynames(7) = &
           (/"Monday","Tuesday","Wednesday","Thursday","Friday","Saturday","Sunday"/)
           CHARACTER(9) :: monthnames(12) =
           (/"January","February","March","April","May","June", &
           "July","August","September","October","November","December"/)
           INTEGER :: daynumbers (12) = (/31,28,31,30,31,30,31,31,30,31,30,31/)
           END MODULE Year

           USE Year, ONLY : monthnames
```

```
11A2        MODULE Constants
            REAL, PARAMETER :: pi = 2.0 * ASIN(1.0)
            REAL, PARAMETER :: e = EXP(1.0)
            INTEGER, PARAMETER :: ipow2(20) = (/(2**k, k=1, 20)/)
            END MODULE Constants


11A4/5      MODULE Sheet
            CHARACTER(12) :: strings(30, 10)
            CHARACTER :: contents(30,10)
                    !           'contents' is blank if the corresponding cell is empty,
                    !                   = "c" if it contains a word
                    !                   = "i" if it contains an integer
                    !                   = "r" if it contains a real number
            CONTAINS
                    INTEGER FUNCTION Number (irow, icolumn)
                    INTEGER :: irow, icolumn, n
                    INTEGER :: ivalue, idefault = 0
                    IF (contents(irow, icolumn) = "i") THEN
                            READ (strings(irow, icolumn), "I12") n
                            Number = n
                    ELSE
                            Number = idefault
                    END IF
                    END FUNCTION Number
            END MODULE Sheet




12A1        RECURSIVE REAL FUNCTION Sinpow(n, x1, x2) RESULT (v)
            INTEGER :: n
            REAL :: x1, x2, value
            SELECT CASE (n)
                    CASE (3:)
                            value = Sinpow(n-2, x1, x2) * REAL(n-1) / REAL(n)
                            value = value - SIN(x1)**(n-1) * COS(x1) / REAL(n) &
                                    + SIN(x2)**(n-1) * COS(x2) / REAL(n)
                    CASE (2)
                            value = 0.5*(x1-x2) - 0.25*SIN(2.0*x1) + 0.25*SIN(2.0*x2)
                    CASE (1)
                            value = COS(x2) - COS(x1)
            END SELECT
            v = value
            END FUNCTION Sinpow
```

```
12B2        INTEGER FUNCTION Mean (n1, n2, n3, n4, n5, n6, n7, n8, n9, n10, n11, n12)
            INTEGER, OPTIONAL :: n1, n2, n3, n4, n5, n6, n7, n8, n9, n10, n11, n12
            INTEGER :: nargs = 0, nsum = 0
            IF (PRESENT(n1))  THEN ; nsum = nsum + n1  ; nargs = nargs + 1 ; END IF
            IF (PRESENT(n2))  THEN ; nsum = nsum + n2  ; nargs = nargs + 1 ; END IF
            IF (PRESENT(n3))  THEN ; nsum = nsum + n3  ; nargs = nargs + 1 ; END IF
            IF (PRESENT(n4))  THEN ; nsum = nsum + n4  ; nargs = nargs + 1 ; END IF
            IF (PRESENT(n5))  THEN ; nsum = nsum + n5  ; nargs = nargs + 1 ; END IF
            IF (PRESENT(n6))  THEN ; nsum = nsum + n6  ; nargs = nargs + 1 ; END IF
            IF (PRESENT(n7))  THEN ; nsum = nsum + n7  ; nargs = nargs + 1 ; END IF
            IF (PRESENT(n8))  THEN ; nsum = nsum + n8  ; nargs = nargs + 1 ; END IF
            IF (PRESENT(n9))  THEN ; nsum = nsum + n9  ; nargs = nargs + 1 ; END IF
            IF (PRESENT(n10)) THEN ; nsum = nsum + n10 ; nargs = nargs + 1 ; END IF
            IF (PRESENT(n10)) THEN ; nsum = nsum + n11 ; nargs = nargs + 1 ; END IF
            IF (PRESENT(n12)) THEN ; nsum = nsum + n12 ; nargs = nargs + 1 ; END IF
            Mean = NINT(REAL(nsum)/REAL(nargs))
            END FUNCTION Mean
```

The above is not particularly elegant and it requires an interface to be provided. A much more elegant version, not needing an interface, could be written if the argument were an assumed-size array instead of a set of scalars. This makes a good supplementary exercise! However, the function would then have to be called with an array name or an array constructor as the actual argument, i.e. the function would have to be referenced by a statement like

```
        klose = Mean((/5,4,8,6,9/)
```

rather than having Mean(5,4,8,6,9).

```
12B4        FUNCTION Cross (v1, v2)
            REAL :: Cross(3), v1(3), v2(3)
            REAL :: x(3) = (/1.0,0.0,0.0/), y(3) = (/0.0,1.0,0.0/), z(3) = (/0.0,0.0,1.0/)
            Cross = x * (v1(2)*v2(3) - v1(3)*v2(2)) &
                  + y * (v1(3)*v2(1) - v1(1)*v2(3)) &
                  + z * (v1(1)*v2(2) - v1(2)*v2(1))
            END FUNCTION Cross
```

```
12B6        REAL FUNCTION Geomean (a, b)
            REAL :: a, b, geo
            geo = SQRT(ABS(a*b))
            IF (a*b < 0.0) geo = -geo
            Geomean = geo
            END FUNCTION Geomean
```

```
        INTERFACE OPERATOR (.X.)
                REAL FUNCTION Geomean (a, b)
                REAL :: a, b
                END FUNCTION Geomean
        END INTERFACE
```

If a and b are of opposite sign, this function copes by defining a 'geometric mean' with a negative value.

13A1   COMPLEX :: xbanks(30)

13A2   LOGICAL, OPTIONAL :: check1, check2, check3

13A3   REAL, SAVE :: matrix_name(20, 20), vector_name(45)

13A4   CHARACTER :: thread(*)

13A5   INTEGER, PARAMETER :: squares(0:99) = (/k**2, k=0,5/)

13A6   CHARACTER(12) :: julius(:,:)

13A7   REAL :: inverse_squares(-100:100) = (/1.0/REAL(m**2), m=-100,100/)

13A8   CHARACTER(*), PARAMETER :: moniker = "Abigail Sara Lemoine"

14A1   (i)   TYPE Species
                    CHARACTER(12) :: name
                    REAL :: weight, extent, height
                    INTEGER :: legs
                    LOGICAL :: marine
                END TYPE Species

        (ii)   TYPE (Species) :: panda, shark, whale, butterfly

        (iii)   TYPE (Species) :: big_cats(15)

        (iv)   whale = Species("cetus_____", 4578.0, 12.71, 2.86, 0, .TRUE.)

        (v)   big_cats(5) = Species("snow_leopard", 46.0, 1.35, 0.69, 4, .TRUE.)

```
```

(vi)   whale%weight = 4287.0

(v)   big_cats(5)%marine = .FALSE.

14A2   (i)   TYPE Vector
                    REAL :: x1, x2, x3, x4, x5, x6, x7, x8, x9, x10, &
                            x11, x12, x13, x14, x15, x16, x17, x18, x19, x20
                    INTEGER :: length
                END TYPE Vector

        (ii)   TYPE (Array) :: qwt = Array(0.0, 0.0, 0.0, 3)

        (iii)   qwt%x2 = 4.12.

14B1   (i)   TYPE Person
                    CHARACTER(40) :: name
                    INTEGER :: nbirthday(3)
                END TYPE Person

        (ii)   TYPE Couple
                    TYPE (Person) :: husband, wife
                    INTEGER :: nmarriage(3)
                END TYPE Couple

        (iii)   TYPE Family
                    TYPE (Couple) :: parents
                    TYPE (Person) :: children(8)
                END TYPE Family

        (iv)   robinson%parents%nmarriage(3)

                robinson%parents%wife%name

14C2   TYPE Fuzzy
                    REAL :: evalue   !   expectation value
                    REAL :: error   !   statistical error
                END TYPE Fuzzy

                TYPE (Fuzzy) FUNCTION Addition (x, y)
                TYPE (Fuzzy) :: x, y, a
                a = Fuzzy(x%evalue + y%evalue, SQRT(x%error**2 + y%error**2))
                Addition = a
                END FUNCTION Addition

                INTERFACE OPERATOR (+)
                    TYPE (Fuzzy) FUNCTION Addition (x, y)
                    TYPE (Fuzzy) :: x, y

```
                    END FUNCTION Addition
                    END INTERFACE

14C4                SUBROUTINE Intchar(n, string)
                    INTEGER, INTENT (OUT) :: n
                    CHARACTER(*), INTENT (IN) :: string
                    IF (LEN(string)==0) THEN
                            n=0
                    ELSE
                            n=IACHAR(string(1:1))
                    END IF
                    END SUBROUTINE Intchar

                    INTERFACE ASSIGNMENT (=)
                            SUBROUTINE Intchar(n, string)
                            INTEGER, INTENT (OUT) :: n
                            CHARACTER(*), INTENT (IN) :: string
                            END SUBROUTINE Intchar
                    END INTERFACE
```

15A1
```
                    chessboard = RESHAPE( SHAPE=(/8,8/), &
                            SOURCE=(/six_rows,(.TRUE.,.FALSE., k=1,8)/))
```

15A2   (i)   (/"a","o","u"/)   (ii)   (/"e","i"/)   (iii)   (/4,5/)
        (iv)   (/"o","e"/)   (v)   (/"ae","oe","ue"/)

15A3   (i)   COMPLEX, ALLOCATABLE :: cmatrix (:,:)
                CHARACTER(12), ALLOCATABLE :: rivernames (:)

        (ii)   ALLOCATE (cmatrix(4,4))
                ALLOCATE (rivernames(200))

        (iii)   IF (ALLOCATED(rivernames)) DEALLOCATE(rivernames)
                ALLOCATE (rivernames(150))

15A4   ALLOCATE (characters(LEN(string))
                characters = (/(string(k:k), k=1, LEN(string))/)

15B1   (i)   (/1,1901,1,0/)   (ii)   (/12,150,20,200/)
        (iii)   (/1,50,20,200/)   (iv)   (/1,2050,20,199/)
        (v)   (/50,20,200/)   (vi)   (/2050,20,199/)
        (vii)   1   (viii) 40000
        (ix)   3   (x)   2
```
```

```
15C2            FUNCTION Snakehead(vector)
                TYPE (Link), POINTER :: Snakehead, beta, gamma
                TYPE (Link), TARGET :: alpha
                REAL :: vector(*)
                alpha%x = vector(1)
                beta => alpha
                DO i, i = 2, SIZE(vector)
                        ALLOCATE (gamma)
                        beta%nextlink => gamma
                        gamma%x = vector(i)
                        NULLIFY (gamma%nextlink)
                        beta => gamma
                END DO
                Snakehead => alpha
                END FUNCTION Snakehead
```

16A1   (i)   Technically this is not a format specification, it is a character string which is a format 'specifier'. But

        (ii)   (F10.4) is a valid format specification. A format specification always includes parentheses around it.

        (iii)   F10.4 is a valid edit descriptor, but not a format specification. The point is that should control all the data that passes when an i/o statement is executed, and in general will contain a list of edit descriptors within parentheses.

        (iv, v) 8(F10.4) and 8F10.4 are equivalent, representing a set of eight identical edit descriptors.

        (vi)   (8F10.4) is a valid format specification.

        (vii)   ((F10.4)) is illegal

        (viii) (F10.6,I8) is a valid format specification.

        (ix)   () is a valid format specification, representing an empty i/o list. It could be used to skip over an input record or to write out an empty record. However, the slash edit descriptor (/) is usually used for this purpose.

        (x)   "3()" is invalid. For three empty records, the format specifier "(3/)" could be used.

16A2   (8X, I4, 3(13X, F7.2), 8X)

16B1   WRITE (*, FMT="(I2,10X,B7,10X,O3)") n, n, n

16B2   (i)   T F   T F   T F
                (this has one blank at the start and two blanks at the end)

        (ii)   Caus   of deat
                (no trailing blanks)

        (iii)   1.4142 1.7321
                (one leading blank but no trailing blanks)

        (iv)   101000 001600

        (v)   0.1414E+01 0.1600E+04
                (two leading blanks)

        (vi)   FATE

16B3   WRITE (*, FMT="(A,TL1,"_",:," ")") (/caption(k:k), k=1, LEN(caption)/)

17A1   (i)   OPEN (UNIT=7, STATUS="SCRATCH")

        (ii)   OPEN (UNIT=3, STATUS="OLD", POSITION ="APPEND", &
                    ACTION="WRITE")

        (iii)   OPEN (UNIT=2, FILE="s_sheet_45", RECL=256, ACCESS="DIRECT", &
                    FORM="FORMATTED")
                CLOSE (UNIT=2, STATUS="DELETE")

17A2   (i)   INQUIRE (UNIT=5, RECL=max)
                OPEN (UNIT=5, FILE="savedata", STATUS="NEW", &
                        ACCESS="DIRECT", RECL=max)
                DO k=1 20
                WRITE (UNIT=5, REC=k) datasave(k)
                END DO

        (ii)   CHARACTER(5) :: i1,i2
                INTEGER :: k1, k2
                        .
                        .
                        .
                READ (UNIT=1, ADVANCE="NO", FMT="(2A5)") i1, i2
                READ (i1, FMT="(I5)") k1
                READ (i2, FMT="(I5)") k2

This reads ten characters from unit 1, and then reads the strings i1 and i2 as internal files to interpret them as integers.

17A3
```
CHARACTER(*) FUNCTION Stitch (c1, c2)
CHARACTER(*) :: c1, c2
INTEGER :: lentot = LEN(c1) + LEN(c2)
CHARACTER(lentot) :: c
WRITE (c, FMT="(A)") c1, c2
Stitch = c
END FUNCTION Stitch
```

18A1
```
INTEGER FUNCTION Logpack(data)
LOGICAL :: data(32)
INTEGER :: i
DO k = 0, 31
IF(.NOT.data(k)) THEN
        i = IBCLR(i,k)
ELSE
        i = IBSET(i,k)
END IF
END DO
Logpack = i
END FUNCTION Logpack
```

FORTRAN 90 STATEMENTS

ALLOCATE	Dynamically allocates memory to arrays or pointers.
ALLOCATABLE	Declares an array to be allocatable.
Arithmetic IF	A switchable GO TO with three alternative statement labels.
ASSIGN	Assigns a statement label to an integer variable.
Assigned GO TO	GO TO with a variable instead of an explicit statement label.
Assignment Statement	= Gives a value to a variable.
BACKSPACE	Moves backwards by one i/o record.
BLOCK DATA	Introduces a block data subprogram.
CALL	Calls a subroutine.
CASE	Specifies a range of values for a case expression.
CHARACTER	Declares a character variable.
CHARACTER FUNCTION	Starts a character-valued function.
CLOSE	Closes an i/o unit.
Comment	! For program annotation.
COMMON	Declares data to be accessible from more than one program unit.
COMPLEX	Declares data of complex type.
COMPLEX FUNCTION	Starts a complex-valued function.
Computed GO TO	A switchable GO TO with several alternative statement labels.
CONTAINS	Heads a set of module procedures.
CONTINUE	Dummy statement

CYCLE	Jump to the bottom of a DO loop
DATA	Gives values to variables
DEALLOCATE	Deallocates a pointer or an allocatable array.
DIMENSION	Declares the shape of an array.
DO	Starts a DO loop.
DOUBLE PRECISION	Declares higher-precision real variables.
DOUBLE PRECISION FUNCTION	Starts a function of double-precision real value.
ELSE	Final catch-all block within an IF construct.
ELSE IF	Alternative block within an IF construct.
ELSEWHERE	Introduces default assignments within a WHERE construct.
END	Terminates a program unit.
END BLOCK DATA	End of a BLOCK DATA unit.
END DO	End of a DO loop.
END IF	End of an IF construct.
END INTERFACE	End of an interface block.
END FUNCTION	End of a function subprogram.
END MODULE	End of a module.
END PROGRAM	End of the main program.
END SELECT	End of a CASE selection block.
END SUBROUTINE	End of a subroutine.
END TYPE	End of a derived-type definition block.
END WHERE	End of a WHERE construct.
ENDFILE	Writes an end-of-file record.

ENTRY	Alternative entry point to a procedure.
EQUIVALENCE	Declares more than one name for one area of memory.
EXIT	Jump out of a DO loop.
EXTERNAL	Declares that a procedure is not intrinsic.
FORMAT	A labelled statement containing an i/o format specification.
FUNCTION	Starts a function subprogram.
GO TO	Jump to another statement.
IF	Conditional statement
IF...THEN	Introduces a block of conditional statements
IMPLICIT	Changes the initial-letter data type convention.
IMPLICIT NONE	Withdraws the initial-letter data type convention.
INCLUDE	Insert here a file of additional Fortran statements.
INQUIRE	I/o unit general status inquiry.
INTEGER	Declares data to be of integer type.
INTEGER FUNCTION	Starts an integer-valued function.
INTENT	Declares if a dummy argument is for incoming or outgoing data.
INTERFACE	Start of an interface block.
INTRINSIC	Declares that a function is intrinsic to Fortran 90.
LOGICAL	Declares data to be of logical type.
LOGICAL FUNCTION	Starts a logical-valued function.
MODULE	Starts a module.
MODULE PROCEDURE	Used to list module procedures in a generic interface block.
NAMELIST	Specifies data to be included together in a NAMELIST group.
NULLIFY	Disassociates a pointer.

OPEN	Opens an i/o unit or file.
OPTIONAL	Declares that a dummy argument's presence is optional.
PARAMETER	Declares a named constant, i.e. a data item of fixed value.
PAUSE	Causes program execution to pause.
POINTER	Declares a data item to be a pointer.
Pointer Assignment	=> Points a pointer to a target.
PRINT	Writes data to a default o/p unit.
PRIVATE	Indicates data not accessible from outside a module.
PROGRAM	Starts the main program.
PUBLIC	Indicates data accessible from outside a module.
READ	General data input statement.
REAL	Declares data to be of real type.
REAL FUNCTION	Starts a function whose value is to be of real type.
RECURSIVE FUNCTION	Starts a function which may refer to itself.
RECURSIVE SUBROUTINE	Starts a subroutine which may call itself.
RETURN	Alternative point of exit from a procedure.
REWIND	Go back to the first record of an i/o file.
SAVE	Declare subprogram data that is to be retained on return.
SELECT CASE	Start a CASE construct, stating what the case expression is.
SEQUENCE	Declare complicated data to be 'sequenced' in memory.
Statement Function	A sort of one-line internal function.
STOP	Halts execution immediately.
SUBROUTINE	Start a subroutine.
TARGET	Declare that a data item may be the target of a pointer.

Type Declaration Statement	::	General data-declaration statement.

TYPE (declaration)   Declares data to be of a specified derived type.

TYPE (definition)   Starts a derived-type definition block.

TYPE ... FUNCTION   Starts a function whose value is of a derived type.

USE   Summons the contents of a module.

WHERE   Starts a masked assignment statement or a WHERE construct.

WRITE   General data o/p statement.

Appendix B

INTRINSIC PROCEDURES

The following is a list of Fortran's intrinsic functions and subroutines. It is a complete list except for what is listed in appendix C. Data types are indicated by the following abbreviations:

I Integer
R Real
Z Complex
C Character
S Character string
L Logical

Name	Argument type	Result type
ABS(A)	R, I or Z	R or I
ACHAR(I)	I	C
ACOS(X)	R	R
ADJUSTL(STRING)	C	C
ADJUSTR(STRING)	C	C
AIMAG(Z)	Z	R
AINT(A,KIND)	R	R
ALL(MASK,DIM)	MASK=L, DIM=I	L
ALLOCATED(ARRAY)	Array	L
ANINT(A,KIND)	R	R
ANY(MASK,DIM)	MASK=L, DIM=I	L
ASIN(X)	R	R

ASSOCIATED(POINTER,TARGET)	POINTER= pointer, TARGET = anything	L
ATAN(X)	R	R
ATAN2(Y,X)	X=R, Y=R	R
BIT_SIZE(I)	I	I
BTEST(I,POS)	I's	L
CEILING(A)	R	I
CHAR(I,KIND)	I	C
CMPLX(X,Y,KIND)	X=I, R or Z, Y=I or R, MOLD=R	Z
CONJG(Z)	Z	Z
COS(X)	R or Z	R or Z
COSH(X)	R	R
COUNT(MASK,DIM)	MASK=L, DIM=I	I
CSHIFT(ARRAY,DIM,SHIFT)	ARRAY=Any array, DIM=I, SHIFT=I	As ARRAY
DATE_AND_TIME(ALL,COUNT, MSECOND,SECOND,MINUTE, HOUR, DAY,MONTH, YEAR,ZONE)	I's	n/a
DIGITS(X)	I or R	I
DIM(X,Y)	X,Y=I or X,Y=R	I or R
DOTPRODUCT (VECTOR_A,VECTOR_B)	Both I, R, Z or L	I, R, Z or L
EOSHIFT(ARRAY,DIM, SHIFT, BOUNDARY)	ARRAY=any array, DIM=I, SHIFT=I, BOUNDARY=ARRAY	As ARRAY
EPSILON(X)	R	R
EXP(X)	R or Z	R or Z

EXPONENT(X)	R	I
FLOOR(A)	R	I
FRACTION(X)	R	R
HUGE(X)	I or R	I or R
IACHAR(C)	C	I
IAND(I,J)	I's	I
IBCLR(I,POS)	I's	I
IBITS(I,POS,LEN)	I's	I
IBSET(I,POS)	I's	I
ICHAR(C)	C	I
IEOR(I,J)	I's	I
INDEX(STRING,SUBSTRING,BACK)	STRING=C, SUBSTRING=C, BACK=L	I
INT(A,KIND)	I, R or Z	I
IOR(I,J)	I's	I
ISHFT(I,SHIFT)	I's	I
ISHFTC(I,SHIFT,SIZE)	I's	I
KIND(X)	Any	I
LBOUND(ARRAY,DIM)	ARRAY=any array, DIM=I	I
LEN(STRING)	C	I
LEN_TRIM(STRING)	C	I
LGE(STRING_A,STRING_B)	C's	L
LGT(STRING_A,STRING_B)	C's	L
LLE(STRING_A,STRING_B)	C's	L

LLT(STRING_A,STRING_B)	C's	L
LOG(X)	R or Z	R or Z
LOGICAL (L,KIND)	L=L, KIND=I	L
LOG10(X)	R	R
MATMUL(MATRIX_A,MATRIX_B)	Both I, R, Z or L	I, R, Z or L
MAX(A1,A2,A3,...)	All I's or all R's	I or R
MAXEXPONENT(X)	R	I
MAXLOC(ARRAY,MASK)	ARRAY=I or R, MASK=L	I
MAXVAL(ARRAY,DIM,MASK)	ARRAY=I or R, DIM=I, MASK=L	I or R
MERGE(TSOURCE, FSOURCE,MASK)	TSOURCE same as FSOURCE MASK=I	As TSOURCE
MIN(A1,A2,A3,...)	All I or all R	I or R
MINEXPONENT(X)	R	I
MINLOC(ARRAY,MASK)	ARRAY=I or R, MASK=L	I
MINVAL(ARRAY,DIM,MASK)	ARRAY=I or R, DIM=I, MASK=L	I or R
MOD(A,P)	A and P both I or both R	I or R
MODULO(A,P)	A and P both I or both R	I or R
MVBITS(FROM,FROMPOS, LEN,TO,TOPOS)	I's	n/a
NEAREST(X,S)	X=R, S=R	R
NINT(A,KIND)	R	I
NOT(I)	I	I
PACK(ARRAY,MASK,VECTOR)	ARRAY=Any array, MASK=L, VECTOR=same as ARRAY	As ARRAY

PRECISION(X)	R or Z	I
PRESENT(A)	Context-dependent	L
PRODUCT(ARRAY, DIM,MASK)	ARRAY=I, R or Z, DIM=I, MASK=L	I, R or Z
RADIX(X)	I or R	I
RANDOM(HARVEST)	R	R
RANDOMSEED(SIZE,PUT,GET)	I's	n/a
RANGE(X)	I, R or Z	I
REAL(A,KIND)	A=I,R or Z	R
REPEAT(STRING,NCOPIES)	STRING=C, NCOPIES=I	C
RESHAPE(SHAPE,SOURCE, PAD,ORDER)	SHAPE=I, SOURCE=any array, PAD=same as SOURCE, ORDER=I	As SHAPE
RRSPACING(X)	R	R
SCALE(X,I)	X=R, I=I	R
SCAN(STRING,SET,BACK)	STRING=C, SET=C, BACK=L	I
SELECTED_INTEGER_KIND(R)	I	I
SELECTED_REAL_KIND(P,R)	I's	I
SETEXPONENT(X,I)	X=R, I=I	R
SHAPE(SOURCE)	Any type	I
SIGN(A,B)	A,B both I or both R	I or R
SIN(X)	R or Z	R or Z
SINH(X)	R	R
SIZE(ARRAY,DIM)	ARRAY=any array, DIM=I	I
SPACING(X)	R	R
SPREAD(SOURCE,DIM,NCOPIES)	SOURCE=any type, DIM=I,	As SOURCE

	NCOPIES=I	
SQRT(X)	R or Z	R or Z
SUM(ARRAY,DIM,MASK)	ARRAY=I, R or Z, DIM=I, MASK=L	As ARRAY
SYSTEM_CLOCK(COUNT, COUNT_RATE,COUNT_MAX)	I's	n/a
TAN(X)	R	R
TANH(X)	R	R
TINY(X)	R	R
TRANSFER(SOURCE,MOLD,SIZE)	SOURCE=any, MOLD=any, SIZE=I	As MOLD
TRANSPOSE(MATRIX)	Any	As MATRIX
TRIM(STRING)	C	C
UBOUND(ARRAY,DIM)	ARRAY=any array, DIM=I	I
UNPACK(VECTOR,MASK,FIELD)	VECTOR=any, MASK=L, FIELD=same as vector	As VECTOR
VERIFY(STRING,SET,BACK)	STRING=C, SET=C, BACK=I	I

Appendix C

INTRINSIC PROCEDURES: 'SPECIFIC' NAMES

This list gives several type-specific names for functions. Strictly speaking these names are inessential since the functions can always be invoked through the generic names in appendix B. In addition, the "double precision" functions DBLE and DPROD have been included in this list. Argument and result types follow the abbreviations listed at the top of appendix B, with the addition of D for "double precision".

Name	Generic name	Argument type	Result type
ALOG(X)	LOG	R	R
ALOG10(X)	LOG10	R	R
AMAX0(A1,A2,A3,..)	REAL(MAX)	I's	R
AMAX1(A1,A2,A3,..)	MAX	R's	R
AMIN0(A1,A2,A3,..)	REAL(MIN)	I's	R
AMIN1(A1,A2,A3,..)	MIN	R's	R
AMOD(A,P)	MOD	A=R, P=R	R
CABS(A)	ABS	Z	R
CCOS(X)	COS	Z	Z
CEXP(X)	EXP	Z	Z
CLOG(X)	LOG	Z	Z
CSIN(X)	SIN	Z	Z
CSQRT(X)	SQRT	Z	Z
DABS(A)	ABS	D	D
DACOS(X)	ACOS	D	D
DASIN(X)	ASIN	D	D
DATAN(X)	ATAN	D	D
DATAN2(Y,X)	ATAN2	Y=D, X=D	D
DBLE(A)		I,R or Z	D
DCOS(X)	COS	D	D
DCOSH(X)	COSH	D	D
DDIM(X,Y)	DIM	X=D, Y=D	D
DEXP(X)	EXP	D	D
DINT(A)	AINT	D	D
DLOG(X)	LOG	D	D
DLOG10(X)	LOG10	D	D
DMAX1(A1,A2,A3,..)	MAX	D's	D
DMIN1(A1,A2,A3,..)	MIN	D's	D

DMOD(A,P)	MOD	A=D, P=D	D
DNINT(A)	ANINT	D	I
DPROD(X,Y)		X=R, Y=R	D
DSIGN(A,B)	SIGN	A=D, B=D	D
DSIN(X)	SIN	D	D
DSINH(X)	SINH	D	D
DSQRT(X)	SQRT	D	D
DTAN(X)	TAN	D	D
DTANH(X)	TANH	D	D
FLOAT(A)	REAL	I	R
IABS(A)	ABS	I	I
IDIM(X,Y)	DIM	X=I, Y=I	I
IDINT(A)	INT	D	I
IDNINT(A)	NINT	D	I
IFIX(A)	INT	R	I
ISIGN(A,B)	SIGN	A=I, B=I	I
MAX0(A1,A2,A3,..)	MAX	I's	I
MAX1(A1,A2,A3,..)	INT(MAX)	R's	I
MIN0(A1,A2,A3,..)	MIN	I's	I
MIN1(A1,A2,A3,..)	INT(MIN)	R's	I
SNGL(A)	REAL	D	R

Appendix D

ARGUMENT KEYWORDS IN INTRINSIC PROCEDURES

A	Numerical argument in many numeric functions; also used as the argument of PRESENT to represent an optional argument of an arbitrary procedure.
ALL	Array of results returned from DATE_AND_TIME.
ARRAY	Array argument in ALLOCATED, CSHIFT, LBOUND, UBOUND, LBOUND, EOSHIFT, MAXLOC, MAXVAL, MINLOC, MINVAL, PACK, PRODUCT and SUM.
A1,A2,A3,...	Numerical arguments in MAX and MIN.
B	Second numerical argument in SIGN.
BACK	Indicates reverse scan in INDEX, SCAN, and VERIFY.
BOUNDARY	Infilling data value used in EOSHIFT.
C	Single character argument in IACHAR and ICHAR.
COUNT	Clock counts in DATE_AND_TIME and SYSTEM_CLOCK.
COUNT_RATE	Counts per second in SYSTEM_CLOCK.
COUNT_MAX	Maximum number of counts in SYSTEM_CLOCK.
DAY	Day of the month in DATE_AND_TIME.
DIM	Dimension parameter used in many array functions.
FIELD	Default data array for UNPACK.
FROM	Source integer in MVBITS subroutine.
FROMPOS	Source bit position in MVBITS.
FSOURCE	Array for the 'false' option in MERGE.
GET	Integers for re-initialising RANDOMSEED.

294

HARVEST	Real argument required for RANDOM.
HOUR	Hours in DATE_AND_TIME.
I	Integer character code in ACHAR and CHAR, exponent in SCALE and SETEXPONENT, and bitstream integer in the bit manipulation functions.
KIND	Specifies the kind parameter for data.
L	Logical argument in LOGICAL (for converting between logical data of different kinds).
LEN	Number of bits moved by MVBITS subroutine.
MASK	Logical array argument used in several array functions.
MATRIX	Argument of TRANSPOSE.
MATRIX_A	Matrix in MATMUL.
MATRIX_B	Matrix in MATMUL
MINUTE	Minutes in DATE_AND_TIME.
MOLD	Indicates desired data type in TRANSFER.
MONTH	Month number in DATE_AND_TIME.
MSECOND	Milliseconds in DATE_AND_TIME.
NCOPIES	Number of repeated string concatenations in REPEAT, and additional array dimensionality in SPREAD.
ORDER	Ordering of elements in RESHAPE.
P	Divisor in the MOD and MODULO functions, and precision parameter in SELECTED_REAL_KIND.
PAD	Array for padding-out in RESHAPE.
POINTER	Argument of ASSOCIATED.
PUT	Integers to initialise RANDOMSEED.
R	Numerical range parameter in SELECTED_INT_KIND and SELECTED_REAL_KIND.

S	Number whose sign indicates direction for NEAREST.
SECOND	Seconds in DATE_AND_TIME.
SET	String of check characters in SCAN and VERIFY.
SIZE	Array size for TRANSFER, and number of integers used in RANDOMSEED.
SHIFT	Number of places that array elements are shifted in CSHIFT and EOSHIFT.
SOURCE	Array of data for TRANSFER, SHAPE, RESHAPE, and SPREAD.
STRING	Character string in character functions.
STRING_A	Character string in LGE, LGT, LLE and LLT.
STRING_B	Character string in LGE, LGT, LLE and LLT.
SUBSTRING	Character substring in INDEX.
TARGET	Argument of ASSOCIATED.
TO	Target integer in MVBITS subroutine.
TOPOS	Target bit position in MVBITS.
TSOURCE	Array for the 'true' option in MERGE.
VECTOR	Supplementary data array for PACK.
VECTOR_A	Vector in DOTPRODUCT.
VECTOR_B	Vector in DOTPRODUCT.
X	Commonly used as a numerical argument in mathematical and numerical functions.
Y	A second numerical argument.
YEAR	Gregorian calendar year in DATE_AND_TIME.
Z	Complex numerical argument in AIMAG and CONJG
ZONE	Time zone, measured in minutes ahead of Coordinated Universal Time, in DATE_AND_TIME.

Appendix E

I/O EDIT DESCRIPTORS

DATA EDIT DESCRIPTORS

These are applicable to generalised data (G), integers (I, B, O and Z), real numbers (F, E, EN, and D), logical data (L) and character data (A). In all cases below the quantities w, d, e, and m are integer literal constants. w must be greater than zero. For any edit descriptor, the range of valid forms for data input is usually wider than the range for output. Any output form would be a valid input form with the same edit descriptor.

GENERALISED DATA:

Gw.d or Gw.dEe G editing can be used with an input or output data item of any intrinsic type. It indicates a field width of w positions. If the data item is integer, logical or character then Gw.d (or Gw.dEe for that matter) will be interpreted like Iw, Lw or Aw described below. If the item is real, Gw.d of Gw.dEe acts like F or E editing as described below. If the item is complex, a pair of G descriptors is required.

INTEGER DATA:

Iw or Iw.m The data item is an integer covering w spaces. For output the parameter m may be present, and causes leading zeroes to be included so that the integer has at least m digits. If present, m must not be negative and must not exceed w.

Bw.m or Bw.m As for I editing, but the data is expressed in binary form as a sequence of 0's and 1's.

Ow or Ow.m As for I editing, but the data is expressed in octal form.

Zw or Zw.m As for I editing, but the data is expressed in hexadecimal form using the digits 0-9 a nd A-F.

REAL DATA:

Fw. d The data item is a real number, covering w positions and including d places of decimals. 'd' must be positive and may not exceed w. Leading zeroes are not included in output, except in the position immediately before the decimal point when the number has a magnitude less than 1. With input, the decimal number may be followed by a multiplying power of ten (exponent), separated from the decimal number by the letter E (or D) and/or by the sign of the exponent, as in 314159265358.E-11 or 2.997924+8.

Ew.d or Ew.dEe   A real number covering w positions and including d places of decimals, and followed by a letter E and an exponent which is an integer consisting of a sign followed by e digits. In fact the e makes no difference for input; and for output the Ee may be omitted in which case an exponent of 2 or 3 digits will appear. Since F editing can be used for the input of numbers with exponents, E editing is only useful to force output into exponent form.

ENw.d or ENw.dEe   EN editing is similar to E editing but is used for what is sometimes called "engineering notation". With output, the number will have an exponent arranged to be a multiple of three, and the number of digits before the decimal point will be 1, 2 or 3. If Ee is absent the exponent has two or three digits, and if it is present the exponent has e digits. For example, EN10.1E3 would display the speed of light as 299.8E+006. Input data is treated similarly to F editing.

Dw.d   D editing is rather like E editing but without the option of Ee to specify the number of digits in an exponent on output. There is no need to use D editing at all.

COMPLEX DATA:

A complex number is always edited as a pair of real numbers, and so a pair of real-number edit descriptors must be used.

LOGICAL DATA:

Lw   On output, this produces the character T or F (for true or false) preceded by w-1 blanks. On input there will again be w places in the field but after optional leading blanks there may be a decimal point before the character T or F, and then other trailing characters. For example, .TRU. is a valid input form.

CHARACTER DATA:

A or Aw   The data item is a character string. If w is specified then it will be the number of characters transferred. If w is not equal to the length of the string then what happens depends on whether the transfer is an input or and output. Under input, if the string is shorter than the input field then only the rightmost characters of the input field will go into the string; while if the string is longer than the input field the w input characters will be left-justified and padded out with blanks to make up the string. Under output, if the string is shorter than the output field, the string will be padded out with blanks to the left to make up the required w characters; and if the string is longer than the output field then the string will be trimmed from the right. If w is not specified, the number of characters transferred is simply the length of the corresponding data item.

Tn   Data transfer is set to proceed from character position n (n being a positive integer) from the start of the current record. In terms of printer or screen output, Tn tabulates to character position n.

TLn   Tabulates n spaces left from the current position. If n is greater than the current position, TLn only goes back to the beginning of the current record.

TRn   Tabulates n spaces to the right.

nX   Leaves n blank spaces (same effect as TRn).

/ or r/   A slash will end data transfer on the current record and moves on to the start of the next. For printer or screen output, the slash goes to the start of the next line. Optionally, several records can be skipped by using the repeat specification r, a positive integer. For example, 6/ is equivalent to //////.

:   The colon will terminate the control of the format specification if (and only if) there are no further data items on the list to be transferred. This can be useful if one format specification is used for different data transfer statements moving different amounts of data.

S, SP and SS   These edit descriptors set switches to determine whether or not optional plus signs shall be put before positive numbers in output fields of numerical data (with I, F, E, EN, D and G editing). SP causes plus signs to appear, SS switches them off, and S restores the processor-dependent default choice.

kP   This edit descriptor sets a scale factor k which must be an integer constant, optionally signed. It can affect subsequent F,E, EN, D and G edit descriptors within one occasion of executing one data transfer statement. On input, if there is no exponent specified in the input field, the scale factor divides the data by 10 to the kth power: for example, using the descriptor -6P, the external numbers could measure volts and the internal number could measure microvolts. On output, with E or D editing (or G editing when it is equivalent to E editing) the data is multiplied by 10 to the kth power (so with -6P internal microvolts would become external volts).

BN or BZ   These switches affect the interpretation of blanks embedded in input numeric fields (I, B, O, Z, F, E, EN, D and G) following in the same data transfer statement. BN sets blanks to be neglected, and BZ sets them to be treated like zeroes.

CHARACTER STRINGS FOR DIRECT OUTPUT

A character string constant which is to be output may be specified directly as an edit descriptor in a format item list. This may be done in either of two ways. The first method is simply to include the string enclosed in quotes or apostrophes, e.g.

format_end = "("You scored ",I3,".   The game is over.")"

but no KIND parameters may be included. The other method, known as H editing (or "Hollerith" editing, after an early pioneer of data processing) gives the string without delimiters following a letter H which is preceded by the length of the string:

format_end = "(11HYou scored ,I3,21H.   The game is over.)"

Hollerith editing is outmoded and unnecessary and should be avoided in new programs. The first method above is common and straightforward for including short rubrics in output, but it is better to avoid altogether the direct use of text in edit descriptors and instead to output named strings by A editing:

format_end = "(A,I3,A)"

with the character strings having been named and spelt out elsewhere.

Appendix F

ASCII CHARACTER CODES

The ASCII code is a correspondence between a set of characters and the numbers ranging from 0 to 127. Since 127 is 1111111 in binary, it is a 7-bit code. Because most computer systems use 8-bit 'bytes', it is usually possible to have additional characters corresponding to the numbers 128 to 511, but they are not specified by the ASCII standard.

Most of the ASCII 'characters' are ordinary printable characters. Those which are not are omitted below, except for some whose usual meaning is indicated in parentheses.

Character	Code		Character	Code
(null)	0		6	54
(bell)	7		7	55
(backspace)	8		8	56
(return)	13		9	57
(delete)	16		:	58
(escape)	27		;	59
(blank)	32		<	60
!	33		=	61
"	34		>	62
#	35		?	63
$	36		@	64
%	37		A	65
&	38		B	66
'	39		C	67
(	40		D	68
)	41		E	69
*	42		F	70
+	43		G	71
,	44		H	72
-	45		I	73
.	46		J	74
/	47		K	75
0	48		L	76
1	49		M	77
2	50		N	78
3	51		O	79
4	52		P	80
5	53		Q	81

R	82	k	107
S	83	l	108
T	84	m	109
U	85	n	110
V	86	o	111
W	87	p	112
X	88	q	113
Y	89	r	114
Z	90	s	115
[	91	t	116
\	92	u	117
]	93	v	118
^	94	w	119
_	95	x	120
`	96	y	121
a	97	z	122
b	98	{	123
c	99	l	124
d	100	}	125
e	101	~	126
f	102	(delete)	127
g	103		
h	104		
i	105		
j	106		

A edit descriptor 221, 298
ABS 34, 45
ACCESS 237
Access code 88
ACHAR 58
ACOS 44
ACTION 238
Actual argument 91
ADJUSTL 58
ADJUSTR 58
ADVANCE 241
Advancing i/o 234
AIMAG 34, 45
AINT 46
ALL 74, 105
ALLOCATABLE 187, 281
Allocatable array 187
ALLOCATE 187, 206, 281
ALLOCATED 189
Alphanumeric characters 20
Ampersand 12, 14, 22
AND 35
ANINT 46
ANY 74, 105
Apostrophe 11, 55
APPEND 237
Argument 90
Argument association 123
Argument keywords 132, 294
Arithmetic IF 281
Arithmetic operators 18
Arithmetic-IF statement 10, 115
Array 8, 63, 181
Array assignment 65
Array constructor 67, 97, 183
Array element order 181
Array pointer 205
Array section 68
Array specification 152
Array-valued functions 135
ASCII 57, 301

ASIN 44
ASSIGN 10, 115, 281
ASSIGN, 10
Assigned GO TO 10, 115, 281
Assignment statement 16
ASSOCIATED 193
Assumed shape 154
Assumed size 96, 155
Asterisk 11
ATAN 44
ATAN2 44
Attribute specifications 144, 149
Automatic data object 148

B edit descriptor 297
BACKSPACE 240, 281
Binary editing 220
Binary operator 18
BIT_SIZE 250
Bits 110, 250
Blank 11, 13, 20, 22, 237
BLOCK DATA 143, 281
Bounds 187
BTEST 250

CALL 29, 93, 281
Capitalisation convention 21
CASE 76, 281
CASE DEFAULT 77
Case expression 76
CEILING 46
CHAR 58
Character 38, 39, 53, 147,
                    281, 301
Character constant 54
Character context 13
Character data 38
Character edit descriptor 221
CHARACTER FUNCTION 281

Character string edit descriptor
      218, 222
Characteristics of arguments 139
CLOSE 239, 281
CMPLX 45
CMS 7
Coding conventions 254
Colon 11
Colon editing 224, 299
Comma 11
Comment 17, 22
COMMON 127, 281
Compiler 3
COMPLEX 33, 146, 281
COMPLEX FUNCTION 281
Complex numbers 33
Computed GO TO 115, 281
Concatenation operator 39
CONJG 34, 46
Connection specification list 235
Constants 20
CONTAINS 120, 281
Continuation 22
CONTINUE 112, 281
Control edit descriptor 218, 223
Core Fortran 90 255
COS 34, 44
COSH 44
COUNT 74, 106
CSHIFT 106
Currency symbol 11
CYCLE 83, 282

DATA 161, 282
Data edit descriptor 218, 219
Data modules 116
Data transfer statements 209
DATE_AND_TIME 43
DBLE 52
DEALLOCATE 189, 206, 282
Decimal point 11
Default precision 32
Deferred shape 154
Deferred-shape array 187
Deferred-shape specification 205
Defined assignment 174

Defined operators 135
DELIM 238
Delimiter 16, 20
Derived types 8, 164
Derived-type definition 164
Descriptor 192
Digits 11, 111
DIM 47
DIMENSION 63, 152, 282
DIRECT 244
Direct access 234
Disassociation 195
Division 18
DO 82, 282
DO WHILE 83
Dollar 12
DOS 7
DOTPRODUCT 109
Double colon 42, 144
Double precision 32, 42, 282
DOUBLE PRECISION
      FUNCTION 282
DPROD 52
Dummy argument 91

E edit descriptor 298
Edit descriptor 217
Edit descriptors 297
Elemental functions 73
ELSE 17, 80, 282
ELSE IF 80, 282
ELSEWHERE 73, 282
EN edit descriptor 298
END 101, 249, 282
END BLOCK DATA 282
END DO 82, 282
END FUNCTION 91, 95, 282
END IF 17, 80, 282
END INTERFACE 131, 282
END MODULE 117, 282
End of record 213
END PROGRAM 17, 282
END SELECT 76, 282
END SUBROUTINE 95, 282
END TYPE 165, 282
END WHERE 73, 282

305

End-of-file condition 236
End-of-record condition 236
ENDFILE 240, 282
Endfile record 233
Engineering editing 221
Enter 16
Entity declaration list 144, 157
ENTRY 100, 283
EOR 249
EOSHIFT 107
EPSILON 48
Equals 11
EQUIVALENCE 232, 283
EQV 36
ERR 249
Exclamation 11
EXIST 243
EXIT 82, 283
EXIT 34, 44
Explicit format 217
Explicit shape 153
EXPONENT 111
Exponent letter 29
Exponentiation 18
Extent 181
EXTERNAL 96, 150, 283
External file 233
External functions 90
External subprogram 5, 258

F edit descriptor 297
File 233, 236
Fixed source form 3
Floating point 29, 217
FLOOR 47
FMT 210
FMT=* 15
FORM 237
FORMAT 232, 283
Format specification 217
Format specifier 210
FORMATTED 244
Formatted i/o 209, 228
FORTRAN 77 1
Fortran 90 1
FRACTION 111

Free source form 9
Full stop 11
FUNCTION 90, 283
Functions 6

G edit descriptor 297
Generic names 114, 138
GO TO 112, 283
Greater than 12
Group name 226

Hexadecimal editing 220
Hollerith data 232
Host association 123
HUGE 28, 48

I edit descriptor 297
I/O 4
I/O edit descriptors 297
I/O item list 210
IACHAR 57
IAND 251
IBCLR 251
IBITS 251
IBSET 251
ICHAR 57
IEOR 251
IF 28, 80, 283
IF 80
IF...THEN 17, 283
IMPLICIT 162, 283
IMPLICIT NONE 283
INCLUDE 249, 283
INDEX 58
Initialization expression 54, 79, 157
INQUIRE 242, 283
INT 30, 46
INTEGER 32, 146, 283
INTEGER FUNCTION 283
Integers 26
INTENT 151, 283
INTERFACE 131, 283
INTERFACE ASSIGNMENT 175

Interface block 131
INTERFACE OPERATOR 136
Internal file 246
Internal procedure 100, 258
INTRINSIC 96, 151, 283
Intrinsic functions 17
Intrinsic procedures 6, 43, 286
IOR 251
IOSTAT 236
ISHFT 252
ISHFTC 252

Keyword 7, 20
KIND function 49
KIND parameter 48

L edit descriptor 298
Label 111
LBOUND 190
Left parenthesis 11
Left-to-right rule 19
LEN 42, 57
LEN 57
Length 39, 53
Length selector 148
Less than 12
Letters 11
Lexical tokens 20
LGE 58
LGT 58
Line 22
List-directed input 212
List-directed output 216
LLE 58
LLT 58
Local variables 123
LOG 34, 44
LOG10 44
LOGICAL 147, 283
Logical data 35
Logical expression 17, 35
LOGICAL FUNCTION 283
Loop index 84
Lower-case 12

Main program 5
Mathematical functions 44
MATMUL 109
MAX 47
MAXEXPONENT 111
Maximum record length 244
MAXLOC 105
MAXVAL 74, 106
MERGE 108
MIN 47
MINEXPONENT 111
MINLOC 105
Minus 11
MINVAL 74, 106
MOD 27, 46
Module 5, 9, 116, 117, 283
MODULE PROCEDURE 140, 283
Module procedures 120
MODULE statement 117
Module subprograms 6
MODULO 47
Multiplication 18
MVBITS 252

Name 20
NAMED 243
NAMELIST 226, 283
Namelists 226
NEAREST 111
NEQV 36
NEXTREC 244
NINT 47
Nonadvancing i/o 234
NOT 35, 251
Null edit descriptor 218
NULLIFY 195, 206, 283
NUMBER 243
Numeric functions 45

O edit descriptor 297
Obsolescent 10
Octal editing 220
OPEN 235
OPENED 243

Operating system 7
Operator 20
OPTIONAL 133, 151, 284
OR 35
Overloading 140

PACK 108
PAD 238
Parallel processing 141
PARAMETER 144, 150, 284
PAUSE 10, 89, 284
Percent 11
Plus 11
Pointer 9, 181, 192, 284
Pointer assignment 193, 284
Pointer-valued function 205
Portability 3
Portability, 3
POSITION 237
Precedence 18
PRECISION 6, 48
PRESENT 133
PRINT 232, 284
PRIVATE 127, 150, 284
Procedures 5
Processor 3
PRODUCT 74, 106
Program 2, 14, 17, 284
Program structure 258
Program unit 258
Program units 5
PUBLIC 127, 150, 284

Question mark 12
Quote 11, 55

RADIX 110
RANDOM 103
RANDOMSEED 103
RANGE 29, 48
Rank 181
READ 15, 209, 244, 284
READWRITE 244
REAL 30, 32, 46, 146, 284

REAL FUNCTION 284
Real numbers 29
REC 241
RECL 237, 244
Record 22, 228, 233
Record length 237
RECURSIVE FUNCTION 284
Recursive procedures 5, 128
RECURSIVE SUBROUTINE 284
Relational operators 42
REPEAT 59
RESHAPE 183
Return 16, 82, 95, 143, 284
Reversion 224
REWIND 237, 240, 284
Right parenthesis 11
Right to left rule 19
RRSPACING 111

SAVE 150, 195, 284
SCALE 111
SCAN 59
Scratch file 236
SELECT CASE 76, 284
SELECTED_INT_KIND 52
SELECTED_REAL_KIND 49
Semicolon 12
SEQUENCE 180, 284
SEQUENTIAL 243
Sequential access 233
SETEXPONENT 111
Shape 181, 191
SIGN 47
SIN 34, 44
SINH 44
Size 181, 191, 241
SIZE function 191
Skip forward 223
Slash 11
Slash editing 223, 299
Source form 21
SPACING 111
Special characters 11
Specific names 114, 292
Specification expressions 188
SPREAD 109

SQRT 6, 34, 44
Statement 7, 22, 281
Statement function 284
Statement functions 143
Statement Label 20, 22, 111
STATUS 236
STOP 82, 88, 284
Stop code 88
Stride 84, 183, 185
String 38
Structure components 168
Structure constructors 166
Structures 164
SUBROUTINE 94, 95, 284
Subroutines 6, 93
Subscript 68
Subscript triplet 185
Substring 59
SUM 74, 106
SYSTEM_CLOCK 102

Tabulate 223
TAN 44
TANH 44
Target 192, 284
TDS 144
TINY 48, 111
TRANSFER 229, 253
TRANSPOSE 107
TRIM 39, 57
TYPE 147, 164, 285
Type declaration statement 32,
                144, 285
Type specification 144

UBOUND 190
Unary operator 18
Underscore 11
UNFORMATTED 244
Unformatted i/o 209, 228
Unit 210, 233, 236
UNIT=* 14
UNIX 7
UNPACK 108
Upper-case 12

USE 117, 285
Use association 123
User-defined operators 135
User-defined types 8

Variables 15
Vector subscript 184
VERIFY 59

WHERE 72, 285
Word 110
WRITE 7, 12, 14, 209, 244, 285

X edit descriptor 299
X3J3 5

Z edit descriptor 297
Zero-length string 53
Zero-size array 64